Constructing Female Identities

SUNY Series, Power, Social Identity, and Education
Lois Weis, Editor

Constructing Female Identities

Meaning Making
in an Upper Middle Class Youth Culture

AMIRA PROWELLER

State University of New York Press

Published by
State University of New York Press, Albany

© 1998 State University of New York

Printed in the United States of America

For information, address State University of New York
Press, State University Plaza, Albany, N.Y., 12246

Production by Diane Ganeles
Marketing by Nancy Farrell

Library of Congress Cataloging-in-Publication Data

Proweller, Amira.
    Constructing female identities : meaning making in an upper middle
class youth culture / Amira Proweller.
        p.   cm. — (SUNY series, power, social identity, and
education)
    Includes bibliographical references (p.   ) and index.
    ISBN 0-7914-3771-X (hc : alk. paper). — ISBN 0-7914-3772-8 (pbk.
: alk. paper)
    1. Teenage girls—Education (Secondary)—Social aspects—United
States.   2. Middle class women—Education (Secondary)—United
States.   3. Women—Socialization—United States.   4. Women-
-Identity.   I. Title.   II. Series.
LC1775.P76   1998
371.822—dc21
                                                                    97-35900
                                                                    CIP

*To my parents, Thelma and William,
my brother, Aaron,
and the memory of my first brother, Maxim,
this book is dedicated from the heart.*

Contents

Acknowledgments

The ethnographic experience is not only an intellectual exercise in social science research but an exploration of the pleasures and risks of intimacy. You find yourself in places that have been carefully guarded and distanced from outsiders, amazed that you have somehow been let in on secrets and into silent parts of individual lives about which most of us will never have the privilege to learn. Risking intimacy as researchers and researched participants as we tell our confessional tales in the field, together we risk betrayal. When I entered the doors of Best Academy in the fall of 1993, I took on the awesome responsibility of first learning how to listen, then hear and retell the narratives of those who had risked breaking their silence and chosen, instead, to come to voice and share their experiences.

To the junior girls of Best Academy who took this risk, I owe my deepest gratitude for their space, their time, and their stories. They let me into the universe of adolescent, female youth culture, knowing full well that intimacy could redouble in betrayals of confidence. But they took the chance, moving in careful and measured steps with me as they slowly folded me into their lives. I am indebted to the Best Academy school administration, faculty, and staff for opening their minds and their hearts during a difficult year of administrative transition that gave everyone pause. Taking me on as a researcher and eventual participant in school life was no doubt one more unnecessary complication in a year of significant change. It is my sincere hope that perhaps, in some small way that I may never know, I contributed to easing that transition. To the parents who granted permission for their daughters' participation in this study and themselves agreed to give their time to my research while they, themselves, were adjusting to a difficult administrative change, thank you.

What begins as a labor of love can all too often be transformed into an academic chore along the way. There are times when your work unravels you to the point that you forget the initial excitement that first brought you to a project. To my friends inside and outside the Academy, I extend the utmost appreciation for intellectual challenge, patience, and love during those moments of faltering confidence and mounting doubt. A special thanks to Julia Marusza for her sustained friendship and intellectual support and for pushing me to take risks when I hesitated to move in new directions. A debt of thanks goes to the School of Education at DePaul University for granting me a course reduction in the spring quarter of 1996 in order that I might complete the final set of revisions. I thank my colleagues in the School of Education for their constant encouragement of my scholarship during my first two years of teaching in a new institution combined with my struggles to forge meaningful connections of my own as a newcomer to Chicago. Their support during the final phase of revising as the book neared completion was immeasurably helpful to the success of this effort. Special thanks to Sandra Jackson, for her careful reading of earlier drafts of this manuscript and to Stephen Haymes, both of whom have helped in significant ways to focus my critical eye with their honed insights and ever-flowing challenges during those moments when things weren't altogether clear and the project's end looked as though it might never arrive. Many thanks also to my co-conspirators from the Women Studies Program and colleagues in other departments at DePaul University who have been a nurturing source of encouragement along the way. In the end, I, alone am responsible for any errors in information and interpretation.

The ethnographic endeavor is remarkably sad. It affords you insight into a slice of life where you have walked and met new, interesting, and thought-provoking people along the way. These folks, for the most part, pass in and out of a researcher's life as one leaves the field and moves into other uncharted territory. The instability of the ethnographic experience is, therefore, unsettling, and the presence of signposts who serve as intellectual and emotional guides along the way is a necessary and welcome comfort. To Lois Weis, colleague and friend, I extend thanks for supporting this project at its inception as a dissertation and now as a finished book, with her undying enthusiasm, pointed sense of risk and critical eye that together helped me tease out the complexities of ethnographic research in ways that have enriched my mind and my soul about the human experience inside and outside school. Her lessons in learning have bridged for me the altogether more important lessons of life. I also owe a debt of gratitude to Hester Eisenstein and Ben Agger whose insights have equally informed the issues this book has taken on. Many thanks to the editorial staff at SUNY Press for recognizing the importance of publishing a work on girls' socialization and identity formation processes in a relatively underexplored educational setting—the private, girls' school—and to the reviewers of this manuscript without whose critical comments this book would have taken that much longer to complete. And finally, my family whose constant love, encouragement, and affirmation have taught me about the fullness that the pleasures and risks of intimacy bring to everyday life.

Chapter 1

Introduction

 This book is an examination of identity formation processes among a cohort of upper middle-class adolescent females set in Best Academy, a historically elite, private, independent, single-sex high school for girls.[1] For close to 150 years, Best Academy has served students from solidly upper middle-class, or, rather, professional middle-class backgrounds.[2] Over the past two decades, the population of relatively privileged youth traditionally served in this private school has been changing to reflect a student body increasingly stratified by social class, race, and ethnicity. A close look at the current demographic make up of the student body points out that the school continues to draw in girls from blue-collar working-class and lower white-collar middle-class families, a trend that began in the early 1980s. Changes in the class culture of the private school do not take place outside of social and political dynamics and are arguably one example of the impact that broader structural shifts in the local and global economy have had on private institutions. The lived effects of economic retrenchment first felt among the working class in the mid-1970s and into the early 1980s have not sidestepped the upper middle class where the relative security a middle class standard of living afforded for much of the post-war period is no longer a predictable part of life (Bluestone and Harrison, 1982).[3] The shift from "Fordism" to intensified capitalist competition on an international scale has spurred the growth of new employment categories and job descriptions, phasing out routine production jobs in the service sector and lower and middle-level management positions and replacing them with the problem-solving services of the symbolic analyst, drawn mainly from the professional middle class.[4] In the tide of corporate restructuring that has defined economic trends from the 1980s into the 1990s, major corporations tapping into the specialized training and skills of the middle class have merged and, in many instances, been forced to close (Reich, 1992).
 Economic retrenchment following from deindustrialization and the shift towards a global market economy has not gone without significant impact on American cities. Best Academy is located in a northeastern, metropolitan

center with a population of 328,123.[5] Typical of many urban areas in the U.S. during the mid-1970s and upwards of that time, it too, has suffered the injuries of structural decline. The city lost its place as an established center of manu-facturing and commercial trade as large-scale plant closings and corporate mergers shifted the bread and butter of American production from manu-facturing to the service sector.[6] Late capitalism has not only indelibly marked the urban underclass and working class, but it has also impacted on the standards of upper middle-class living as this group lives out and suffers its own forms of social and economic dislocation. New job categories and work rela-tionships inside the American culture of work have an obvious impact on the organization of social relations inside school. An increasingly stratified class culture in Best Academy, for example, forces new tensions that arise at the intersection of competing class strata to the surface. In the main, this dynamic has not been part of this school's history. Forty-seven percent of the thirty-four girls that I shadowed in the junior class receive financial assistance in the form of grants-in-aid based on financial need. Only sixteen students are full tuition payers.[7] Of the total student sample represented in this study, sixty-two percent attended public grammar schools. While only one indicator of the changing class culture at Best Academy, the early public education backgrounds of these students suggests that parents across class strata are interested in providing their daughters with a private education at substantial cost to their families.

In his comparative ethnography of three all-American high schools, Philip Wexler (1992) describes students' varied responses to class-based norms and expectations of who they should be in the context of a working-class, a professional middle-class, and an urban underclass high school. Through collected narratives and observations of youth across these three settings, he discovers that schools, by and large, do not support the development of relational communities but, rather, discourage and block the production of meaningful relationships among school-age youth. Students respond to the fractured organization of school culture by working to "create a visible, differentiated and reputable self" in opposition to the felt emptiness of school life in each of these sites (p. 132).[8]

> In their own words, students are trying to "become somebody." They want to be somebody, a real and presentable self, anchored in the verifying eyes of friends whom they come to school to meet. . . . [T]heir central and defining activity in school is to establish at least the image of an identity. "Becoming somebody" is action in the public sphere, and this is what life in high school is about (p. 155).

Inside classrooms and corridors, youth engaged in the project of "becoming somebody" are working to shape felt notions of self across multiple and intersecting discursive fields through which meanings are organized, mediated, and filtered (Foucault, 1980; Weedon, 1987). Socially constituted identities of social class, race, ethnicity, gender, and sexuality form in/through discursive fields that map out meanings and social practices and set limits and possibilities for social relations in schools.[9] As systems of representation, they organize and mediate culture as lived experience through a range of subjectivities that form within and against structure, culture and ideology in educational contexts. The relationship between knowledge and power is at the heart of questions about identity formation and asks that we examine the "complex ways social, economic, political tensions and contradictions are 'mediated' in the concrete practices of educators as they go about their business in schools" (Apple, 1990, p. 2). For students no less, the project of "becoming somebody" is a matter of negotiating structures and embedded meanings as they make sense of who they are daily in schools. As schools bear the marks of structural change, so, too do shifts in the economy imprint on and complicate the production of youth identity in educational contexts.

This book adds a missing link to existing culturalist critiques of identity construction through close examination of the ways in which upper middle-class, adolescent girls organize and problematize daily life in school within and against their experiences in peer culture, family life, and broader social dynamics. Individually and collectively, they continue the struggles that social analyses of identity have described over two and a half decades of research on youth cultural forms in schools. The difference between this volume and foregoing discussions is cast in the context, characters, and conditions that private schools face in this current historical moment. While public and private schools cannot avoid feeling the effects of changing market conditions, it is very much the case that the specifically market-driven character and near total dependence of the private school on private sources of funding leaves schools like Best Academy that much more vulnerable to economic downslides than their public school counterparts.

The crisis of public life brought about by a newly aggressive market economy has introduced real challenges for upper middle-class adolescent girls that speak to a need for more sustained and focused research on girls' identity formation processes. To that end, this study is based on a number of central questions. To what extent does the shift to a post-industrial, global economy impact the organization of social relations in the private high school? How do adolescent girls negotiate messages about class, race, and gender privilege structured into their educational experience and what forms do social relations of class, race, and gender take in this context? What accommodations do these youth make as they shape new identities? What types of counter-hegemonic strategies do they draw on in opposition to institutional arrangements and embodied ideologies?

That the bulk of research on identity formation in context has centered on the public school makes a strong case by its absence and omission for studying this issue in a relatively unexplored site—the private high school. As suggested earlier, the private school is more vulnerable than the public school to downward economic trends that threaten to further destablize what has been, up until now, a relatively stable class base. This reality is not only an argument for the significance of this study but also for the timeliness of research conducted in this site at this historical moment. Given the inextricable relationship between school and society, there is no doubt that identity formation wil be inflected by broader social change. Ethnographic snapshots of girls' subcultures at Best Academy set their project of "becoming somebody" against these conditions, deepening our understanding of the contradictions that structures introduce around meaning-making in an upper middle-class youth culture.

On Identity Formation: Sociological Theories in Context

Structuralist critiques of socialization dominating theoretical discourse in the sociology of education through much of the decade of the 1950s on up through the early 1970s, argued that youth identities reflected existing school structures and broader social relations (McCarthy and Apple, 1988). Research in this genre tended either to ignore narrative accounts of lived experience altogether or to privilege structure over cultural forms. Up until the last fifteen years, research on identity formation processes in schools has been squarely located in reproduction theory.[10] Attributing to schools a direct role in stratifying the labor force, reproduction theory holds simply that schools are socializing agencies that reproduce the norms, values, and ideologies of the dominant culture by outfitting students with the skills for work roles important to the maintenance of social inequalities on which the balance of a capitalist economy and society depends.[11] Structuralism would shape the direction of debate in the field significantly, beginning with the influential work of Samuel Bowles and Herbert Gintis (1976). Working from a class-reductionist model, they propose that schools are agencies of transmission that stand in a one-to-one correspondence with the social relations of production in a capitalist economy and society. Through class specific forms of training, power is unequally allocated to youth who are prepared for work roles appropriate to their class background. Not unlike structural frameworks that tend to cloak analysis of school culture in class models, economic reproduction theory frontloads examination of processes of transmission in schools but fails to consider the ways in which social actors articulate with existing institutional forms and practices.

With the rise of the New Sociology of Education in the early 1970s, first in the United Kingdom and shortly afterward in the United States, research in the sociology of education turned toward study of the organization and stratification of school curriculum.[12] Sociological examination of school knowledge raised questions about the ways in which knowledge is presented in schools and the differences in the content and delivery of information to different groups in school. The shift in focus to curricular form paralleled the emergence of cultural reproduction theories in education and helped to extend understanding of the relationship between schools and the class structure. Cultural reproduction theory moves beyond the strict class analysis of economic reproduction models to examine how school knowledge embeds class differences in cultural forms, patterns, and styles of communication (Bennett and LeCompte, 1990). In this regard, Basil Bernstein's (1977) important work put forward the notion that specific linguistic codes reflect the structures of family life based in different class cultures. Children from middle class backgrounds will adjust more easily to school since middle class patterns and styles of communication tend to dominate in schools. Children from working-class families, on the other hand, have the opposite experience. Different linguistic competencies funnel children in different directions, overwhelmingly training working-class youth for skilled or semi-skilled waged labor while preparing middle-class youth for more specialized professions. In short, children's school experience is influenced by the social and cultural resources and linguistic competencies that they bring with them into school, and the school plays a central role in reproducing inequalities along class lines.

Pierre Bourdieu and Jean-Claude Passeron (1977) built on Bernstein's notion of linguistic codes with the concept of cultural capital. Cultural capital extends our understanding of the role that schools play in cultural repro-duction from one generation to the next. Upper-class children are said to inherit more cultural capital, meaning general cultural background, knowl-edge, tastes, and skills, than do children from working-class backgrounds. As sites for the transmission of class interests and ideologies, schools sort and select children by rewarding the cultural capital of the dominant classes. While public schools claim to be democratic spaces committed to providing equality of educational opportunity, some children do arrive in school with a distinct cultural advantage, and schools tend to recognize and develop middle class competencies. Distributing power differently, though, by sorting and selecting students, effectively contributes to the marginalization and silencing of children from relatively less privileged backgrounds (Weis and Fine, 1993). The knowledge and competencies that middle and upper middle-class children bring into school are summarily reinforced, passing class status onto them and securing their place in the class continuum.

Despite a shift in focus, the cultural dynamics of schooling still tended to be narrowly treated through class analysis and the overdetermined logic of reproductive frameworks. Categories of race, ethnicity, and gender were virtually missing from discussions of school form and practice. Analysis based mainly on class inequalities privileged structure over culture and failed, once again, to narrow the gap between them. In recent years, however, sociologists of education have begun to re-examine the longstanding divide between structure and culture and have chosen to reframe their analysis of identity construction in culturalist terms that foreground the complex and creative work of school-age youth around the project of "becoming somebody." Redressing this imbalance, Michael Apple and Lois Weis (1983) exploded the boundaries of cultural reproduction theory, pushing new theoretical models to the center of debate. Cultural theorists speculated that schools *could* be sites for semi-autonomous identity production where social actors do more than simply mirror and accommodate themselves to dominant structures. From a site of uncontested socialization, schools were refashioned at this critical moment as spaces for the creative production of self. As culturalists, they forced structures to take a disciplinary back seat to culture and refocused their analytical lens on the dynamics of school culture as lived experience. Identity formation analyzed through a culturalist lens catches youth in the act of making the everyday problematic as they configure meaningful lives in the context of shifting social relations inside and outside school (Smith, 1987). Given this disciplinary seachange, it was no longer possible to speak of identity formation in terms of "additive models of double and triple oppression" (McCarthy, 1988). Instead, identity production was newly reconceptualized as a complex set of interlocking processes based in multiple social relations that closely articulated with defining structures inside and outside schools. Culturalists had substituted dimensionalized and fluid accounts of school life based in conflict, contradiction, and contest for overdetermined analyses of socialization. Students, teachers, administrators, and parents were now restored as subjects and agents of knowledge production in context.

Contradictions in Culture

One of the earliest attempts at theoretically unpacking the lived effects of class culture in school appears in Paul Willis' narrative of identity construction among white, working-class lads in a British comprehensive school for boys (Willis, 1977). In his now classic study, Willis illustrates that working-class schools are reproductive as well as productive sites of self-determination. For these working-class lads, shop floor culture celebrates manual labor which they associate with masculinity while school culture values mental labor which they link with femininity. Against the backdrop of shifting economic trends in Britain, formal school culture promises little in the way of maximizing life chances for a group of young men destined, like their fathers before them, for factory jobs. That school knowledge has no intrinsic or extrinsic value for them becomes the basis for their strategic resistance to formal school culture. Through a meaningfully constructed set of discursive practices that finds them taking schoolwork less than seriously, these working-class lads actively contest middle-class norms and values central to offical school culture. Countercultural forms of resistance raise levels of class consciousness for the working class but are only partly successful in bringing about real changes in the conditions of their working-class lives. In the final analysis, the responses of the working-class lads serve only to "partially penetrate" offical school culture, and their location of structural subordination in the British labor market is reproduced.

Up until a decade ago, research on school socialization and identity formation processes were almost exclusively focused on boys' school experiences. Feminist social theorists roundly criticized Willis for privileging male cultural forms and failing to examine the virulent and pervasive sexism of male subcultures (McRobbie, 1991). This emergent critique drew attention to a missing piece in the literature on socialization, identity construction, and school engagement. In the early 1980s, feminist researchers began to redress this imbalance through questions about the relationship between class and gender and its impact on the organization of social relations in schools. Socialist feminists understood that patriarchy and capitalism combined to produce and legitimate the sexual division of labor, restricting women's activities to the private sphere and men's responsibilities to the public domain (Deem, 1978; Eisenstein, 1979; MacDonald, 1980; Wolpe, 1981; Arnot, 1982).[13] Linking together gender and social class, feminist theorists found that schools distributed messages about normative gender roles reflecting inequalities in the social relations of production responsible for blocking women's full participation in the market economy. Findings along these lines seemed to indicate a general willingness by female students to fold in and internalize roles for women based in the traditional sexual division of labor.

While there is much to suggest that schools are implicated directly in reinforcing structural inequalities along gender lines, studies on girls' school experiences begun in the early 1980s provided empirical support for their active resistance against and negotiation of dominant school forms and practices. Gail Kelly and Ann Nihlen (1982) found it interesting that girls, although proportionately fewer in number than boys, continued onto college and university in spite of prevailing school messages that urged more circumscribed experiences and roles for women in the private domain. What these findings implied for these researchers was that somehow, there were girls who were rejecting dominant ideologies and managing to find their way into higher education. Reproduction paradigms had evidently overlooked equally salient expressions of resistance among a significant part of the youth population. While not unproblematic, Kelly and Nihlen's analysis importantly directs those in the field to take serious account of girls' cultural forms that have been overlooked consistently, in part, because of the limitations of reproduction frameworks. With inroads into the possible forms of creative contestation among school-age girls yet to be explored, critical feminist researchers began in earnest to examine schools as sites where girls, and not boys alone, were actively engaged in counter-hegemonic moves both in accommodation of and resistance to school structures and sex stereotyped messages.

Work focused on critique at the level of girls' lived culture would reshape the direction of research on socialization in school. Formative analysis of anti-school movements among girls would come in the pioneering work of Angela McRobbie (1978) whose ethnographic examination of female subcultures in a comprehensive high school in working-class England would provide strong evidence for the development of counter-hegemonic sub-cultures among adolescent females. Like Willis' working-class lads who opposed formal school culture by "having a laff," these girls enacted a set of discursive practices tightly wrapped in an ideology of romance played out through the reappropriation of feminine forms. In their preoccupation with fashion, beauty, dating, and marriage, they were, in fact, rejecting the official school culture of middle-class norms and belief systems. For these girls, counter-cultural expressions of opposition to school came directly out of feminine ideologies so that the anti-school culture they forged was specifically female. Not unlike the lads who valorized masculinity in connection with shop floor culture, working-class girls strategically draw on and use sexuality in opposition to formal school culture and its middle-class valuing of *acceptable* forms of femininity. Angela McRobbie finds that the production of working-class, female counter-cultures ultimately depends on the partial rejection of ideologies undergirding the historical subordination of working-class women. Strategic resistance to formal school culture among working-class females in school contexts is consistent with this early study (McRobbie and McCabe, 1981; Thomas, 1980; Lees, 1986).

Critical ethnographic research on girls' subcultures in working-class schools carried out in the 1980s would extend our knowledge of the central place that domesticity continued to hold for girls in their decisions about coursework and future work roles. That the form, content, and distribution of knowledge in working-class schools has typically encouraged reproduction of marginalized labor identities among school age students has been well documented (Anyon, 1980; Apple, 1982, 1990; McNeil, 1983). High school clerical training programs, for example, tend to attract working-class girls and guide them toward entry-level jobs after graduation (Gaskell, 1985; Valli, 1988). Girls are discouraged from educational and professional avenues that might open the possibility for them to enjoy greater personal and financial autonomy in their futures. This does not necessarily mean that working-class schools are not contested sites of identity production for school-age girls. On the contrary, research has documented that girls are not as oversocialized into dominant ideologies as reproduction theory suggests in analysis of working-class settings. Working-class girls do choose, in some instances, to enroll in business courses rather than undertake coursework in the academic track (Gaskell, 1985). In part, they participate in reproducing the traditional sexual division of labor. What is important, though, to extrapolate from these studies, is that girls' identity formation is more complex and contested than earlier thought and that girls might engage in accommodation and resistance at one and the same time (Anyon, 1984). Lois Weis (1990) presents somewhat of a departure from earlier studies of girls' identity processes by pinpointing an emergent "moment of critique" among working-class girls who begin to construct primary identities around a culture of work. Facing the harsh economic realities of urban de-industrialization in the mid-1980s, girls recognize that they can no longer depend on their future husbands for financial support in the wake of urban displacement, factory shutdowns, growing unemployment lines, and rising divorce rates. Projecting the very possibility that they will be forced back on their own resources, white, working-class girls begin to narrate, instead, the importance of centering waged labor in their lives not only for themselves but, more importantly, for the welfare of their families.

The cultural forms and expressions of youth of color have received attention in a number of studies of the social construction of race. In her study of racial identity forms among a cohort of black youth at urban, public Capital High School, Signithia Fordham (1988) found that black students adopt strategies of racelessness perceived as a way of increasing their chances for vertical mobility in school and in their future work roles. Racelessness is arguably a form of accommodation to dominant racial and class structures in the public school. Interestingly, James Stanlaw and Alan Peshkin (1988) discovered different cultural responses in their ethnographic investigation of black youth culture in a predominantly white, public high school. At Riverview, conditions were in place for black students to integrate themselves fully into school culture, enjoying what these researchers described as a "positive black visibility." John Ogbu (1988) documents that racial stratification of black youth, based in their historical exclusion from the opportunity structure, is largely responsible for the emergence of cultures of opposition in predominantly white school contexts. That black youth tend to reject school meanings and formal knowledge is based, he argues, in a history of collective struggle against white, supremacist culture and is in contention with their desire to be academically successful in school. The double-sided nature of oppositional cultural forms among black youth underlines the contradictions of racial identity formation for this group.

For youth of color, research on racial identity formation to date has emphasized the experiences of the black male, although this, too, is a piece that has yet to be rounded out in the socialization literature. Mary Fuller (1980) helped to balance the equation with her formative study of the identity development of girls of color, a gap in the relational construction of race that Ladner (1971), Grant (1992), Fordham (1993), Hemmings (1996) and others have begun to fill. Having interviewed and observed African-Caribbean and Asian girls in a London comprehensive school, she learned that these British West Indian girls resisted existing school structures through non-conformist behavior that masked academic competence and their desires to achieve in school. Fuller's findings suggest that the cultural strategies that girls of color adopt are both gender and culturally specific. Working across multiple locations of race, class, ethnicity, and gender, these girls engage identity production differently than has been found to be the case for white girls and boys of color as well.[14]

Until very recently, research on racial identity formation has focused exclusively on youth of color. For the most part, race has been neatly categorized and delimited in terms of the black experience. Equating race with blackness overlooks the fact that identities are relationally constituted and that the production of racial identities among folks of color has historically depended on negotiation of forms and practices specific to the white, western Self. Whiteness is not recognized as a social and political category of experience but remains unnoticed and unnamed as the invisible cultural center (Frankenberg, 1993; McLaren, 1997). Where the socialization literature takes up identity construction among youth, "white" as a racial referent is typically neither named nor decoded as a symbolic marker of power and privilege. Best Academy enrolls a largely white, European-American student population. Statistics documenting the racial and ethnic composition of the student body indicate that eighty-five percent of the school population consists of white, non-Hispanic Americans. The remaining fifteen percent articulate at nine percent African-American, one percent Native-American, four percent Hispanic-American, and one percent Asian-American. Of the thirty-four students constituting the study sample, four are African-American, one is Hispanic American, one identifies as Native-American and one is the child of a bi-racial marriage. As a predominantly white high school, Best Academy is a site of structural dominance where those located at the cultural center are blind to their own condition of "raceless subjectivity" (McLaren, 1991; Frankenberg, 1993; Gallagher, 1994). Studies of identity construction among white girls have fundamentally *assumed* whiteness, taking it for granted as an identity dimension, without taking critical steps towards detailed investigation of how being white informs ethnic, gender, and class subjectivities. Joining an emerging body of research on the social construction of discourses of whiteness in context, this study of private school culture fixes attention on the racial center, asking much needed questions about what it means to be white and the ways in which a dominant yet strikingly invisible racial location informs human behavior (Fine, Weis, Powell, Wong, 1997).

Studies of student performance have mined the private school for its proven effectiveness in raising levels of student achievement, providing rigorous instruction, and enhancing educational opportunity, access, and outcome (Coleman, Hoffer, and Kilgore, 1982, 1991; Coleman and Hoffer, 1987). With the turn away from outcome-based measures toward detailed investigation of cultural forms in school, research to date on the relationship between class and education has focused on the linkages between the content and authority structure of working-class schools and the production of working-class identities (Willis, 1977; Everhart, 1983; MacLeod, 1987; Weis, 1990, McLaren, 1994). Absent from this discussion is any in-depth examination of elite culture, particularly around middle and upper middle-class youth cultural forms.[15] Richard Connell (1982) provides a missing piece early on in his comparative study of working-class, state and private, ruling-class secondary schools in Australia.[16] Through detailed ethnographic work, he gathers strong evidence to support the fact that private, ruling-class schools, by design, transmit ruling-class capital from one generation to the next. This is hardly surprising, given what Bourdieu (1974) explained as the conserving role of the upper-class school. Where Connell shifts direction from others in the field at this moment is in his contention that ruling-class schools reflect and respond to structural changes on the outside. As a market driven institution responsive to shifts in the local and national economy, it was increasingly problematic for educators to continue to see the private school as a homogeneous and static class culture. Rather, he argues for the importance of revisiting the private school as a dynamic space that moves with and against broader structural ebbs and tides. Connell lands squarely on what we now know to be the case in the class and education literature, that class relations fluctuate continuously and take multiple forms in school contexts. This is not to suggest that the private school does not continue to play an important conserving role because it does. It is simply to add that it is also a complex and interactive space, more dynamic than ethnographic studies have portrayed up to this point in time.

Along similar lines, Peter Cookson and Caroline Persell (1985) find evidence for the maintenance of upper middle-class power in college preparatory high schools.[17] Such private institutions depend on a student body that sees itself as part of an elite collective shaped in the shadow of the organization and mediated messages of class status, prestige, and resources. A shared cultural identity around which students and faculty rally encourages the development of cohesive school communities based in commitment rather than compliance (Hannaway and Abramowitz, 1985). This is not to suggest that private school culture does not suffer the realities of social dislocation among its students as Wexler (1992) finds to be the case in his comparative ethnographic study of three public schools differentiated by social class. What he uncovers is a growing sense of social disaffection and loss of meaningful relationships among youth in three different schools whose expressive forms illustrate the emptying of the social center and the extent to which the crisis of American public life has crossed and penetrated class cultures.

Close to fifteen years earlier, Ralph Larkin (1979) traced the emergence of the loss of a felt sense of legitimacy and promise for the future among white, suburban, middle-class youth in Utopia High School to the conditions of monopoly capitalism—surplus absorption and coerced consumption. On the threshold of entering the decade of the 1980s, middle-class suburban youth began to notice the growing competition they faced for scarce resources. Their anxiety was a clear signal that the fortunes their parents before them were able to secure in the post-war years were potentially unattainable for their generation, now facing downward shifts in the marketplace. While these studies do not center on youth subcultures in the private school, they do spur questions about the nature of identity construction in an educational setting driven by market trends in an urban context that has and continues to suffer the effects of de-industralization and inclining levels of unemployment.

From the post-war period on, educators hailed co-education as the most natural approach to children's schooling (Tyack and Hansot, 1990). Claims that co-educational schools are gender-neutral have been undermined seriously by a spate of research findings that question the educational and social benefits of mixed-sex schools for girls.[18] Over the past two decades, support for the economic and social benefits of co-education has been challenged by feminist researchers and others who have argued that co-educational schools emphasize social interaction over academic achievement and block girls from achieving at levels competitive with their male peers (Jones, 1990). Research to date on gender and schooling has found that girls generally perform at higher levels in single-sex schools (Finn, 1980; Jimenez and Lockheed, 1989; Riordan, 1990) and that these types of institutions directly promote increases in levels of confidence, self-esteem, and locus of control (Cairns, 1990; Foon, 1988; Gilligan, 1990, 1992). Positive effects on women's affective development play themselves out in the form of higher educational aspirations, committed political involvement, and increased satisfaction with academic and social dimensions of college life (Lee and Marks, 1990). Altogether, studies index the single-sex school as an environment that is strongly supportive of academic and social opportunities and outcomes for girls because they are less conditioned by sex stereotypes and gender-based norms for academic performance and school engagement (Keohane, 1990).

Toward Re-definition of Identit(y)-ies

Shifting attention to girls' experiences in private, single-sex schools names and locates gender as a fundamental organizing principle of everyday life (Lather, 1991). Gender identities are shaped out of a particular location or positionality, where "the identity of a woman is the product of her own interpretation and reconstruction of her history as mediated through a cultural discursive context to which she has access" (Alcoff, 1989, p. 324). Subjectivity or identity is a matter of local positioning or, as Donna Haraway (1988) suggests, partial or situated knowledge where women validate their subject status as agents, themselves, of knowledge production. Nancy Lesko (1988) and Dorothy Smith (1988) remind us that the discursive construction of femininity is often a matter of the ways in which girls and women reappropriate and mediate cultural icons of femininity that sweep across popular culture in television, magazines, and newspaper advertising. Femininity is constructed by way of negotiating meanings about what it means to be female that swirl through these representational forms.

The public spectacle of an idealized, fictionalized, popular female self seriously threatens meaningful identity work for adolescent girls and adult women alike. Given these conditions, it is no longer possible to speak of identity as constituted in one-to-one correspondence with the logic of school culture and society. Borders of self-definition are unclear as students living in the midst of the postmodern condition struggle daily to build lives with and against a sexy, hyper-saturated and -mediated culture.[19] Mapping their way toward self-definition involves continuous negotiation of the lived contradictions that class, race, ethnicity, sexuality, and gender present against a challenging urban backdrop. Because identities are not unitary and static, changing in relationship to the contexts that individuals find themselves participating in, students are forced into the uncertain terrain of the borderland, that space that Gloria Anzaldua (1987) describes as "a vague and undetermined place created by the emotional residue of an unnatural boundary" where one "is in a constant state of transition" (p. 3). Different from the familiar usage of the "borderland" by post-colonial feminists who write about negotiating multiple identities at the interface of European and American cultures, I reappropriate this concept to describe the active repositioning of identities inside a school site of structural dominance.[20] Renato

Rosaldo (1989) reminds us that the borderland is that invisible site where a closer look reveals creative acts of cultural production. The narratives that Best Academy students, school officials and parents offer, take us into this newly named territory. As a predominantly white, upper middle-class, all-girls' high school, Best Academy is a site of dominance where discourses of whiteness, privilege, and femininity presume an undifferentiated school culture. Where dominant discourses define a united school front, conflict and contradiction remain virtually invisible to the naked eye. Put another way, the prevailing culture and ideology of private schooling filtered through dimensions of whiteness, privilege, and femininity paradoxically combine to create a site of absence. This complication introduces the possibility of complex and strangely meaningful identity productions where those at the historical center now find themselves actively decentering class, race, and gender locations as they work at becoming somebody. Whether girls' responses to the organizing codes of life in Best Academy involve reproducing or creatively producing existing structures and ideologies will decide the extent to which the content and authority structure of the private school shapes who they are. Their work opens up the possibility for critique and creative cultural production in multiple borderlands where none was thought to exist before.

To this end, chapter 2 works its way through school structures, curricular forms, and practices that organize social relations in the private, single-sex high school, looking for evidence of social class as one of the principle organizing codes of social relations at Best Academy through which other equally important and interrelated dimensions are filtered. As I point out, class dynamics are particularly difficult to see, a condition further complicated by the fact that class is generally unspoken and tends to be accessed through alternative categories of social analysis like gender, race, and ethnicity (Ortner, 1991). For those inside a class structure that is seen by most Americans as the universal class location, meaning that the middle class has come to be seen as representing everyone, it is difficult to uncover a dimension invisible to most people. Once brought to the surface, it is possible to raise questions about the conserving and constructing role class culture plays in the private school and the resulting implications for girls' identity formation.

Having sketched the broad outlines of life in the private, girls' high school, chapter 3 moves to the lived voices and experiences of Best Academy students as they begin to narrate and elaborate class identity processes. In a school whose historical mainstay has been the children of upper middle-class families, it is most likely that one would find youth accepting of class-based norms, values, and expectations. A diversifying class culture has, however, introduced competing forces and new dynamics among girls in the private school, planting the seeds for complex and conflicted articulations of class identities to develop along the way. To this end, I make a case for class as a border zone, where girls are actively reshaping what it means to be classed and gendered, repositioning themselves as upper middle-class girls in relation to meanings and social practices that have been presented to them.

Chapter 4 explores the constitution of race identities inside a predominantly white school where white girls engage their own particular struggles around what it means to be white in an otherwise "white-washed" educational site. In this chapter, I take seriously the notion that whiteness is a racial category that structures girls' lives—white girls as well as girls of color. Like class privilege, whiteness is a site of absence, doubly difficult to see because this discourse *whites out* racial difference, tension, and conflict (Fine, 1997). Among girls of color, a relatively underrepresented but vocal group in Best Academy, steps taken to guard as well as cross color lines emerge from the data. Students of color at Best Academy will narrate dual struggles around visibility and invisibility, positioning themselves at once separate and different from but also part of the dominant cultural codes in the private school. White girls also engage their own unique forms of borderwork. As they move into consciouness of what it means to be white, they begin to unearth the lived contradictions of race privilege in a school site that has worked hard at managing and containing difference.

Girls' future projections along trajectories of career, marriage, and family laid out in chapter 5 need to be situated at the frontiers of post feminist ideology and broader structural shifts in the economy. Internalizing messages around girls' academic potential and professional development for the future, girls educated in the private school tend to center salaried labor in their projections for the future. They begin to see that their plans for marriage and family might conflict with professional expectations, and find themselves raising questions about the viability of being able to have it all, in spite of messages floating through school and society that tell women they can have it all. We will also hear a remarkable realism in the voices of these girls who cast their desires for marriage in the shadows of separation and divorce, sounding strikingly similar in substance and tone to working-class girls who are looking to develop themselves as resources for their own survival in a moment of structural decline.

In chapter 6, we hear the voices of parents around issues of school choice and expectations for their children's future. Their narratives will be contextualized in terms of the lived effects of a changing economy on the upper middle class who begin to see that the benefits of relative privilege that they remember a generation earlier are no longer guaranteed in a time of economic dislocation and delayed gratification forced by a narrowing job market. This discussion will bring into sharp relief the felt descent of upper middle-class parents and their hopes that their children will be able to exercise control over the conditions of their lives in spite of very real dynamics that have the potential to limit the possibilities that membership in upper middle-class culture traditionally guaranteed. These chapters are pieces of a bigger story that come together in chapter 7 with a review of the main findings and implications of this study along with recommendations for meaningful work that has yet to be done as we continue to broaden and deepen our understanding of the complex realities of girls' lives in school contexts.

Chapter 2

Inside Best Academy:
Socialization in the Private Girls' School

In the history of American education, schools, both private and public, have performed a number of important functions, chief among them being the transmission of social norms, values and dispositions for the purpose of preparing school-age children for appropriate roles and interactions inside and outside school. Unlike the public school, the structure and coherence of the private, independent high school depends on building a collective cultural identity that draws students, faculty, and administration together in a common educational mission. The wide range of independent schools prevents one single definition that would be inclusive of the varieties of institutions from which families interested in sending their children for private education can choose. Despite characteristic differences, private independent schools tend to be organized around a set of cultural forms and practices based in a common history, traditions, and mission critical to the development of a spirit of community (Deal, 1993). Tight-knit relationships between individuals and institutions growing out of these cultural bonds shape the context for understanding youth socialization in the private school in ways notably different from processes of educational transmission in public education.[1] In her analysis of the educational project of Australian private schools as compared with public, state schools, Julie Kapferer (1981) observes that rituals and ceremonial practices play a central role in forging a solid school identity and strong commitment among students and school officials to the guiding mission of private instruction.[2]

> A comparison of the stated aims of public and private schools suggests that not only do the latter provide a complex framework for the socialization of their pupils into what might be called the cultural bourgeoisie, and public schools do not, but also that private schools regard the provision of such a framework as fundamental to the working out of their overall education project, in which socialization constitutes a recognized element of importance

17

equal to, but not greater than, instruction in academic skills. By the term "cultural bourgeoisie," I refer to the fraction of the ruling group that controls, dominates, and, in an important sense, owns (partly through consumer patronage, but also through public, professional activity) the means of educational production—the dissemination of knowledge, ideas, opinions, and judgments (p. 263).

Notwithstanding the fact that Kapferer centers her discussion of institutional culture in Australian schools, it is arguable that her description can be translated to analysis of socialization in American private schooling. Material and representational forms embed certain cultural codes that link social and cultural resources first distributed in the upper middle-class home with the cultural capital that is developed and rewarded in the private school. While socialization in the private school is geared toward building a conceptual bridge between the individual and their surrounding social context, it is oriented differently from transmission processes operating in the public school. Emphasis in the private school is on instruction in culturally specific norms, values and attitudes first made available in the middle-class home that are meant to develop those competencies that will equip students with the cultural capital for class-appropriate roles and social networks. As a conserving force, private institutions are deeply invested in the transmission of class privilege and exist as a primary socializing agency for reinforcing the aesthetics of middle-class family life (Bourdieu, 1974).

A commitment to the maintenance of class privilege is central to the socializing project of Best Academy. While social class is a salient structural dimension of life in the private school, I make no claim for its being the single most influential element of lived culture at Best Academy. I will argue, however, that it is the structure through which other constitutive discourses of gender, race, ethnicity and sexuality are filtered, mediated, and distributed daily.[3] Broadening the socializing mission of the private school to mean more than simply providing instruction in academic skills, this discussion will locate social class at the center of "an overall education project." In this chapter, I examine the formal and informal curriculum-in-use of class culture at Best Academy, looking closely at material and representational forms that inscribe and institutionalize class identity on school walls, in classrooms, rituals, and routines.[4] The fact that this analysis is categorically divided into a discussion of social class and gender frames organizing school culture is in no way meant to suggest that these are separate and distinct sites of identity production. Rather, I will argue that gendered forms and practices need to be re-viewed through a class lens in order to make sense of the ways in which female students are en-gendered by definition of the prevailing class culture.[5]

Socializing a Gendered Elite

Class Frames/Framing Class

The cultural reproduction of a class elite is as key today to social relations, meanings, and practices at Best Academy as it was at the establishment of this female academy over 150 years ago. Best Academy was founded in 1851 as a female academy, the first and only non-sectarian, private, independent high school for girls in this region.[6] In an 1852 address to the patrons and students of the academy, the first school principal, Dr. Findlay, noted that the school was "erected by the munificence and enlightened policy of the citizens [of the city], who have felt that something ought to be done for the education of their daughters.[7] Situated in the exclusive Parkway District, the school is an imposing, three-story, stone-colored building whose Gothic facade mimics the architecture of the medieval English college.[8] The school and its grounds occupy the greater portion of a long boulevard, where affluent homes extend downward in the direction of a nationally recognized art museum not far from the school. Entering the school doors on the morning of my first appointment with Mrs. Nicholson, the Head of School, I stood in a space where bourgeois privilege had been captured in time.[9] To the left of the front entranceway is the library, one of the largest rooms in the school, similar in prototype to the drawing rooms typical of nineteenth-century bourgeois homes. Portraits of former headmasters and headmistresses and mounted plaques dedicated to the memory of important alumnae dot the library walls, giving students the sense that they are part of a community that has long stood committed to educating girls.[10] Connections with the past branch out into classrooms, corridors, and administrative offices where students can feel themselves part of a legacy of class privilege through class photos, dotting school walls, of the "daughters of society" that have been collected over time.[11]

The appeal that Best Academy holds for the larger public lies in its history of providing a rigorous education for daughters of the ruling classes, and it continues today to draw its students mainly from a set of private, elite feeder and magnet schools within city limits. For an outsider like myself, the "community of memory" (Bellah, 1985) among Best Academy faculty fills in important gaps as teachers narrate their own experiences with the school and their perception of the role that it has historically and continues to play today for the surrounding community.

A.P.: What kind of community did the school historically serve?

Mrs. Berson[12]: Pretty elitist.

A.P.: Pretty elitist?

Mrs. Berson: Children of the leaders of the community and people with money.

A.P.: For how long would you say that it continued to serve that community?

Mrs. Berson: Well, when I was here, and it had broadened its base considerably or I wouldn't have been here, but I still think that it served the elitist community because all of the young women from certain families did come here. There just were additional women here, and I'm not sure for how many years that had gone on. It's just very, very different now. Now it really does serve a diverse community. When I was here, I think there were people from certain families who always had the expectation that their daughters would come here. They would have been at least half of each class of fifty girls, and the other half would have been sort of a rag-tag bunch of people who came for different reasons but very few on scholarships. They didn't get much aid then.

A.P.: What did their fathers do? Do you have any sense of that?

Mrs. Berson: Well, they were certainly businessmen, bankers, doctors, lawyers, and this was really the only choice then. There were Catholic schools, but I guess they were not considered of the same caliber, and this was *the* [my emphasis] school for women.

*   *   *

Mrs. Lewis: I went to St. Sophia's three blocks away. I graduated in 1965 from St. Sophia's. When I was at St. Sophia's, this [Best Academy] was the school where the debutantes went, the society, [the daughters of families that belonged to] the Park Lane Club and the Arista Club, and fathers of the Westwood Club.

A.P.: These are people who you would say lived in the immediate neighborhood of the school?

Mrs. Lewis: Well, I would say that the money in the city is in the Parkway District. I would say that the power in the city is in the Parkway District in that period of time. Some may have been in Whitehaven, some of it may have been out in Knoll Park, but primarily the power structure, the power in the city was centered in the Parkway District. This was, in effect, a neighborhood school for debutantes or for the children of the wealthy, and it was a first class school. You just, I mean in my growing up, Best Academy was never a possibility for me. Number one, because I was Catholic, you went to a Catholic school, [and] this was definitely a WASP school, and a Catholic didn't go to a WASP school. So, you know, this was never a possibility. As I said, three years ago was the first time I ever walked in the building. This school was . . . in the spring, you would see all the debutantes' pictures [in the newspaper], you know, that was the yearbook for Best Academy.

*   *   *

Mrs. George: [. . .] this school has always been rigorous, but it was also for a long time a society school, and I think the perception of it as a finishing school just hangs on. I know the city news will seldom publish an article about us unless they put it on the society page. And they don't do that to Hartford School [a neighboring, elite, private, co-educational high school in the local community].

***

Mr. Taylor: [. . .] I think our clientele has changed a good deal. When I came to Best Academy, there were people who actually said to me—"Oh, that's that snob school over on Knox Drive." And in the pre-70s, uh, most of our clientele came from one school, one [social] class. There were, they came from Eastmeadow School [a neighboring, private, elite, co-educational grammar school]. Eastmeadow girls graduated in the eighth grade. They had no choice. They had choices, but if they wanted to stay in town, their main choice was to come to Best Academy. They could go off to boarding school. Some of them did come to Best Academy for freshman year and then went off to boarding school.

Several female faculty had been educated in single-sex schools, and it was through this experience that many of them received firsthand knowledge of upper middle-class privilege. As an alumna of Best Academy, Mrs. Berson remembers that the school "served the elitist community because all of the young women from *certain* [my emphasis] families did come here." As a young girl, Mrs. Lewis attended St. Sophia's, a prestigious Catholic high school for girls that has historically existed as local competition for Best Academy, and explains that her religious and economic background prevented her from enrolling in "a neighborhood school for debutantes or for the children of the wealthy."

Students whose families live in the neighborhoods surrounding Best Academy have grown up knowing it as a competitive, prestigious private high school for girls. Girls from outlying neighborhoods and suburban areas, within and outside city limits, tend to hear about the school either through word of mouth or informational meetings with Best Academy Admissions staff who visit local schools throughout the year to recruit students.[13] Since independent schools, unlike other private schools, do not depend on church funds or on tax dollars for their operation but, rather, rely heavily on tuition dollars and alumnae contributions, they actively solicit qualified candidates whose families will have the financial resources to purchase a private high school education, or at least a sizable part of it, as well as individuals who would be likely to continue to support the school after their children have graduated. Structurally dependent on and highly responsive to market forces, private independent schools need to protect themselves against potential fiscal losses, and they do this through rigorous recruitment of middle-schoolers from competitive public and private schools in the local area. As part of these efforts, eighth graders at area sending schools are encouraged to spend the day "shadowing" at Best Academy with the expectation that their experience will inform their decision about what high school they would most like to attend and ultimately persuade them to apply here.

Reflecting on their experiences as "shadows," a number of junior students recall initially positive impressions of their first visit to the school because it reminded them of their own homes or provided them with a felt sense of community belonging. For several of them, the school either extended or substituted for the safety and protection they felt at home with their families. For others who saw themselves as privileged although somewhat less so than their more affluent peers, Best Academy offered them the possibility of association with a class culture that they saw being different from their own.[14]

A.P.: How did you first hear about Best Academy?

Dina: I didn't. Actually, St. Sophia's was my first choice for high school. And my mother said, come on, we are taking you to this open house at Best Academy. I was like—Best Academy, where is that? As soon as I like walked in the door, I like fell in love with the school. It just looked so exclusive, and I am that type of person. I love the exclusive stuff, like the carpet, the sculptures, the [grandfather] clock really struck me. I thought—wow—this isn't an ordinary school.

A.P.: What do you remember your mother telling you about this school [when she first mentioned it to you]?

Dina: She didn't. It was one of those days . . . they usually have open houses on the same days [as other private schools in the local area], and I think we went to St. Anne's, St. Sophia's, St. Mary's, and Best Academy on the same day, and Best Academy was the last stop. I was just like—wow.

A.P.: Did you meet some of the girls at that time?

Dina: Yes I did. But they are graduated now.

A.P.: How did they come across to you?

Dina: They spoke well as compared to other schools. The girls [at the other private schools I visited] seemed very timid and shy. And the girls at Best Academy were just very confident and were dressed really well, and they were polite. And they would just answer anything that I had asked.

A.P.: You mentioned earlier in our conversation that you like exclusive things. Why do you like exclusive things so much?

Dina: I don't know. I can't give you an answer for that. It is just in me.

A.P.: What else felt exclusive to you?

Dina: The [grandfather] clock, the population, the big study hall, the gourmet chef. Just the image that came across just from going through the open house made me want to shadow. And once I did, I was just like wow— because the classes were just so nice. The teachers weren't stuffy. They were like your best friends. They were really nice which really impressed me.

A.P.: Now when you say exclusive, what exactly do you mean?

Dina: The atmosphere and just the look of the school. I think if you stand across Knox Drive on the other side, and you look [at the school], it doesn't really look like a school. It looks like a house, a big mansion, maybe an apartment building. At first, I thought it was a boarding school. But then, of course, it's not. I don't know why. I just really like the carpets. You will never find carpets at a public school. Like I said, I had been at St. Sophia's [to visit], and they have tiles. Those places are dark. They seem like small, like the hallways are narrow. It just seemed like Best Academy was a big, wide, open community of love.

*   *   *

A.P.: When you first came to Best Academy as a shadow, what attracted you about the school?

Randi: Well, I came to shadow during the spring, so they had like signout Parkway privileges [students are free to sit on the Parkway Boulevard across from the school during their free periods when classes are not in session], and so I thought that was really neat. I like the idea that during your frees [free periods], you could pretty much do anything that you wanted to do. In my old school, you have to like sit around, and it wouldn't be productive, you know. I don't know what else. I liked the lunches. I like the small classes. Like now that I think about it, it's a lot more to look forward than look back. I am thinking when I am choosing colleges, I want pretty much what Best Academy is like. What I like about Best Academy is the small classes, the atmosphere basically, like small and like a family. I like the fire.

*   *   *

A.P.: What did you like about the school on the day that you came to shadow?

Wanda: The fireplace.

A.P.: Why did you like the fireplace, especially?

Wanda: It seemed like such a warm and cozy thing to have in a school, and you don't think of a school having that kind of thing.

For Dina, Best Academy takes on the aesthetic qualities of an upper middle-class home with its sculptures, paintings, grandfather clock, and carpeting covering the floors of the main interior vestibule. Girls, like herself, who describe themselves coming from upper middle-class families, see the school as an extension of their privileged lifestyle. Unlike Dina, Randi privately portrays her family as blue-collar, working-class whose standard of living decidedly contrasts with the relative affluence of her upper middle-class friends from school. While Randi draws clear borders between who she is, as different from the students represented in the school, she is able to imagine herself becoming *part of* the school, the class culture, and capital that it potentially offers. Irrespective of where students might fall in class affiliation and membership and the *habitus* that one's class background provides, Best Academy holds the promise that students from a range of class backgrounds can access the social and cultural resources valued most by the official school culture. Provided one gains access, once inside, students come to believe that they each have equal opportunity to compete and will be justly rewarded on the basis of deserved merit (Conforti, 1992).

Unlike the public school where community is regulated through a set of explicit rules, the private school encourages positive relationships among individuals through an implicit, organic commitment to collective solidarity (Deal, 1991). The sense of community fostered at Best Academy is spearheaded by routine rituals that punctuate daily life, reminding students of the specific educational project driving private school instruction. Bringing individuals together under the umbrella of a common mission, rituals create culture through shared meanings that have the effect of strengthening identification with and commitment to the school as a community. As they pass the norms and values of the official school culture on, rituals create and refashion cultural ties that link the past with the present and carry the school as a unified whole into the future (Bernstein, 1975; Henry, 1991).[15] At Best Academy, the school day begins each morning with the mandatory ritual of Morning Meeting, historically called Chapel.[16] Morning Meeting was reinstated the very same year that I began field work and became a daily practice from that point on.[17] For no longer than fifteen minutes at the start of each school day, the entire school gathers in the auditorium to hear a spate of announcements from students, faculty, and staff that cover scheduling changes, special events, and discussion of problems in the school. Morning Meeting often includes a student presentation organized around a specific theme like Women's History Month or Black History Month and most of these assemblies end with an obligatory sing-in led from the front of the room by the music teacher. While drawing students together for a few minutes before the hectic school day begins, this common time doubles as vocal practice for the school graduation in June in which all students participate. But most importantly, time is set aside each day for creating a sense of shared purpose and collective identification, basic to transforming a school into a community (Bryk and Driscoll, 1988). Faculty impressions of the purpose of Morning Meeting assemblies speak to the importance of building solidarity in private schooling through community.

> Mrs. George: It's [Morning Meeting] to bring the whole school together, to provide a moment of community at the beginning of the day, to reinforce some of the things we're trying to do around here. Sometimes it's educational. [. . .] And up until, through last year, we had Chapel, but only on special days, only when it was declared a Chapel day. The rest of the time, we weren't together in the morning. Attendance was taken in the study hall, and the girls went right to classes. So the point was to get together, to sing, to have some fun together, and so forth. [. . .]
>
> *   *   *
>
> Ms. Nelson: . . . the whole feeling of having the whole school in a room to catch up and to make your announcements. This is the first place that I have ever been where this is the way that the announcements are made. In an average high school, announcements are made over a PA system, an entity, a voice from somewhere. And there is a really great feeling about having everyone in this town meeting hall. That sort of feeling, as much as people may have not seen it because it's changed over the year [reference to the faltering sense of community among students and faculty directly attributed to this first year of a new administration], I think that's a really good feeling for a school.

As the first organized meeting of faculty and students each day, Morning Meeting provides, as Mrs. George see it, "a moment of community at the beginning of the day to reinforce some of the things we're trying to do around here." Her comment draws attention to the class codes that are distributed through these rituals, valued early on in order to shape a school community of "cultivated persons" described in a school catalogue published in 1852.

> Reliance is placed rather upon the mutual regard which naturally springs up between cultivated persons than upon any system of penalties for the violation of rules. The pupil is treated with confidence. She is encouraged to exercise self-control and to cultivate those graces of heart and manner which give lustre to the cultivated and refined woman.[18]

This statement suggests that there are "natural" values and norms that implicitly regulate social relations, styles of communication and interaction among upper middle-class students. Consideration, self-control, self-reliance and independence are attributes that are widely upheld by the middle and upper middle classes, and the customary singing of the school Alma Mater, written by an alumna of the class of 1910, captures core values that have remained constant throughout the school's history (Kohn, 1977; Brantlinger, Majd-Jabbari, and Guskin, 1996). Two junior students, Donna and Amanda, tie rituals like Morning Meeting and singing the Alma Mater to the reproduction of class privilege. Asking them about the ways in which class culture is emphasized in school, they quickly point to the Alma Mater as one of the strongest illustrations of the material and representational forms that class can take in the private school and around which much of school life is organized.

> Donna: I think like at Best Academy with [social] class, I mean, like they want us all to be upper class. Like look at the song—"lift us to better things, to worthy living" [a line in the Alma Mater] like the Alma Mater [reads]. As though everyone [who attends Best Academy] is like rich and has a country house.
>
> Amanda: That's the stereotype.

Along parallel lines, dress and displinary codes must also be contextualized in terms of the fundamental *class* project of private schooling. School codes for student dress and discipline decide appropriate behavior for students at *this* school and instill in them a commitment to an elite collective where they are taught that individual actions cannot be separated from a larger ethical responsibility to the school community as a whole. All entering students receive the student information bulletin which spells out the wider implications of individual actions.

> Each student at Best Academy is expected to be honest and courteous, to show respect for the rights and opinions of others and to conduct herself as a lady at all times. This often means going beyond a simple commitment to abide by written rules. In all situations, on or off campus, Best Academy students are encouraged to display the good judgment in behavior, attitude and speech that is the cornerstone of constructive relationships with others and which reflect positively on the entire school community.[19]

Norms and dispositions consistent with the cultural capital of the upper middle class run through this statement where school officials hold expectations for students to behave honestly, courteously and respectfully. While students are not required to wear a school uniform, the school information bulletin indicates that student dress should be clean and tailored, meeting standards of "common sense, neatness and good taste" that take into consideration "the needs and the rights of the community as well as those of the individual." School codes and policies teach students that individual actions can directly impact others. Aside from the fact that explicit codes for appropriate dress and conduct create a more serious context for school work, they are importantly part of a deeper investment in having students build positive relationships and a sense of belonging to an elite group.

Unlike many urban public schools where surveillance and silencing frame students' lives on a daily basis, private school structures are based more on implicit forms of social control that naturally grow out of the communal sense found there than on explicit regulatory practices (Deal, 1991). The student handbook spells this out clearly by emphasizing the centrality of social and community honor in relationships and interactions at Best Academy.

> The Social Code demands consideration for others, openness and honesty in all matters, politeness, respect for peers and adults and for their differences— high standards of human behaviors. The Social Honor Code forbids the taking, use or abuse of another's property without his or her permission, forbids the use of foul language, unkindness or rudeness to another. It demands sportsmanlike conduct in and away from school. It expects to give students in return for the acceptance of this responsibility, the personal freedom to make choices during the school day about how and where to spend free time—studying, socializing, working on a project with faculty permission—unmonitored—as long as that trust is not violated.

The social code regulating interactions in the private school grows out of an implicit contractual relationship between students and school officials where students who act responsibly in ways that reflect well on the school community and, by implication, their social class, are vested with the privilege of "personal freedom to make choices during the school day about how and where to spend free time." Along with access to most spaces in the school, Best Academy students have more freedom with their time than is now the case in most public high schools.[20] Free periods are structured into the school day, and students are able to decide how they want to distribute and dedicate this time.[21] The library, the main study hall formally named the Study Center, the computer room, and the dining room remain open throughout the school day for student use. During free periods, students are free to use the library for school work and leisure reading. I would often see cliques of students gather around the library fireplace mining the pages of magazines, trading impressions of the latest teenage fad, or simply stealing a few moments of sleep in an otherwise tight school routine. They also had the option of wandering into the Study Center which doubled as both a social and academic space. On any given day, students move in and out of both of these rooms throughout the day, with the expectation that they will "not be roudy or distracting to anyone who wishes to read or study there" (Best Academy Student/Parent Handbook, 1993–94).[23] Virtually all of the junior girls describe the relatively unrestricted use of school space as a privilege falling to students who attend a private school and link these "gifts" to the benefits of class privilege.

> Cleo: I think one thing the school didn't lie about is that they teach you to be like self-reliant because they give you a lot of freedom here. Like you are able to walk around during your frees [free periods] unless you've got proctored which I do now.

*   *   *

A.P.: What do you like best about attending Best Academy?

Mandy: Probably the freedom, like frees [free periods]. You can do whatever you want, sleep in the library. In Grant School [my public grammar school], I had a fifteen minute lunch, and a lot of the time a teacher might sit with you. So I really like the freedom here.

A.P.: Have you experienced this kind of freedom consistently over the past three years as a student here at Best Academy?

Mandy: Yeah. I mean, you can use anything in the school anytime you want to—use the computer lab, the library. Whereas in Grant School, you couldn't use the library normally. [. . .] We can use whatever we want in school. That's why I came to the school because I like the freedom so much.

*   *   *

A.P.: Briana, you said that one of the reasons that you like attending a private school is that you have freedom here. Tell me a bit more about that.

Briana: You couldn't, like here, you can have a free period. First of all, you drop your major subjects [most classes meet four times a week which allows for rotating class preparation for students and teachers], except for math and chemistry one day a week, and you get to do that. And when you have a free period, lunch or . . . you can go wherever you want. You can go to the library. You can go to another teacher's room, and you don't need a pass. If you would get caught in the halls in a public school in Knoll Park School [a public school], you would have to have a pass, and if you didn't, you would get detention.

*   *   *

A.P.: What do you think the school provides you with?

Shelby: Independence. When I came from Eastmeadow School, I was shocked at how much independence they gave us. It's like if you're doing well, you gain independence, and you gain responsibility and freedom. But if you're not doing well, you still have a bit of independence. But they [the faculty] put you, they put whatever restraint on you to make sure, to let you know that—listen you, you're not doing well, you're not going to get all these freedoms that everyone else does—and I think that's good. I, you know, a lot of people are like—I can't believe I am in proctor this week. I don't resent proctor. It helps me to get my work done. And I just don't complain about it because I don't mind it.

A.P.: How do you define independence?

Shelby: During our free periods, we're allowed to go wherever we want, you know. They trust us in this school. They don't think we're gonna be, you know, in the bathrooms, writing on the walls or whatever. And that we're just given freedom to roam around the school as we wish. And a lot of schools don't do that. I don't know of another high school who does that. They give you like a hall pass if you have to go to the bathroom or something. Our school just has a lot of freedom when it comes to being able to like, be at the school, like by ourselves or whatever.

*   *   *

A.P.: What do you like about attending Best Academy?

Diana: Um, let's see. I like hope we don't have to, like if we have a free period, we can do what we want. We don't have to like report to a study hall. People don't have to know where we are and what we're doing constantly. I like how they [the faculty] at least trust us enough to have like freedom and [to] control ourselves instead of having like, all the time, having someone watching us or something like that. And, um, I like the openness, like the open discussions in class. Like we don't have our chairs in rows, in all our classes. Like we don't have our chairs in rows. In all our classes, we have the chairs in circles so that everyone can talk to everybody and like get it all out.

As these narratives suggest, the broader socializing project of the private school frames the organization of space and time. Best Academy students openly value relative freedom to move through and appropriate school space and school time as free space and free time.[23] Not unlike Cleo, Mandy and Briana separate the private from the public school on the basis of these privileges. If students fulfill their end of the contractual bargain, then school officials follow through, as Shelby states, by "trusting[ing] us enough to have like freedom [. . .]. Unrestricted freedom to move through school is instrumental in teaching students to make decisions about the appropriate use of space. Help in making such decisions, though, is less a matter of explicit regulation and more an effect of internalized cultural codes. In other words, Best Academy promotes certain standards for best behavior and practice, and students are held to the exercise of self-restraint and self-control within the terms of appropriate socialization in an elite, private school and class-specific expectations for model behavior.

Freedoms around the use of space and time in school can introduce unexpected challenges for students who have to learn how to negotiate these privileges. Between scheduled class periods, students often populated the Study Center where they would typically slip into identities that double-crossed school expectations for behavior appropriate to "the cultivated and refined woman." Knowing full well that their freedoms are contingent upon their contractual responsibilities, Best Academy students still don't always follow the rules. Girls would often trade sexual jokes and innuendos otherwise not allowed into the formal classroom. "Acting out" typically consisted of teasing, innocent pranks, gossip and rough play where girls were able to forget for a moment *who they were expected to be* according to social codes and institutional policies. What this behavior suggests is that youth inside the private, independent high school are, at some level, challenging both written and unspoken cultural codes. By "acting out," they re-appropriate and transform school space and time to fit other identities that school officials have ruled out as inappropriate to the intentional world (Shweder, 1991) of the private school.

In the above narratives, students speak glowingly of the privileges they enjoy in an institution where academic and social responsibilities carry over into increased trust of students by school officials. A student population numbering under 120 in a small, contained school building makes it rather difficult for students either to purposefully violate school rules or, at the very least, to get caught in the act of breaking them. While there is strong evidence to support the argument that the structural organization and physical layout of Best Academy inhibits misbehavior, it is arguably the case that students have certain freedoms because of the expectation by school officials that youth from upper middle-class backgrounds can be trusted to "play by the rules." Faculty and staff are relatively confident that students are able to exercise self-control and self-restraint in their interactions with each other and with faculty. Free use of time and space in school is, in effect, implicitly monitored through assumptions of class-appropriate behaviors first learned and acquired at home and then reinforced in school.

Curriculum in Context

The academic program at Best Academy is based on a traditional core of subjects in the humanities and sciences, a liberal arts program designed to situate students well to compete for prized slots and scholarships in academically competitive colleges, to be successfully achieving students, and finally, working professionals. All students at Best Academy are required to take four years of English, three years of history, a foreign language, mathematics, and laboratory science, two years of physical education, a half year of health and visual arts, and a single year of training in the performing arts. The curriculum is dedicated to a cross-section of the western, humanist tradition around which students have available elective coursework. Like the curricula of private independent high schools in general, it provides an academic program geared toward shaping intellectual ability and moral character through rigorous academic standards and social service. The student information bulletin given to all entering students includes a message from the Head of School that captures the broad-based educational project of this private school:

> They [our students] find their voices in these critical years in a supportive environment in which they are asked continually to think for themselves and speak for themselves. They are accomplished and multifaceted young women who, when they leave us for higher education in college and beyond, have discovered and developed individual interests and skills through wide exposure to the performing and visual arts, athletics, and a myriad of co-curricular, leadership, and service opportunities to others. They have developed their critical thinking skills and are well prepared for the next level of education, their college years.
>
> Best Academy students are participants in social service activities and are leaders and participants in student government. They are team players and concerned citizens reflecting values of the school community. Emphasis on values and the importance of community is pervasive here.

Best Academy's commitment to developing critical styles of learning across the curriculum is consistent with the stated goals of independent education.[24] In her study of the stratification of school knowledge across five, class-differentiated elementary schools, Anyon (1981) finds marked differences in the content and delivery of curriculum and attributes variations across schools to the class orientation and clientele served in each educational context. Best Academy most closely approximates Anyon's description of the affluent professional school which she describes as a public institution serving a student population whose fathers are employed in professional capacities as doctors, advertising executives, and other occupations that fall squarely within the professional middle class. Annual family income in this school generally ranges from 40,000 to 80,000 dollars. However, the form, content, and presentation of knowledge at Best Academy most nearly articulates with her analysis of knowledge production and distribution at the executive elite school which she describes as a public institution consisting of students whose fathers tend to hold positions in the upper levels of corporate management. Annual family incomes in this population generally exceed 100,000 dollars. Classrooms in this school context emphasize the development of reasoning and problem-solving skills that translate what is learned in school into maximal educational returns for the future. Faculty perspectives on teaching students to be critical and independent learners deepen our understanding of the relationship between the curricular form, content, and presentation of school knowledge and the overall educational project of the private school as it is tied to class reproduction.

A.P.: As a math teacher, what do you think is the most appropriate knowledge for the girls sitting in your classroom to be learning?

Mrs. Adams: Well, this is changing. We have to deal with content because they have to take standardized tests. And they have to take achievement tests, and when you take achievement tests in math, on those achievement tests, there are certain topics. But more and more, I'm beginning to think that what we should be teaching is a process of thinking. And it doesn't matter whether I'm teaching it by using circles or whether I'm using a trapezoid, if I can get them to work with numbers and get them to understand numbers and have a feeling of how numbers work, if sometime later in life they want to study ellipses, and they never studied ellipses let's say, they could go to a book and understand how the math worked in order to do something with an ellipse. And they would know about substituting in equations and that sort of thing. But I really don't think an ellipse, let's say, by itself, is something you have to know. But you need to know the general techniques for working with math. And I'm beginning to do that more in class too.

*   *   *

A.P.: How do you define knowledge?

Mr. Fischer: [. . .] Sort of the things that you, sort of like the clay that you have to play around with. I mean, everybody can sit there with this big lump of clay in front of them, and that's the knowledge. What one kid does with it, doesn't really matter with the clay as much as what kind of kid they are. Do they come to it with a degree of creativity, thoughtfulness. [. . .] You need the knowledge, but the knowledge is just a start. [. . .] Really, it's my goal as a teacher to try and show them what to do with it, to try and fire a little bit of creativity, a little bit of thoughtfulness with it so that when they come up on lumps of clay later in their lives, when they pick up a book, or they're listening to campaign ads [a reference to the 1992 presidential campaign], then they can sort of look at that and make some astute judgements about it for themselves. I don't think that I am supposed to tell them what your clay looks like or what you should do with it. It's like I hopefully, I want them just to try and be thoughtful with it and decide what you want to do with it.

*   *   *

A.P.: As a history teacher, what do you feel to be the most appropriate knowledge for the girls in your classes to be learning?

Mrs. Lewis: How to find what they need to know. Finding. And to become an independent learner, that's my goal. To make these children independent learners. My goal is not to teach them the Declaration of Independence.

A.P.: Would you say that your goal is to give them a sense that they, too, have a participatory role in creating knowledge?

Mrs. Lewis: That everything is within their capabilities. Learning anything is within their capability. You just have to know how to go about it.

*   *   *

A.P.: What would you say is the most appropriate knowledge for the girls in your chemistry class to be learning?

Ms. Donohue: What I really care that they learn from Science I is that they are capable of doing real science, not half-way science, that they are capable of real, genuine, scientific investigation. That they leave here with that confidence—I'm pleased as pie. I don't particularly care if they can remember how to balance nuclear equations. The other thing that I would like them to leave with is knowing that science is process, not product.

Best Academy faculty overwhelmingly see learning as a process, shifting the focus in the classroom away from an emphasis on output alone in the form of measured achievement onto input of school forms and practices. Mrs. Adams understands that mathematics instruction should be geared toward developing critical thinking processes in her students, but admits that this change from a stronger framed curriculum and pedagogy where students have diminished control over the presentation and delivery of school knowledge to weaker framed forms for the presentation and delivery of school knowledge is only recent in her classroom (Bernstein, 1977). With this goal in mind, the social construction of curriculum and pedagogy in her classroom tends to be more "critically" oriented. After introducing students to a concept, she encourages them to work with a single partner or with a larger group on problem-solving. Shifting power relations in the classroom from a more strongly framed pedagogical relationship between student and teacher to a weaker framed learning context creates certain space for students to negotiate received knowledge, a practice that appears more in line with the curricular possibilities that private education seems able to put into practice because of the autonomy faculty in the school have over curriculum development and implementation. That students should be taught to question the underlying assumptions of received information in the classroom, particularly in science where information tends to be linearly presented to them as fact, is the driving force behind Ms. Donohue's insistence that students come to understand science as a process and not simply as a product. Much of the faculty believes that students need to be taught to question and challenge received information. Mrs. Lewis reflects this in her concern that her Advanced Placement American history class produce independent learners over the course of the year, a goal Mr. Fischer follows through in his English class in the way that he shapes his instructional role as teacher-facilitator. While it is not possible to generalize this finding across the curriculum, it appears to be a relatively consistent goal for much of the school faculty.

As is typically the case with independent schools, the curriculum at Best Academy is not subject to state regulation.[25] Teachers have relative autonomy over curriculum development and instruction. Despite salary levels that rank consistently lower than what public school teachers generally receive, they single out the freedom they have over curricular decisions as one of their main reasons for taking a teaching job in a private school.[26]

A.P.: How would you compare your experience as a teacher in the public school system with your current experience in an independent high school?

Mrs. Adams: [. . .] There's much more autonomy. I can teach pretty much what I want, because around here, we teach what we want and then we test on it. And so you don't have to prepare them for Regents [state-wide, subject-based tests] or anything, which makes it, makes it wonderful in that sense. Because if I don't like a topic anymore, I don't think it fits in the curriculum any more, I just take it out. You can't do that in a, where you're in a system where there's great hierarchy, and, well, you just couldn't do that [where] you teach what somebody else imposes on you.

                    *   *   *

Mrs. Harrington: [. . .] they give you the freedom to do things if you want to do them. It's so nice. I'm trying to work technology into our math program here. And instead of finding resistance, which is normally what you do when you are trying to do something different in a school, especially if you have a lot of faculty and administration that have been here a long time. [. . .] If I want to do something completely different that has never been tried before, they say—go ahead, do it, we will go with it, we have confidence in you.

                    *   *   *

A.P.: What do you especially like about teaching at Best Academy?

Mr. Schultz: Well, I especially like being able to play with the curriculum and being able to go with what the girls' needs are rather than well, you will study A-B-C. There was one class that the choreography was so incredible, that we spent probably almost two months on choreography, and we really delved into it. It was very, very exciting. And I could watch . . . the moment where I see that it stops and is not being contributed to, when it begins to become silly and a game, then we don't do it anymore.

                    *   *   *

A.P.: Would you say that you really enjoy autonomy here as a teacher?

Mrs. May: Absolutely. That is one of the things that I enjoy about this school. There is no one telling me what to teach and what not to teach.

An administrative infrastructure that supports teacher autonomy over the development and implementation of school curriculum should lend itself to greater possibilities for integration of critical pedagogy in the private school classroom. Giroux (1981), Apple (1983), Kincheloe and Steinberg (1995), and other critical educational theorists argue that educational reform depends on disrupting top-down, instrumental styles of learning and instruction typically found in U. S. public schools today, a condition that is especially prevalent among schools catering to working-class and lower middle-class populations. A strongly framed curriculum highlights the tight relationship between power and control exercised in schools (Bernstein, 1971), placing undue limits on student voice while undermining student ownership over knowledge production. The relative absence of critical, transformative pedagogies has sadly contributed to the marginalization and silencing of broad representations in American schools, both public and private (Giroux, 1993). Re-envisioning schools as public spheres where students are encouraged to exercise critique as a democratic right moves students to the center of educational process. At that same moment, teachers are forced to take the lived accounts of others more seriously just as they are directed toward inter-subjective examination of the contradictions in their own lives (McLaren, 1988; Ellsworth, 1992; hooks, 1994).

Across the curriculum, faculty *seem* vested in more critical approaches to instruction.[27] While autonomy over curricular development is a hallmark of independent schooling, it is also the case that teachers at independent schools tend not to take risks in their teaching. Since the private school seeks to prepare students to compete effectively in the college admissions game, it is worth speculating that school officials want students to master those skills that will maximize their educational and occupational attainments for the future and so they would tend toward more traditional instructional approaches that have stood the test of time. School forms and practices in Best Academy classrooms, however, raise questions about the extent to which independent education in Best Academy is *truly* independent in terms of creative, progressive and critical approaches to instruction. To begin with, the arrangement of physical space in most classrooms appears to work against democratic practices of student-centered teaching and student-directed learning. With the exception of English and foreign language classrooms where student desks are generally arranged in circles, most classrooms follow patterns that reflect teacher-centered forms of instruction. Speaking with Mr. Fischer, he offers a rather pragmatic rationale for choosing to seat his students in a circle.

> Mr. Fischer: For the juniors, I do this [arrange them in a circular format]. For the freshmen, I need a little more structure. For the juniors, they have a little more maturity, and they can deal with it. I almost want it to be that I am part of the circle, rather than I am sort of at the front of the class. I know it

sounds like I end up saying more than I should or even when they are giving presentations, I try to make it a point not to sit behind my desk but to sit looking at them or to sit beside them in a desk. I think those kinds of things make kind of subtle statements that maybe students don't notice consciously. [. . .] They like to be in a circle. They like less structure. Of course, they like more freedom the better when you're a teenager. [. . .] [But], I think it really facilitates discussion because you can see the people you are having discussion with. If you are in a circle, you can see them and talk to them.

Mr. Fischer reasons that the junior girls are mature and, therefore, do not have to sit in straight rows. They are able to *discipline* themselves, in effect, to exercise self-control and do not require orderly rows of desks to help them do that. He admits to wanting to sit inside [as part] of the circle with his students, a decision aligned with his perceived role in the classroom as teacher-facilitator. His example reflects attempts at rejecting top-down models of instruction that locate the teacher at the center and sideline the student as a passive learner. Arranging desks in a circle attempts to disrupt traditional forms of power that have historically structured social relationships in schools, leading to more schooling than education in American public schools (Spring, 1996) and private institutions. On the surface, it looks as though more democratic approaches to learning are ongoing in private, independent schooling. In Mr. Fischer's English class, this does, in fact, translate into more creative lessons that integrate student experience and validate student voice. Junior students make weekly journal entries where they respond to class readings in addition to critical and analytical essays that punctuate routine assignments throughout the year. Class discussion dominates most class periods where small classes and student-centered instruction encourage student voice and independent thinking based on the understanding that knowledge is co-produced, negotiated, and contested. These dynamics are played out in an in-class discussion of the film—*I've Heard The Mermaid Sing*—included in a unit on women in literature.

Mr. Fischer: What is the movie about?

Amanda: Finding yourself. Polly [the film's protagonist] is unsure of herself, but at the end of the movie, feels better about herself and sort of finds herself.

Mr. Fischer: Is Polly happy at the beginning of the movie?

Wendy: At the beginning, Polly is pretty settled, but she is not sure about it.

Mr. Fischer: What do you think Polly wants out of life?

Shelby: She wants to be invincible.

Lucy: Walking on water [reference to one of the fantasy scenes in the film] shows that she wants to be like a deity, to be able to take care of herself and everybody else.

Mr. Fischer: She is like a deity. Do you think that talking about art like the curator is something to be valued? Is it something that we should aspire to?

Victoria: That's just something she wants to do, her vision of being tres chic.

Shelby: No. What people don't have, they strive for. That's what they're saying in the movie.

Lucy: I don't know if I think Polly is happy. If she could, she would be like all the other characters. I don't know if that is happiness or not.

Mr. Fischer: I like your ambiguity about the film. Why does there have to be an absolute? Can't things be relative? In relation to gender, Polly questions whether it has to be right for other people what she decides to do—to sleep with a man or a woman. Inside of Polly, she, for instance, feels things more than people but is afraid to take chances. She does this with her photographs [by not displaying them publicly but only within the private space of her one room apartment]. She is not sure that she wants to lay things out on the line for people or not.

As the students work with their teacher to decode the film, it seems that students are being taught through this example that knowledge is open to a range of possible meanings, that there "does not have to be an absolute." Mr. Fischer makes clear to his students that the film is not reducible to one interpretation but that there are multiple ways that viewers can read it. That there is continuity between the presentation and distribution of school knowledge in some Best Academy classrooms and the *explicitly stated* curricular goals and orientation of private schooling goes without saying in this example. There is real doubt, however, as to the sustained commitment of school officials and faculty to critical pedagogy and its uniform implementation and integration across the curriculum.[28]

The presentation and delivery of knowledge in Mr. Fischer's junior English class is decidedly different from the structured packaging of information in American history class. In this class, students have daily reading assignments from one main class text where material tends to be presented as brief and fragmented facts strung together.[29] Information is distributed in lecture formant, while important names, dates, and events are outlined on the blackboard, giving students the impression that history is made up of an uncontested set of facts that unfold in chronological progression. The *form* of knowledge encourages students to respond in routinized ways by copying information verbatim into their notebooks. Multiple-choice questions dominate unit tests, giving the illusion of choice, where students mechanically identify terms, people, and events by matching descriptors in the "left-hand column" with corresponding descriptions in the "right-hand column." As part of their unit tests, they are typically asked to complete one or two short essays that require some synthesis and analysis of information.

Throughout most of the classroom situations that I observed over the year, faculty tended to emphasize the substance of knowlege rather than a concern with form. Instances where information was distributed in highly instrumental ways bear striking parallels with the technocratic form, content, and delivery of school knowledge found in working-class schools (McNeil 1983; Apple, 1983; Weis, 1990). In the Advanced Placement American History class, for example, there is decidedly less evidence of this as opposed to the general American history class described earlier. Under the direction of another faculty member, instruction there is less regimented by informational outlines, and students are more inclined to challenge received information, integrate personal experiences into class discussion, as well as to make independent decisions about what material to include in their notes.[30] Instructional material is, however, framed by the standardized Advanced Placement test administered to all junior students in college preparatory courses in public and private school systems and, therefore, is largely focused on factual information in preparation for the test. In this example, "teaching to the test" restricts the independence and creativity that might otherwise be operating in the independent school curriculum (Wilson, 1992).

Across the curriculum, there emerges a persistent tension between teacher-directed, technocratic models of instruction and more critical examples that emphasize substance while encouraging students to take a more central role in knowledge production in the classroom. Because teachers in the private school exercise greater autonomy over the curriculum, it is more likely that one would find a greater range of instructional styles and modes of presentation in the classroom. That there is striking evidence of attention being paid more to form than to substance in some classrooms, though, raises questions about the types of students that are being shaped in a school that holds out the promise of preparing critical and independent learners for future professional and leadership roles. As students talk about what and how they learn in school, the contradictions between the educational project of the private school and actual classroom practices begin to emerge.

A.P.: What is your favorite subject?

Shelby: Probably English because it's not just the fact that I like the class. English is like my favorite class. It's not like it's a better class. It's just that I'm more interested in it.

A.P.: Why do you find it more interesting?

Shelby: Because I like writing a lot, like creative writing. I think it's so much better when you can write than stuff like memorizing facts and things like that, so I like it a lot better. It's less like facts and things like that. It's more philosophy.

A.P.: What kind of knowledge are you presented with in your English class?

Shelby: Analytical. He [Mr. Fischer] likes to analyze, and he would like us to be able to analyze and to . . . like, when we read a book, not to just see what's on the outside but to see what's underneath it. He wants us to be analytical, philosophical about what we think, and he just doesn't want us to see what's on the outside. He wants us to see what's there in books, [not just] what's obvious and what's on the cover.

*   *   *

Dina: History is definitely a class that presents facts, and you have to learn those facts very well especially in AP History because you have to learn like in detail. [. . .] This year is very factual, and I just feel like we are learning facts. You can lock them away in your mind, but you can't really go further on them unfortunately.

*   *   *

Hannah: English class is more of a like—what do you think [class]. History class is "this is what happened." But, yeah, I think, I guess you'd say you make knowledge in English class. There's definitely more discussion, and even if Mr. Fischer has a different opinion than yours, he'll listen to you, and he might not think you're right, but he can see where you're going with it.

*   *   *

A.P.: Do you create knowledge in your history class or is it given to you?

Marlene: In Mr. Peoples' class, I think it's given to you.

A.P.: In what sense?

Marlene: Well, you have to read this chapter and learn this. I mean, we discuss things but not like how we discuss things in English class. It's very different. That's why I do so much better in English than I do in history just because I feel that I can relate to a book or a character in a book more than I can someone who maybe lived a long time ago. I am sure they had a personality, but their personality just doesn't come across at all in a history book.

*   *   *

A.P.: How would you compare your English and history classes?

Donna: History is more straightforward. Well, history is kind of like we are given information, and we learn it. There is a little bit of discussion on it, you know, the facts. You can't really like input and say—well, I think that's wrong [in reference to a fact] because that is not true. What happened, happened. And in English, it is more like loose interpretation, like um, you get into more discussions and have to put in your own input. Like there's a lot more discussion because there is a lot more to be discussed. It's kind of like it can go either way. [. . .] I guess it's kind of like ideas. He [Mr. Fischer] gives you ideas just like about life and some books like stories . . . you read about different people's lives, not just your own, so you are aware of other people. [. . .] You could get an essay wrong if it's about facts like history. Like you could have the history of an author, and you could be [either] right or wrong. You can't have right or wrong about your ideas or his ideas. You can interpret them in your own way. History, you can't really interpret in your own words.

What student commentary points out is that students draw borderlines between different subjects, describing history knowledge as uncontested fact and English knowledge as more conceptual and open to interpretation and debate. Donna sketches the differences in the way knowledge is presented in discrete content areas, describing history as a class where "we are given information, and we learn it" as opposed to English where learning is "more like loose interpretation" and students have space for their own ideas. It is worth speculating that this dichotomy grows out of the strong framing of knowledge as discrete content areas that seem to dominate in the private, independent high school. The discipline-centered nature of the curriculum qualifies it as a collection code curriculum where students study discrete subjects with very little interaction within and across separate content areas (Bernstein, 1977).[31] Across content areas, faculty are honest about the structural limitations of a small private school where little leeway in scheduling and a relatively small student body limit course offerings and present real obstacles to interdisciplinary work within content areas and across departments. While there is support for interdisciplinarity from the current Head of School, generalized resistance to collaboration across the faculty is not only related to constraints on faculty time but also grows out of vested interests in developing curriculum in their individual disciplines.[32]

It is also possible that more democratic forms of learning and innovative modes of instruction are less evident throughout the curriculum because of changed attitudes toward schooling among contemporary American youth (Wexler,1992). Faculty observe a decline in the pursuit of academic excellence, not only among Best Academy students, but among youth culture at large both in public and private schools, which tends to discourage them from adopting more progressive approaches to classroom instruction. Teachers note that a felt sense of entitlement swirls through student culture at Best Academy, an effect with striking parallels among youth in public schools.

Mr. Vogel: Um, the students are, they're lazy people, which is part of our . . . my job is to try to inspire them to work harder and expect more of themselves and perform better. But I think they have an—it's good enough attitude. If I'm getting a B, I'm getting a B+, my parents aren't going to gripe. I can go out on the weekends; it's good enough. Learning for learning's sake doesn't seem that important to most of the kids. There are some that are great. [. . .] There are some other students that are the same way. They really want to know.

A.P.: Do you think that this laziness that you have described is just something here at this school or, as a teacher having taught in other schools, do you see this as a current trend among students in general?

Mr. Vogel: It's a more general, I think, feeling in teenagers because I don't have any idea why other than because, um, I don't know, they seem to just expect to get good grades and do well and expect to just move through and have fun.

*   *   *

Ms. Donohue: [. . .] There are some students who are pretty borderline in whether or not they should be here because some of them are pretty borderline incapable of doing the work. And that's just not a good match because it's real discouraging to have to keep turning back D's and F's to a child who is trying. Students in general have academics much lower on their priority list than they used to. Way low. It scares me. It aggravates me, frustrates me. But they're still kids, good kids. Every year, they've got harder choices to face outside of school.

A.P.: What kinds of academic differences have you seen?

Ms. Donohue: I would say that there's a substantial lessening in the quest for excellence. We have a few kids who want the A, but they're not obsessive about it. And generally, if we can squeak by on the minimum amount of work, if we can pull a 70 on the reading quiz without having done the reading, that's okay. Next time, I'll do the reading, and it'll work out. That's very different from at least the first group of children that I taught here. And yet you have individuals who spend a vast amount of time perfecting violin playing or whatever it is. But overall, there isn't a passion, there isn't a drive for excellence, for mastery, for that deep level of enjoyment when you really immerse yourself in something, lend yourself to it, taken some risks in it, wrestled with it. I don't see that. And I wouldn't care if it didn't happen in [class]. But I would like to see it happen some place. And I don't hear them coming in and telling me that that's happening in other parts of their lives either. It's not just my [class] that doesn't turn them on, but neither does English and neither does what they're doing on the weekends and neither does, you know, nothing seems to have really set very many of these girls on fire.

A.P.: Nothing?

Ms. Donohue: Nothing. That's the concern. I mean, if they had a burning passion for something, anything, I would feel much happier about their futures. And . . . but again as I say, I have spoken with colleagues who teach in a variety of different schools, and they, they have generated that thought, before it was actually hearing them say it, that I recognized it as being part of what wasn't feeling right—why I didn't feel the same, why I wasn't able to do the things with my kids that I wanted to do.

*   *   *

Mrs. May: When I first started teaching here, if a student was absent one day, for a test, the next morning before school, she would come to me and say, Mrs. May, I know I missed the test yesterday. I can make it up today, third period, or something like that. The responsibility that the students took 19 years ago, or were willing to take, was far greater than the responsibility that they're willing to take now. And they, they were willing to do more, they were more willing to accept the consequences for what they did or didn't do. On top of that, they were motivated. They, I mean, if I gave an assignment, every kid in the class did it, and every kid did it thoroughly. [. . .] And I now find that the attention isn't there, the interest [isn't there]. Now, of course, I'm generalizing. There are students that don't do this...but the interest isn't there. The motivation isn't there. The willingness to do the work isn't there. The willingness to accept the responsibility for not doing the work isn't there.

*   *   *

Mr. Schultz: The youth culture. It's not just our school. I think most of what I am saying is true all over. They are a different student today.

A.P.: In what way?

Mr. Schultz: I think they have the expectation that they deserve it[things] whether they work [for it] or not.

These faculty articulate a waning sense of responsibility and desire for the pursuit of knowledge for knowledge sake among students who simply appear to "do school" without the goal of academic excellence driving them from behind. Changing commitments inside student culture at Best Academy are not terribly different from more general attitudes towards school engagement that faculty identify as a larger social problem across American youth culture at large. While teachers at Best Academy generally fix their teaching on honing students' critical and analytical skills around the independent pursuit of knowledge, it is possible that the changing nature of American youth culture, in part, forces a more instrumental presentation of information in the classroom than would otherwise be the case.[33] To a student population that is showing growing signs of rejecting academic excellence in favor of more technocratic and linear forms of learning because of its perceived exchange value, it is possible that Best Academy faculty are left with no other alternative than to strike a careful balance between technical and critical approaches to curricular form, content, and delivery in the classroom.

With an institutional commitment to reproduce an upper middle-class clientele of future professionals who will wisely manage and control knowledge production and distribution, it is no surprise to find values and standards directly associated with upper middle-class professions erected to contain the upper middle class while keeping others on the periphery of this class culture out. Tracing the historical rise of and importance attached to the professions among the middle class, Barbara Ehrenreich (1990) points out that the professions served as a protective hedge, containing this group while providing it with an economic strategy for upward economic mobility in the face of shifting market forces.

> Through professionalization, the middle class gained purchase in an increasingly uncertain world. Henceforth it would be shielded, at least slightly, from the upheavals of the market economy. Its "capital" would be knowledge or, more precisely, expertise. Its security would lie in the monopolization of that expertise through the device of professionalization. Its hallmark would be higher education and, with it, the exclusive license to practice, consult, or teach, in exchange for that more mundane form of capital, money (p. 80).

Inside the music room hangs a banner that reads—"Responsibility, Dependability, Promptness, Be Professional." A banner on the top of the blackboard in Mrs. Harrington's Course II mathematics classroom has this to say: Determination + Hard Work = The Way to Success. Both signs embody the broader educational thrust of private schooling, promising students that individual efforts can either result in outcomes of individual success or failure. The point is that all students have open to them the opportunity to compete for maximal outcomes in school, reflecting liberal principles of individualism, equality, and equity that have secured the meritocratic ideal of equality of opportunity in American education systems. As I have argued up to this point, the private, independent school plays a key role in transmitting the norms and values that define upper middle-class cultural capital. By acquiring training in math, history, and English, students develop and hone the competencies that they bring with them into school, transferring valued cultural capital meant to prepare them to satisfy the demands of new work roles in a diversifying economy (Riech, 1992). As one teacher put it,

> What we are also teaching in terms of our subject matter is dealing with just what you have to do from day to day. Getting your assignments done. There is a knowledge that you are trying to teach them that here is what you have got to do, so get it done for tomorrow. That's a practical kind of thing—you

have to be on time, you've got to be organized, put together. So there is a kind of knowledge that comes out of school that is the dealing with what you have to deal with today. Maybe it's homework here, or it's outside activities or in-school activities or sports, and that's a practical kind of thing. When you get out to college, you know, when you get out into the world, you have to go to work and be prepared for work, and that's part of the knowledge that we are trying to get across.

Students understand that if they work hard, follow through on assigned tasks in mathematics class and risk open competition with other students, then they will be recognized for their efforts. Despite coming to school with unequal social and cultural resources, once inside the school, all students come to believe that individual success will be fairly rewarded, reflecting a class reproduction model that argues that students internalize the just and equitable distribution of opportunities inside and outside school which institutional arrangements, themselves, legitimate (Cookson and Persell, 1977).

In earlier narratives, Best Academy students point out that while the norm of independence is typically valued among the upper middle class, it can create conflict for students who face the challenge of effectively managing schoolwork and other responsibilities in a college-preparatory high school. A junior class meeting with Mrs. Nicholson brings this felt tension into sharp relief. The fact that the meeting is convened in the library, a space that doubles as a site of learning and leisure, is an interesting context for discussion of the balance private school students need to learn to strike between school work and play. Among the many issues shaping the conversation that day is an emergent concern voiced by students over what they perceive to be a contradiction between the expectations of school officials and their understanding of what constitutes constructive use of school time. Ruth, one of the first students to address the issue, observes that "too much stress is placed on school work at Best Academy." Her peer, Lucy, elaborating on Ruth's argument through a pointed critique of her own, takes on the form and content of classroom instruction at Best Academy by criticizing the fact that students "are memorizing dates and facts [in school] instead of learning." Lucy's complaint is that the school seems to value breadth over depth of information by overloading students with too much knowledge in a con-centrated period of time.

Without wholly ignoring student comments, Mrs. Nicholson moves to her concerns over what she perceives is a decline in the level of student participation in the school extra-curriculum and is sharply critical of the tendency among Best Academy students to involve themselves in musical and sports programs at other local schools rather than invest in their home school. At that moment, Yvonne, a junior class officer and a rather vocal student, articulates what most of the students appear to be feeling from the annoyed looks on their faces: "this school is full of contradictions—there is so much to do but not enough time in which to do other things and develop a sense of commitment to the school." From Yvonne's perspective, school officials lack real understanding of the contradictions that can arise out of the institutional culture of the private school. Students are left with the responsibility of squaring these demands with the privileges that they had been trusted with by school authorities.

In a year of administrative transition marked by subtle expressions of student resistance to change, the new administrative regime had simply mistaken student efforts to negotiate and balance out school expectations for the emptying of school identity among what looked to be a disaffected student population. While the school administration and faculty believed that the students would be able to negotiate these challenges, their vote of confidence did not make the resolution of these emergent tensions any easier. Students did manage, though, to begin working through these conflicts by rationalizing the disproportionate amount of time they felt they had to spend on their school work. As they saw it, heavy acdemic demands and high standards would prepare them for educational and occupational success, maximizing life chances for them after graduation. In the final analysis, they valued a rigorous school experience because they were confident that it would lead to positive personal and professional outcomes in the future. Important to the argument being made here is that the scope of the educational project of the private school reaches beyond simply providing "instruction in academic skills" to a broadened investment in socializing the upper middle class to an appropriate set of norms, values, and dispositions that will secure their place in the prestige continuum. Attending a private school is seen as the first important step in this direction, and students who meet the challenge have no reason to believe that they will not be educationally and professionally rewarded for their hard work.

A.P.: What do you think Best Academy prepares you for?

Beth: I think it prepares you for college because this school is not the same as regular high school you know. They give you, it's harder. They give you more work, and that's preparing you for what you will get in college because college and high school are not the same. It's harder. They give you more work. They expect more of you, and that's what I think Best Academy is doing, so you can be prepared when you go to college.

Tess: Yeah. I think this school prepares you for just about anything you want to do. I know my friend Monica who went to Michigan State, she graduated from here. She came back, and she is like—this school really prepares you. She says especially like if you go up in the levels of work, like she was in calculus and stuff. She said it's harder in college, but it's not really that much more different when you first go. She said that this school really prepares you for it.

*   *   *

A.P.: What do you like best about Best Academy?

Dina: I think it's a great education, I really do. I think that anyone who graduates from Best Academy can go on to be whatever they want to be because it's such a name. It's like a presence, like colleges know who we are. I mean, I am sure . . . I don't want to offend anyone who has ever gone to a public school, but I think it's more prestigious to say—oh, I graduated from Best Academy, than to say—oh, I graduated from West High. You will get in better universities, nicer colleges or at least you have a better chance. And I think one hundred per cent of our girls go to college, and I think that's just great. Education is really important to me. My grades are really important to me.

*   *   *

A.P.: Do you think the school prepares you to be able to meet your goals?

Glenda: Yeah, I think so. I think it teaches you that you don't have to be afraid of what anybody else is going to think, that you should really express yourself. I think the school basically rewards hard work, so I think that they teach you that you need to work in order to get somewhere. You need to work to get somewhere.

*   *   *

A.P.: How do you think you've changed since you've been a student here?

Nina: Um, I think that I've learned to put up with a lot more than I used to. Um, a lot of times, I'm just like—oh, I can't take this. But I'm sort of used to it in a way, put in a lot of work and stress. And um, the only, one of the few, if not maybe the only good things I've really gotten out of coming here is that I've learned how to handle a lot of work and get it done under a lot of time restrictions. I mean, it's not always easy, and it's very stressful, but I can do it, and I know you have to do that in college too, so at least I'll be ready, unlike maybe some of these kids who go to public school who are just like— eh, you know, who cares. And then they get to college, and they're like—oh my God, we actually have to do work, go to class and stuff. So, that's one thing I think I've learned to do since I've gone here.

*   *   *

A.P.: What do you think you are learning in school here?

Shelby: Um, I think it's mainly, it's like preparing us for college and when we get on our own. Because if we went to, um, although the school's like there for you when you need help and stuff, it's also, it gives you a lot of responsibility which I think is good. Which, because when you go to college, there's no one going to be there, you know, if you haven't handed in an assignment. You know, and there's not going to be any one there that says that [to you].

And here they don't do that either. So it really prepares you for like, when you go to college.

These six students attach market-value to rigorous academic preparation and construct a rationale for hard work in school around projected outcomes for the future. In other words, they expect that a competitive academic program in high school will translate into educational and occupational opportunities in later life. As Nina points out, a rigorous daily workload and the ability to complete assignments under pressure in high school will ease the transition to more difficult academic challenges that lie ahead. Dina draws attention not only to the academic preparation but the prestige that follows from private high school training. Confident that she will be competitive in the college application game, Glenda joins many of her peers in believing that hard work will pay off.

At the same time, some students articulate that the struggle to strike an effective balance between schoolwork and other responsibilities risks blocking important dimensions of youth identity formation:

> A.P.: If you could change anything about this school, what would you change?

> Casey: I would change the amount of work that we get because I do honestly think that it is too much. Because at this point in our lives, we don't need . . . it is important to know what we want to do in order to prepare for college and things like that. But school should not become our total lives right now, I really don't think. We are at a point where we need to discover who we are as individuals, and school, being in the way all of the time with it, makes it really difficult.

What Casey identifies are very real contradictions that grow out of the socializing project of the private school. At the moment that the formal schematization of the private school holds out long-term educational and professional opportunities, students, in the short-term, criticize the school for blocking critical work around identity production. As Casey sees it, school knowledge has its limits and does not always stretch down to broaden and deepen students' felt notions of self, giving them a clearer sense of who they are becoming as a gendered elite.

Framing Gender: Through the Looking G-[C]lass

Lived culture in the private, girls' school arises through the close articulation of gender with class forms. Feminist materialists have cogently argued this point, attributing systemic inequalities based in the social relations of class and gender to material structures and conditions that impose limits over and create possibilities for women's lives (Jaggar, 1983; Apple and Roman, 1991; Roman, 1993). Centering issues of power and the structural organization of inequality in their work, they have raised important questions about the conditions of women's experience of oppression. As field work progressed from the time that I first entered Best Academy, it became increasingly clear to me that gendered meanings and social practices were bounded by prevailing class forms in educational context. In order to understand what adolescent females speak and act on, I turned to class as a meaningful lens through which to decode the educational project of socializing *girls* in the private, girls' school.

In a school where enrollment scarcely reaches above 120 students, it is possible for students to develop close-knit relationships with their teachers. Demonstrably warm towards a number of faculty, they frequently embrace favorite teachers, many of whom they see as more friends than distant, disembodied authority figures (hooks, 1995). The culture of the single-sex school encourages students to build close relationships with teachers and peers based on an ethic of care, not unlike research findings that support girls' tendencies towards relational and communal styles of learning and social interaction (Noddings, 1988; Gilligan, 1990; Riordan, 1990). As I walked the halls and sat in classrooms throughout the year, not a day would pass that I would not see girls comfortably walking arm and arm, hugging and sitting on each other's laps. The importance that adolescent girls' attach to female friendships has been widely discussed over the past two decades, particularly around the benefits of friendships for adolescent girls' social and psychological development (Epstein and Karweit, 1983; Gilligan, Lyons, and Hanmer, 1990; Leadbeater and Way, 1996). When one student asked Lucille Clifton, a noted African-American poet, who spent a day at the school as a visiting artist, for her thoughts on girls being educated together, she spoke to the sense of relatedness and connectedness that girls' schools nurture.

> Most places, schools included, give you what you are allowed to take. In a school with all women, one doesn't have to worry about male-female chemistry taking over. The strength of school is in learning something about bonding.

In my conversations with students throughout the year, they repeatedly pointed to their female friendships as defining parts of their school experience, in some instances naming these relationships as more important in their education than in-class instruction.

> A.P.: How is what you learn from your friends different or the same as what you learn from your classes?

Shelby: From your friends, I think everything that you learn is more, you remember it, it's more important to you because your friends, to me at least, my friends are the most important things right now, and school is obviously not the most important thing. But what you learn from your friends is more what you are going to be using in life, I think. What you learn in school, you are like, uh, I don't think I will be using that. Just put that way back in your head. But what your friends teach you is gonna like stay right there and be used and remembered.

A.P.: What do your friends teach you?

Shelby: In my classes . . . I feel like life, I learn more from them than I do from my family, than I do from my teachers. We learn more together because we experience things together, and you know, we learn more because we are experiencing things. At school, we aren't experiencing things. We are writing things down, you know. We are just having them talked at us.

*   *   *

Donna: I think I found love like with my girlfriends, I would say, more than [with] boys.

A.P.: Do you mean you found a deep connection with your girlfriends?

Donna: Yeah, like they are like part of me. I can't imagine living without them. Like if one of them, like if I am without them, because we spend every, like every minute of my life, I am with one of them, it seems. Like we live with each other. If I do something, I'm thinking about—oh, what's she doing.

*   *   *

A.P.: Is there anything else that you like best about attending an all-girls' school?

Michelle: I think the close friendships that I have, even though at times, a lot of times, it's really annoying. But still I probably have a group of twelve people, that I am really close with. I think in a public school situation or a co-ed situation, the people are more like measured in how they act around you all the time because there are always guys there. There are some girls who are always flirting. And here you don't have that kind of superficialness that you always have. It makes you almost more honest. I've got a lot of friends at Whitehaven and my friend [there] is a guy, and he hangs out with probably seven girls all of the time. All of the girls are like flirting all of the time.

*   *   *

A.P.: Why do you feel that your friendships are more important than school?

Marlene: Well, because friendships with other people last a lot longer than school does. And, you know, if you like can't get a job or something, it's more

important to have friends who support you than to have all of this knowledge and just be out in the middle of nowhere with nothing to do and be
homeless.

*   *   *

A.P.: As women, are friendships important to you?

Casey and Lucy: Uh hum.

Casey: Because I think that women need the support from other friends.

Lucy: From other women because women can tear down other women so
easily. And that's just the mentality of this country which I will say is run by
old, white men. They are going to sit there, and they are going to perpetuate
this against us. And it's awful when women fight against women. Women
just really need to be [to stand] together.

For Shelby, her peers are the most meaningful part of her school experience,
seeing them as a group with whom she is able to share intimate dimensions of
her life and to learn more about herself through others' realities. Cultivated
friendships are invaluable, she observes, because we "learn more because we
are experiencing things together." Book knowledge acquired in the classroom
leaves less of a lasting impression on girls than their friendships during these
school-age years. For Donna, female friendship is equated with love which she
understands as a deep and abiding connection that cannot be found and
duplicated in male-female friendships and relationships.

Since girls don't feel pressure to compete for boys' attention in a girls'
school, a climate of trust and honesty is fostered and encouraged. The fact
that there are no boys sitting next to them in class keeps girls like Michelle
from being distracted from their school work, at least in the immediate
classroom context. This is not to argue that girls were not interested in
fashion, cosmetics, boys, and dating. Magazine clippings of the latest adored
teen idol or fashion model—the underworld of female fantasy—littered
students' desks in the Study Hall, and talk about fashion and boyfriends
peppered girls' conversations in the Study Hall and library during free periods
and the cafeteria during lunch. Without exception, junior students share a
vision of the single-sex high school as liberating for them. Describing what
most attracted them to attending a single-sex school for four years, they
collectively agree on a felt sense of having been emancipated, however
temporary, from the close and constant scrutiny of their male peers in ways
that allow them to imagine the conditions of their lives stretching beyond
traditional roles and expectations.

Bella: I guess I like the fact that you can come to school, and you don't have
to worry about what you look like. That's good. And it's true what they say

about less competition. Since I have gone to school with boys, teachers, especially like female teachers, tend to favor like boys. And I mean, boys are always like louder than girls too, you know. So usually, they get most of the attention in classes. And I think that I am doing better, that I am learning more in an all-girls' school because I can also, I can focus more on learning.

*   *   *

Lucy: I like that I can come to school looking awful, and there's nobody that's going to say anything about me. Or no one's going to be, you know, talking behind my back because everybody else looks the same way. Um, and I like that this school isn't, it doesn't have to be policed because it seems like when it's a co-educational school, you know, you have to say no running in the halls and all of this. And I don't know anyone really at this school who wants to run in the halls or wants, you know, I mean, we're just very . . . we take care of ourselves. And if there were boys here, I don't think it would be that way.

*   *   *

Donna: Well, when we had vacation awhile ago, we had a Friday off or something. I went to Clinton High School [a public, co-educational high school] with one of my friends just for the day. And it was really interesting because like, you know, between classes, the girls go to the bathroom and do their hair and their make-up and everything. And I kind of found it funny because I couldn't imagine myself doing that here.

A.P.: You never see girls in the bathroom at Best Academy doing any of that.

Donna: Yeah, and if they are, they are changing from their pajamas into their clothes [laughter]. [This refers to one of several specially scheduled theme days at school that involved students going to school in their pajamas].

A.P.: That's right.

Donna: But really, you don't have to worry about the image thing so much. Because if you want to look nice, you wait until you go out. I mean, you can look nice for school if you feel better about yourself doing that. But it's not a thing where you have to always look perfect, and you have to worry about what the guys are going to think of you . . . things like that. I mean, in classes, I was never one of those people that would be afraid to say what I was going to say because there was a guy or something like that who would disagree with me. Like that never bothered me, you know. But I can see that in a lot of the classes, it did bother a lot of the girls. I guess that is eliminated by coming here.

*   *   *

Hannah: [. . .] There's no guys here. It's like, that's the best part, and it's also the worst part.

A.P.: What effect does having boys in school have on girls, do you think?

Hannah: I don't know. It affects girls. I mean, there's a guy sitting over there. Whether he's cute or not, he's still a guy, and he's like, I mean—what if he's looking at me, what if I don't say something right, what if I stumble, and he laughs at me. And it's worse if you do like him, and what if he doesn't like smart girls, you know. I mean, I don't think I'd get into that kind of thing. But I think some girls would. I mean, I know some girls would. But it's easier. And another thing—I keep hearing that teachers pay more attention to guys. You don't have to worry about that here because they have to pay attention to you.

                    *   *   *

Randi: Um, being able to get up at quarter to seven and getting here at like 7:30 a.m. and not having to worry about the way that you are dressed, whether you've got make-up on or if your hair is done. That's pretty much it. You are more relaxed. We were talking in English [class] the other day. We read a poem. I can't remember who it was by, but it was called "Pretty," and it was all about female issues. If we were in school with other guys, we probably would be able to say that [some of the things that we talked about], but we would have to defend ourselves versus them, against the guys. We wouldn't be able to talk freely because they would be like—well, no, that is not true.

Best Academy students are not unlike adolescent girls in general who tend to be consumed by dating, hair, clothes, physical appearance, and sexuality that typically organize girls' adolescent subcultures. Around these issues, they are no different from their female friends in both private and public co-educational schools. Yet they separate themselves from their female peers in mixed-sex schools, who seem to them, hostage to the cultural artifacts of romance. Their perceptions reflect the importance that adolescent girls invest in their appearance, because of and not simply in spite of boys, in their school experiences where attractiveness comes to represent a "commodity of value in an ongoing 'sexual auction'" (Holland and Eisenhart, 1990, p. 96). Best Academy students do speak about the importance of "looking nice" when they "go out," but their identities as young women do not appear to be as dependent on their bodies as studies of the relationship between body image and gender identity formation have shown to be the case (Gilligan, 1992; Fine, 1992). Attractiveness is no doubt valued in and of itself, but it is not a necessary condition for having a relationship and developing self-esteem and self-worth. As Donna describes it, attending a girls' school is different from being a student in a co-educational school "where you have to always look perfect, and you have to worry about what the guys are going to think of you." What Best Academy girls suggest, in contrast, is that the single-sex school undercuts the material commodification of girls' cultural forms, leaving them feeling more in control of who they are and less a reflection of who they have been made up/out to be as girls in social and cultural context. Girls' struggles around coming to voice do not completely disappear in the single-sex school, but they are noticeably diminished as girls' move into the center of the school universe (Gilligan, 1992). Comparing what she knows of all-girls' schooling with her own firsthand experience in a co-educational, public grammar school, Bella points out that the absence of boys in the classroom eases the struggles that girls typically wage around having their voices heard and validated in the mixed-sex classroom (AAUW, 1993). Her sense of relief is echoed time and again in interviews with other junior students who reflect on the liberal amounts of attention and intellectual validation they see students receiving, and benefitting from, in an all-girls' school. As Hannah reminds us, "you don't have to worry about that [teachers paying more attention to guys] here because they have to pay attention to you."

Given time off from the reifying practices that have historically positioned females as objects of the male gaze, Best Academy students are able to point to the academic and social advantages of their school experience, distinguishing it from their peers' education in public and private co-educational settings. Separating themselves from *other girls* who go to school with boys, they define a Best Academy student through constructed notions of *difference*.

A.P.: What do you think you are learning here at Best Academy, not only in an academic sense but more broadly speaking?

Donna: I think that you are learning like to be a strong person and like not afraid of anybody or anything or let anybody tell you what you can't be. I mean, it sounds like a brochure, but it really is true. It really does sound like—we will teach your daughter. We will give you a leader. I think it does, though. You know, I was telling you during lunch how people think that we are like different. We are different from other girls.

*   *   *

A.P.: How are you different?

Donna: Well, because it teaches you, like, you know, you have to raise your hand and stuff. It forces you to participate. First of all, it teaches you that you can't be like antisocial or like not answer. You can't . . . it's impossible. And then like it teaches you to be part of a community. So it's not like you are going to go into the real world and have no idea how to relate with other people even though we are kind of secluded from everyone else. You still get a general feeling for relationships, I guess. [. . .] When we go out sometimes, like look at us now [referring to her peers at a focus group interview]. We are all [look like] scumbags. All the girls we know, like they get jazzed up [for a baseball game]. We are like different [in that way]. Guys look up to us in that sense. I think guys respect us a lot more. They look at us like positive girls;

like with the other girls [girls who attend co-educational institutions], they are like—I want to hook up with her, oh, she is sexy.

*   *   *

Casey: I like the attention that is put on us. I like the fact that we don't have to compete against guys for attention, for, you know, can I answer this question, raising hands in class. I think also just because of the nature of women. It's easier to just speak out and not have to sit there and be like—should I say this. People just speak, you know. I like that. It's interesting because when I went to visit Central High just for the day, I remember sitting in class, it was an English class, and they are all sitting in a circle, and then they were talking about this book that we had already read [in our English class here at Best Academy], the *Scarlet Letter*, and I was like, and I opened up my mouth and started blabbing away. People were looking at me like you didn't raise your hand. I was like—I'm sorry, I didn't know that I had to. It was interesting. But it's a lot more free and easy, I think, here. And then again, people don't come into the school trying to look all dressed up and everything for the guys. [. . .] You are not looking good for anybody. So, it's easy in that way, in terms of how you look. There's no stresses on that [. . .].

As adolescent girls narrate themselves being *different from* other girls, they script a culture of femininity that sees no contradictions between being female, feminine, and high achieving students. A context that nurtures girls' positive school engagement gives rise to a stronger self-concept, such that Donna can argue that "guys respect us a lot more" and "they look at us like positive girls." Educated girls are "positive girls," young women who *model* restraint, strength, independence, initiative, and leadership. Donna goes on to explain that "they [guys] look at us like positive girls; like with the other girls [girls' who attend co-educational institutions], they are like—I want to hook up with her, oh, she is sexy." When I asked Donna's friend, Shelby, whether she sees herself as a woman or not at this point in her life, her response is straightforward, seeing herself as a woman because of her sense of independence and tracing this to the ideology driving the culture of single-sex schooling.

Independence. I'm not going to back down like when a guy, um, I'm not intimidated by men. I have three brothers, so I understand that they are human beings, and that, you know, they're not better than women. And so I think it has a lot to do with school, that . . . with this school. That, you know, that they've taught us that being a woman isn't inferior to being a man. So, yeah, I'm not like intimidated by men at all.

Adolescent girls' identities take shape not only in opposition to boys but also in ways decidedly different from girls in co-educational public and private schools, where it appears that a female identity is constructed on the sexual auction block, in direct relationship to traditional requirements for attractiveness that have been defined for women by men (Holland and Eisenhart, 1990).

Wide-ranging support for girls' intellectual and moral development is knit into the cultural fabric of the school through a variety of iconographic forms and images. Entering the library, it is impossible to miss the stately portrait of Ms. Lyons, headmistress of the school for 49 years of its history, hanging over the fireplace. Her portrait embodies the moral character of nineteenth-century bourgeois women educated for the purpose of being able to instruct their sons, but it also captures the historical shift from the cult of true womanhood to the ideology of access and equality of educational opportunity driving the movement for girls education in the mid-nineteenth-century and beyond (Bloch, 1978; Woloch, 1984). Signs directing young women towards future opportunities that have been historically closed to them stand out in many classrooms in support of girls' intellectual and moral growth. Posters reading "Famous Mathematicians" dot the wall of a mathematics classroom where girls can read about accomplished women in a traditionally male-dominated field as they run through theorems and mathematical problem-solving exercises on the blackboard. In that same classroom, decals on windows at the back of the room name reputable women's colleges like Smith, Barnard, and Vassar among a host of other schools that Best Academy students might compete for places in after graduating high school. Signs that read "Celebrate Your Own Uniqueness," "Great Visions Often Start With New Dreams," and "Women Worth Knowing About" cover the walls of a chemistry classroom. These are the words and images that female students hear and see built into the structure and daily routines of life in a girls' school, whose explicit messages are reinforced throughout the year by female authors, poets, artists, performers, and politicians regularly invited into the school to share their talents with students and faculty during scheduled Activity Periods. While each of these accomplished women have individual narratives to tell, they unite around the common theme of equal access and opportunity, modeling opportunities for girls to exercise the cultural capital they have acquired as a gendered elite.

During one celebrated event honoring a distinguished alumna of the school, a Justice of the Appellate Division Supreme Court, students, faculty, alumnae, and patrons of Best Academy heard her speak to the imperative of women taking the lead in building a more just and equitable world as part of a larger vision of corporate restructuring. The judge attributed incipient changes in the culture of work to women's leadership styles which she suggested could bring about effective change on a broader scale. Women taking on leadership roles in their professional work and through volunteer work in their communities is typical of what Ostrander (1980) found among the upper middle-class women she studied. Single-sex education stands ready to develop in girls these particular kinds of skills. A segment of radio publicity issued for the 1992–93 academic year speaks to this, sounding the intellectual, social, and moral advantages of all-girls' schooling in order to attract prospective candidates for admission.

> You provide the daughter, and we will provide the educational opportunity to excel. Best Academy provides the education necessary to send young women onto higher education and into the world with the knowledge, skills, and attitudes required to become leaders. A study conducted by the American Association of University Women documents that girls receive significantly less attention from teachers than boys when they share a classroom. Best Academy is a non-sectarian, independent high school for girls. Scholarship, leadership, and sportsmanship for young women is our top priority. Our graduates continue with higher education, attending colleges such as Princeton, Yale, and Georgetown Universities. Visit Best Academy and see how a young woman's intellectual, social, moral, and creative strengths are recognized, supported, and appreciated.

Best Academy advertises a curriculum that provides girls with certain "knowledge, skills, and attitudes" that can translate into access to a wide array of opportunities where women are able to exercise power through voice and action. Socializing a gendered elite lies at the heart of this school advertisement, a sure indicator of the educational project of the upper middle-class girls' school. The organizing principles of girls' education cannot be understood apart from a class frame where those on the outside looking in see socialization as the transmission of appropriate attitudes and behaviors toward the maintenance of upper middle-class power and privilege. As the radio voice goes on to explain, "graduates continue with higher education, attending colleges such as Princeton, Yale, and Georgetown Universities" which promise wide opportunities for women to achieve positions of leadership and power in their future adult roles.[34] Admission to Princeton, Yale, and Georgetown Universities are likely outcomes of the reproductive models that shape private school interests. Gender identity formation in school context is, in part, a matter of priming adolescent girls to represent and carry the partial interests of the upper middle class forward into the future.

While girls' intellectual, social, and moral development factor into the formal schematization of the girls' school, it is also interesting to see the extent to which gender remains a muted category of social life. As one teacher describes it, past attempts by faculty to integrate the study of gender-related issues into the formal curriculum have fallen short, generating rather benign interest from students.

I don't see that [an interest among the students]. We tried to introduce in the history curriculum, a women's studies component. We tried whenever we could in the history department to emphasize the role of women. It was tough because there wasn't much material that wasn't radical or extremist at that point to do [present in class]. There was no initial interest in the first place, and what interest there was dwindled and waned, and we dropped it. [. . .] I recognize the need for it. I try to do what I can. [This teacher refers to an assignment that he had given to the class in which he had asked the students to put themselves in the positions of two notable women in history that had been featured in class lectures and to write a brief essay from the perspectives of these two women in relation to their circumstances]. They handled that assignment pretty well. But did they like it? No! It was just another thing they had to do, and so lighting the fires under them takes awhile.

The students' lack of interest in this classroom exercise reflects on some level how easy it becomes to take gender for granted as a social and political cateogy of analysis in a girls' school. Students are not unaware of women's historical exclusion from the mainstream history of Western civilization since their narratives suggest just the opposite. It is simply to point out that gender can slip into invisibility, just as being white and upper middle class can, at times, be relatively unnoticeable dimensions in a largely white, upper middle-class, all-female school. On several occasions, students mention that gender is an "unspoken thing at school." As they see it, the very fact that they attend an all-girls' school eliminates any need for formal discussion of this category.

A.P.: Do you think the school deals enough with gender issues?

Cara: Um, well, we're doing a whole, I mean courses, the English courses are very to the feminist side, with its female writers and, um, I think it's dealt with the right amount. I don't think it should be overly stressed.

A.P.: It shouldn't be overly stressed? What do you mean by that?

Cara: No. Because it's not the point to say . . . like when we did our race, our racial unit in English [class]. I think it was overly stressed. But the feminists, it's just, the view in this school is that we're all here to go to college and make something of ourselves. It's kind of an unspoken [issue] that of course we can do it.

A.P.: As women, you mean?

Cara: As women, I mean, it's not even said. You don't think—oh, well, we're women, and it's really great that you're in an all-girls' school because that'll make you better than men or something. That's not the feeling. It's just that, well, you're here, and the fact that you're women has nothing to do with the fact that you're going to go out, but it's great that you are [women] anyway.

A.P.: Do you think gender issues are discussed enough at school?

Lucy: I don't understand, what do you mean?

A.P.: Do you think in your classes that you discuss gender issues enough, issues centered on feminism and the women's movement, for instance?

Lucy: There is no reason to.

Casey: Yeah, I don't feel the need for it.

A.P.: Because you attend an all-girls' school?

Lucy: [Shaking her head—Yes]. And there is no person to compare us to. Like he [some boy] is getting better treatment than men, because there are no guys at Best Academy.

Because boys are not around as part of the daily school routine to remind girls of the ways in which patriarchy has historically and continues to organize gender relations between boys and girls at home and at school, their place of work, gender paradoxically pales as a key structural dimension of life in the all-girls' school. When I asked for teachers' input on how teaching in an all-girls' school influences their approach to teaching, they tended to attribute more individualized forms of instruction in their classrooms to small class size and the virtual absence of disciplinary problems than to conscious intention on their part to tailor instruction to learning styles that have been found to be most effective in teaching girls (Belenky, 1986; Burke, 1989; Mickelson, 1989).

> Ms. Adams: Uhm, in my subject, I think the girls part of it, is more the style of the classroom. I mean, I . . . in English, they try to, in authors, and in history, they try to deal with people. Maybe Pythagoras but not many other people who came up with the theorem about something or other. Nor does it matter whether it was a man or a women or even in what century it happened. So, uhm, but to tell you the truth, I don't know how much of what we do around here has to do with girls as opposed to smallness. I mean, I think if I had a class of seven boys, uh, I might run it very much the same way that I run a class of seven girls. I'm not sure—I've never had a class of seven boys, but I think some of the letting them work together, well, you've seen how I sort of stand in the background too, and I think the size of the class more than the fact that it's all-girls, that that works. Uhm, I think maybe that girls are maybe a little more willing to cooperate, maybe stand back and let others take a lead than boys would be. [. . .] I think that a girls' school . . . I think in math and science and computer, girls are probably less intimidated, not probably, I know they are, dealing with just other girls, than they are if they had boys in the class. But I don't know, as far as my teaching role, whether that plays a big, a big role.

*   *   *

A.P.: Has teaching in an all-girls' school had any impact on the way you present material in your classroom?

Mrs. London: I don't think so. Uhm, I always have an argument when they [educators] start talking about gender differences and how you should present things differently. The only thing that might be different is, I know, that girls learn better in group situations. So I might do more group work. But I ask myself that a lot, and I think that boys benefit from that equally as well. As long as you make sure the girls are in on the presentation of the topic. Well, I'm not sure that in my particular field that really changes an awful lot.

*   *   *

A.P.: Has teaching in an all-girls' school had any impact on your teaching?

Ms. Donohue: Not profound, in that it does not alter the subject content. There's a certain woman thing, bonding, that is possible in an all-girls' setting that simply cannot happen in a co-ed setting. I went to a co-ed high school. I've taught in co-ed situations.

While faculty have a general awareness of existing research supporting more effective instruction for girls in single-sex schools and point to the unique bonds that are possible between students and teachers in a school context conducive to the development of solid and meaningful relationships, they do not necessarily link their teaching styles to the educational project of single-sex education. Pedagogical practices seem to correspond more to the structural characteristics of a small, independent, private school like class size, for example, than they do to conscious attention to the documented ways that have been determined to increase girls' achievement outcomes. While faculty do not deny that open classrooms, relational modes of interaction, and less directed forms of communication are conducive to girls' learning styles, they argue that these practices are in place not *because of* but, rather, *in spite of* the fact that Best Academy is a girls' school. As they reflect on their classroom practice, teachers suggest that their teaching and interaction styles with students seem to dovetail more with the features of private schooling than with the documented ways in which girls have been shown to learn best.

As students receive valuable instruction in academic skills, they are also the focus of a larger educational project to socialize a gendered elite. The emphasis here is on the production of a *class* elite, where students receive daily lessons in class appropriate norms, values, and dispositions. Acquired resources then translate into upper middle-class cultural capital that benefit them now in school and hold out promises for educational and occupational attainments in the future. The educational project of single-sex schooling as it takes shape in the private, historically elite, independent high school for girls, speaks to the production of self-reliant, independent young women in defiance of school practices that have historically blocked girls' achievement, silencing their voices and deflating sensibilities of self-worth in the process. While schooling specifically for girls aims at their intellectual and moral growth, it also reflects the particular investments of private education in the repro-duction and maintenance of class power and privilege. Analyzing girls' social-ization simply in terms of the educational mission of the single-sex school fails to capture the extent to which social class frames the production of female youth identity at the intersection of school and society. The institutionaliza-tion of class privilege through school structures, practices, and circulated meanings is only one part of the equation, though. On the other side of things, the overall educational project gets worked through by students in their identity work as narrated experiences and sensibilities that arise at the intersections of self, school and society shape school culture in spaces of contradiction and moments of critique. Chapter 3 takes us to that place.

Chapter 3

Class Identities in the Borderlands

The question of identity has resurfaced as part of the vast cultural transformation of meanings and social practices in the West. Through discovery of other cultures and inclusion of the voices and experiences of those who have been historically displaced and silenced, multiculturalism, for example, has played a heavy hand in redirecting social discourse and creating the conditions for transformative social change.[1] Challenging the rationalism of western sensibilities and practices, multiculturalism has interrogated invisible systems of power and privilege that have institutionalized and legitimated unequal social relations and brought questions of difference and exclusion into the center of cultural discourse and analysis. Cultural transformation on this scale, however, cannot be contextualized apart from the epochal shift into postmodernity which has likewise had the effect of de-centering discourses of social identity.[2] Having disrupted the apparent seamlessness of white, western culture, postmodernity has contested the boundedness of identity, displacing the unitary, transcendental, modernist Subject with a destabilized, fractured and fragmented Self in perpetual motion. Stuart Hall (1996) expands on this critical revision of identity in the postmodern condition.

> Precisely because identities are constructed within, not outside of discourse, we need to understand them as produced in specific historical and institutional sites within specific discursive formations and practices by specific enunciative strategies. Moreover, they emerge within the play of specific modalities of power, and thus are more the product of the marking of difference and exclusion, than they are the sign of an identical, naturally-constituted unity—an 'identity' in its traditional meaning (that is, an all-inclusive sameness, seamless, without internal differentiation) (p. 4).

As Michel Foucault (1970), Chris Weedon (1989), Madan Sarup (1996) and others have pointedly argued, identities are socially constituted within discursive fields of power and exclusion across which multiple and different modes of subjectivity(-ies) are possible. Together with Hall (1996), they capture the relational qualities of identity formation, where identity(-ies) re-present(s) the Self apart from and against an Other (Grossberg, 1996). Identity production pivots on exclusions and borders where relations between Self and Other are elaborated across multiple and intersecting dimensions of power and privilege. In their multiple and varied forms, identities are constituted along borders that separate who one is from who one is not.[3]

Earlier, I point out that ethnographic studies of working-class youth have dominated the socialization literature, finding social class integral to adolescent identity work in schools. Within this genre, particular attention has been paid to within-class differences in youth perceptions of working-class culture and its effects on their lives (Willis, 1977; McLaren, 1986; MacLeod, 1987). Only within the past fifteen years do we begin to see a shift within this literature toward critical examination of the varied and highly complex strategies that youth draw on in opposition to the "structuring of silence" that has remained largely invisible within the organization of public and private school forms and practices (Weis and Fine, 1993; McLaren, 1994; Davidson, 1996). Noticeably absent from this body of research are studies of the lived experiences of middle and upper middle-class youth. Studies conducted with these populations have analyzed the cultural match between middle-class schools and pro-academic identity development among middle-class youth but have done little in the way of examining the class implications of within-school processes that add to our understanding of the tight fit between middle-class homes, schools, student competencies and broader class dynamics (Varenne, 1976; Sieber, 1982; Brantlinger, 1993).[4] As Wexler (1993) points out, educators need to turn their attention to examination of school structures as they impact on meaning-making processes among youth *across* class cultures [my emphasis].

In chapter 2, I explored the material and representational forms and practices texturing school culture at Best Academy and made the case that social class is a salient organizing dimension of social relations in the private school. Upper middle-class codes define school policies and practices that students largely model as a reflection of dominant class norms, values, and dispositions. I pointed to those moments where we begin to glimpse students' attempts at disrupting the prevailing class order, providing evidence for the contradictory ways that adolescent girls engage schooling. Against the backdrop of postmodernity and changing notions of identity, expressive forms of class identification and solidarity in student culture are cast differently. On the surface, the population served at Best Academy seems continuous with generations of privileged students before them. Over the past two decades, however, the demographics of private school populations have changed to reflect the shifting dynamics of late capitalism. Once exclusive only to the upper middle class, the private school is now stratified increasingly along vertical and horizontal class divisions.[5] Pearl Kane (1991) speaks to this in her description of the changing culture of private, independent education, in general, throughout the United States.

> Critics of independent schools have argued that these schools are nothing more than "status" seminaries that furnish upper-class youth with the cultural capital they will need to assume elite membership. Traditionally, independent schools have served a homogeneous, affluent stratum of the population, but there are indications of change. Perhaps in response to public sentiment, or a desire to set up a more socially equitable school community that reflects American society, or to the threat that public school reform is imposing, or simply to the economic imperative to fill seats at a time when demographic shifts have created a precipitous drop in the number of school-age children, independent schools are accepting the challenge to open their doors to a more ethnically and socioeconomically diverse student body (p. 402).

With the structural reorganization of relations of production in late modernity, the characteristic class divide separating the public from the private school appears to be narrowing as the socioeconomic, racial and ethnic make-up of the private school student population widens in scope. At Best Academy, there are visible indicators that the student body is diversifying along class lines as students from traditionally blue-collar working-class and lower white-collar middle-class families, although disproportionately fewer in number in relation to the dominant class culture, have seeped into the representative population of students from solidly upper middle-class or, rather, professional middle-class backgrounds. Faculty who have had a long history with the school note this gradual movement toward a more class-differentiated population of students over the past three decades.

> A.P.: What social class would you say that they [students] came from [in the past]?

> Mr. Taylor: [. . .] Now, we, a lot more, a lot of our clientele, because we have changed over the years, is a more, certainly a more middle class [clientele]. It cuts across, just kind of, um, kind of a slice of society at this point. We still have a few whose parents came here, went to Hartford School, but by and large, we have got girls who, uh, whose parents didn't come, didn't come here [to Best Academy], didn't probably think when they were born that their daughters would be going to a private school other than a Catholic private school, a religious private school, so, now it's perfectly acceptable to be going to places like Queen of Peace, and, it doesn't, to go to one of the name New England schools, or New York schools or one of the Seven

Sisters, and all that stuff isn't really as important as it used to be, I think, and that's healthy. I think it's a much better cross-section of society that we have here now.

*   *   *

Mrs. George: . . . and certainly the social class composition of the school is very different. I like that in a way. Some of these girls are ruling-class girls. A lot of them are sort of middle of the middle-class girls. They are not upper class and lower upper class. They are middle of the middle class, and it's wonderful.

In their history with the school, both of these teachers have seen the class culture at Best Academy change to reflect a broadened representation of professional middle-class constituencies. Where up until a decade ago the ruling-class was arguably the representative student population, teachers now describe the class catchment at the school as students who are sort of "middle of the middle-class girls," neither "upper class and lower upper class," a clientele that is "kind of a slice of society at this point." The professional middle class is a social and economic stratum, divided among a number of social spheres and purposes that include those in business services, applied sciences, culture and communications, civic regulation, and human services (Brint, 1994).[6] The professional middle class has been aligned with a newly emergent work category of symbolic analysts who enjoy semi-autonomous control over knowledge production and distribution of information. These "knowledge controllers" are typically college-educated wage earners whose work involves problem identification, problem-solving and strategizing plans for arriving at the most effective way of solving a problem.[7] As college graduates who often hold advanced degress through post-baccalaureate training, this group typically has within its reach expanded professional opportunities. Examinging a list of parents' occupations among the junior class, it appears that close to 88 percent are employed in jobs whose descriptions and anticipated incomes fit the wide range of occupations that fall into the category of the professional middle class.[8] The remaining 12 percent of girls have parents who work in what have been traditionally described as blue-collar working-class and lower white-collar middle-class forms of employment, although it is possible, given these parents post-secondary schooling in either community or four year colleges, that these families could well be included among the professional middle class as it has been newly reconfigured.[9]

As the urban poor and working class have felt the effects of a newly aggressive market economy, so too have the middle classes suffered their own form of social and economic dislocation in the decade of the 1990s. Experiencing intragenerational downward mobility, those within the "middling classes" have slipped from the relative security of earlier decades, losing their ground through job loss and escalating rates of unemployment, stagnant income levels, and declining social status (Ehrenreich, 1989). The old monied elite historically served at Best Academy has fled the urban center for suburban comforts and resource rich public schools.[10] This demographic shift has significantly impacted the fiscal stability of the private, independent school, effecting sharp declines in school revenue as a result of cuts in tuition dollars. Structural shifts in the economy provide a blueprint for class changes showing up across the Independent School Movement, more broadly, and at Best Academy, more specifically, where competing class cultures dot the school landscape.

> Mrs. Nicholson: And I feel the absence of it [a sense of community]. I guess I have, I feel the absence of it very strongly. I think it leads to some of the anomie that, we're looking at here [in Best Academy]. Now look, we have, in the outside world, a social, a process of social disintegration, which may be at a point of total emptiness for girls. Dual-working families, the divorce rate combined with life patterns of fast food, television, the quick grab, there is no . . . families aren't providing . . . there isn't time for the church, the synagogue, in the same way there used to be. I mean, this is really, I [will] know at the end of this year what managing diversity really means.
>
> A.P.: Talk a little bit more about this.
>
> Mrs. Nicholson: I think—I thought—it had to do with the social and economic class, the eclecticism that's come into independent schools over the last twenty years that really wasn't part of our lives before. Most of us are not equipped as educators, by background, by training, by anything, to deal with this. It is macro-cosmically echoed by what's going on in the economic world, in the geo-political world, the global market economy, the connection with it, it just, every single thing that has happened in the world is just expanded, in recent history. What I think, after being here for a year, is that it's really class. It is really a class phenomenon. [. . .]

Mrs. Nicholson sums up the challenges that Best Academy students now face as a "class phenomenon." Only a decade earlier where class strata were more narrowly and clearly defined, struggles around class identification and solidarity would not be as complex an element of socialization as they would prove to be at this moment. Forced to diversify its student population, Best Academy now gathers a range of students from different class backgrounds whose relationships to institutional power and privilege will be played out in complex and highly differentiated ways. The fact that social class has emerged as a principle organizing code of social relations in Best Academy does not necessarily mean that students in the private school will adopt a uniform class discourse that directly corresponds to the prevailing codes of upper middle-class culture in school and in their families. Richard Connell and his associates (1982) remind us that social classes are constantly recreated in response to broader structural shifts.

> [. . .] this points to the fallacy of assuming any class to be a homogeneous group of people with the same character or culture or class being, from which we can read off educational consequences. Classes are always complex and internally-divided groupings, composed into a class by a dialectic between their own activity and its circumstances. And that, of course, never goes on in isolation; it proceeds in the context of a class system. To understand the relation between class and schooling, we have to understand the ways in which the education system shapes, and is shaped by, the processes of class construction and division (p. 189).

Social class relations are not simply reproduced in school cultures but are, arguably, reconstituted in institutional settings in response to internal class dynamics that articulate with economic trends in the larger society. In a historical moment that has issued a challenge to stable identities in schooling and society at large, Best Academy students give voice to a set of struggles uniquely their own giving those of us on the outside looking in an understanding of just *"how* deeply the differences of class run in the lives of high school students" (Wexler, 1992, p. 18).

In an age of destabilizing identity production where identities are continuously shifting and being redefined, it is questionable whether we can argue anymore for the formation of homogeneous class cultures in schools.[11] While upper middle-class codes decidedly organize school forms and practices at Best Academy, this does not mean that the class identities that students enact will necessarily reflect a logical coherence within and across the professional middle class. Renato Rosaldo (1993) powerfully argues for the "fiction of the uniformly shared culture" (p. 207), claiming that it is no longer viable to think of the social borders that frame and organize our daily lives as fixed, discrete, and "empty transitional zones" (p. 208). Instead, he reconfigures social zones like class as sites of creative cultural *production* that capture the fluid and dynamic quality of identity formation that class-reproductionist frameworks have traditionally denied. For Anzaldua (1987), a Chicana lesbian of Mexican descent, the borderland is a site where differences growing up at the intersections of salient borders and border zones of class, race, ethnicity, gender, and sexuality, are continuously negotiated and worked through. Appropriating the notion of the borderland in analysis of class identity formation among adolescent youth subcultures creates space for re-(en)visioning identity production as a charged and contested process that challenges the "fiction of the uniformly shared culture" commonly attributed to the private school (Connell, 1982; Henry, 1993). It carves out conceptual space for theorizing more than one dimension of difference at a time, recognizing multiple and varied meanings of the Self in the postmodern condition.[12] This chapter chronicles class identity production among Best Academy juniors who are not only constructed at the cultural center as upper middle-class students but are themselves actively engaged in decentering class power and privilege. Through student narratives, it explores the ways that adolescent girls understand what it means to be objectively located and subjectively positioned in the professional middle class as a function of their family backgrounds but also in terms of private school socialization. It hinges on a total reconceptualization of the private school as a borderland site where possibilities exist for new identities to take shape and emerge.

Class Culture and the Peer Group

The peer group is the primary form of individual and collective identification during adolescence and provides a legitimating space for youth to try on and adopt attitudes and behaviors that test the limits of adolescence on the threshold of adulthood. Investigation of peer group affiliation and stratification has focused mainly on the impact that societal and community forces have on the development of peer networks, leaving the regulatory processes of group formation and cohesion within and across peer subcultures largely unmined in the youth socialization literature (Eckert, 1989). For young girls who have historically gone underground in search of connectedness, validation, and self-determination, the peer group marks off a safe space for them to forge common ground around shared identities (McRobbie, 1982; Lees, 1986; Gilligan, 1990, 1992; Holland and Eisenhart, 1990).

Junior students at Best Academy tend to identify with three distinct peer groups around which social categories of membership and friendship networks are established early on in their high school careers. The first of the peer groups, which I refer to as PG1,[13] is made up of twelve girls, ages sixteen and seventeen. Half of these girls attended private, non-sectarian and parochial grammar schools, and the other half public schools, four of which are designated magnet schools, before coming to Best Academy.[14] Nine of the girls are white, two are African-American, and one is of mixed ancestry. They are largely from families with professional parents whose occupations are represented heavily in the applied science and human services spheres of the professional middle class.[15] Some of the students in this peer group receive substantial grants and merit scholarship monies relative to students in the other two peer groups in the junior class, most of whose members are close to or full tuition payers.[16]

A second peer group that I have named PG2, consists of nine girls, ages sixteen and seventeen, five of whom attended private, non-sectarian and parochial schools earmarked as the main feeder institutions to Best Academy, with the remaining four from public or magnet schools in the local area. Several of them are longtime friends, having developed relationships through the shared contexts of elementary and middle school, their neighborhoods, and families. Largely daughters of entrepreneurs, lawyers, and doctors, they are from families whose parents' occupations put them in the top income bracket of the professional middle class.[17] Most of them live in or very close to the historically reputed upper middle-class neighborhood surrounding the school. Several of them have strong ties with Best Academy through earlier generations of family that attended the school. Being able to trace family ties back to the school over more than one generation is not part of the experience of the girls in the other peer groups. The members of PG2 are all white and represent the class catchment of upper middle-class students that has traditionally passed through Best Academy up until the last two decades.

The third peer group, identified as PG3, is made-up of fourteen girls, ages sixteen and seventeen and integrates the largest number of under-represented racial and ethnic groups in the junior class. Among their number are girls of Native-American, African-American, and Hispanic ancestry. This peer group most closely approximates the class indicators of PG1, including in its number students whose parents' occupations include but are not limited to teacher aide, factory worker, and truck driver. This peer group was by far the most eclectic of the three, able to knit itself into a coherent network in spite of wide ranging differences in class, racial, and ethnic backgrounds. Of the fourteen girls in this peer group, twelve of them came to Best Academy from public schools and two from private Catholic schools.

Studies have concluded that peer subcultures tend to be relatively class homogeneous, forming around shared class identification (Shimahara, 1983; Brantlinger, 1993). Among the junior students, peer groups do tend to organize around common class backgrounds, although there are variations within groups that reflect the scope of professional middle-class affiliation. Social class is integral to the definition of separate and distinct peer networks. Close examination of peer groups in the junior class suggests that they are not all class homogeneous, but, rather, reflect a range of professional middle-class backgrounds. In a small private school where community hinges on a common school identity, it is likely that peer relationships will form and cohere in spite of class differences within groups.[18] This dynamic stands out in PG3 where students from a variety of professional middle-class backgrounds and others on the periphery manage to shape tight social arrangements. As their narratives and those of students belonging to PG1 and PG2 will illustrate, class culture at Best Academy is far from seamless as students forge class indentities in the borderlands, along constructed boundaries and border crossings, that pivot around the "play of power and exclusion" (Hall, 1996, p. 5).

Class in the Border Zones

While class is a central category of social analysis inside American culture and society, it remains a relatively unspoken descriptor, commonly filtered through discourses of gender, race, and ethnicity. The "myth of classlessness" is notable among Americans in general who tend to describe themselves as middle class because they see the middle class as a *universal* class with *universal* membership (Ehrenreich, 1989; Ortner, 1991). As Katherine Newman (1988) reflects, "the middle class is a category so broad that it encompasses everyone from white collar executives to elite unionized labor, sometimes called the labor aristocracy" (p. 15). That is, the middle class seems to feel that it represents everyone, everywhere. A subset of American culture, adolescent youth pattern themselves after these same terms of class identification.[19] When asked about class background, junior students tend to describe themselves as either middle or upper middle class, providing evidence of the persistence of the "myth of classlessness" in American culture and consciousness.

A.P.: What social class would you say you belong to?

Cara [PG1]: Meaning like the middle class?

A.P.: Yes.

Cara: Middle class, good old right down the middle of the road—middle class.

A.P.: Why do you say that?

Cara: Both of my parents work. They, um, my mom's just a part-time teacher. My dad just works at, in housing [office of student residence at a local university], and he's in the army [reserve].

A.P.: Do you like the middle class lifestyle that you lead?

Cara: Yeah. It's, it would be nice to, I mean, I know the people here that just go to the store and buy things and don't even try it on first. I mean, it just boggles my mind. I went out and bought shoes last night, and I never buy anything for myself.

*   *   *

A.P.: What social class do you feel you belong in?

Gwen [PG1]: Middle class.

A.P.: Why do you say that?

Gwen: Well, we live in the suburbs, and it's kind of like a middle class neighborhood. Everyone is kind of the same.

A.P.: What do mean by that—that everyone is kind of the same?

Gwen: People mainly make the same amount of money, I'd say. I'm not deprived of anything, nothing like that.

*   *   *

A.P.: What social class would you put yourself in?

Sarah [PG2]: Like, um, lower, upper, or middle?

A.P.: Right. Where would you locate yourself?

Sarah: Um, probably middle.

A.P.: And what is it about your lifestyle that leads you to say that you are middle class?

Sarah: Oh, I don't know. When I think of social classes, I think of like money. So, I, when I think of lower [classes], I just think of like, people like, not poor but less fortunate than other people. Um, when I think of upper [class people], I think of like wealthier people and people that, um, I don't know. I think of big houses, too. I don't know why.

A.P.: You think of big houses?

Sarah: Yeah.

A.P.: Among people of the upper class?

Sarah: Well, not, I don't know, not like big houses, but I guess I'm kind of a materialistic person. I just think of like wealth when I think of upper class. And middle class, I think it's just like average, you know, just like an average person.

A.P.: What is it about your lifestyle that leads you to say that you are middle class?

Sarah: Well, I feel middle class. Both my parents work so that, you know, brings some stuff. I mean, [I live] in a nice like environment with my home and stuff. I, we have a really nice house. Um, we drive cars. Um, we, I don't know, we go away sometimes.

A.P.: On family trips?

Sarah: Yeah. On family trips, we're like by ourselves. I mean, we have a nice Christmas and like stuff like that.

*   *   *

A.P.: What social class do you think you belong in?

Lisa [PG3]: Like financial? Me or me and my family?

A.P.: You in relation to your family and their lifestyle?

Lisa: Me, myself, I have no social class just because I am still in school, and I am not working. But my family, I guess, is middle class.

A.P.: What does it mean for you to say that you are middle class?

Lisa: There is food in the house. You don't go home and look in the fridge and there is nothing there except for like a bottle of ketchup or something. There are two working cars in the garage. You don't come home and then have to fiddle with the engine of your one car for a twenty person family. But at the same time, you don't go overboard. Like you don't walk into a middle class family's house and find statues, elaborate paintings, rugs hanging on the walls just to look impressive.

*   *   *

A.P.: What social class would you locate yourself in?

Beth [PG3]: I wouldn't say that I am poor because I am not. I am in the middle. We get going with what we have. So, you know, if you need anything . . . sometimes, you know, we can't get it; we have to wait until we have money or something. But I wouldn't say that we are low, in the low social class. [We are] around the middle.

Students signify middle-class status in terms of the dual-income family, the comforts of a family home, one or more family cars in the driveway, and food on the table. Even Beth, a first-generation Hispanic whose father works in a factory and whose mother is employed as a classroom aide in a local public school, states proudly that she is not in the "low social class" but, rather, is "around the middle."[20] That middle-class families model restraint separates them from more affluent families, as Lisa is quick to point out: "You don't go overboard, like you don't walk into a middle class family's house and find statues, elaborate paintings, rugs hanging on the walls just to look impressive." The fetishization of material values swirls through her comment, strategically using this moment to critique the symbolic and material investments of the dominant class.[21] Lisa's father is a well-known attorney in the region, and several of her sisters attended Best Academy before her. Although I had no knowledge of family income, it is possible to gather from conversations with her about her family and lifestyle that she is from a characteristically upper middle-class background. Still, she identifies herself as middle class.

Drawing lines between themselves and the "wealthier" people, Best Academy students describe a status hierarchy that parallels the complex stratification of the professional middle class. A number of students from professional middle-class families provide insight into the ways in which they sort and select themselves out from their peers on the basis of certain behaviors that they link with class culture. Cara distinguishes herself from other students who can "just go to the store and buy things and don't even try it [them] on first." Coming from a family whose father works in the administrative offices of a local university and whose mother teaches part-time at a local private school, she recognizes that how she shops and what she shops for are delimited by her social class. In other words, she understands that she is not as free as her more affluent friends to buy material items, a feeling shared by Beth, who self-identifies as middle class and, on the same breath, observes that "if you need anything . . . sometimes, you know, we can't get it; we have to wait until we have money or something." The convergence of Cara's and Beth's statements is particularly striking since Cara is from a solidly professional middle-class background while Beth, a first generation Latina, is from a blue-collar working-class family where financial hardships are substantially greater.

American adolescents are typically unfamiliar with objective measures of class and generally tend to name appearance and attitude as predictable measures of class status. Narratives from across all three peer groups identify dress, jewelry, and automobiles as important class indicators in much the same way that they index class standing in the broader society. Attention to appearance within girls' subcultures has been attributed to their projected desires for intimate relationships with boys, parading femininity across the sexual auction block in pleas for male attention (Holland and Eisenhart, 1990). In contemporary capitalist cultures, girls have used such market goods as dress and jewelry to signify femininity (Haug, 1986; Canaan, 1991; McRobbie, 1991). Adolescent females have, however, moved one step beyond this to link feminine commodities with social class. Inside female peer subcultures, adolescent girls appropriate these signifiers as a way of highlighting class differences within and between peer groups. Instead of constructing a culture of femininity in relation to an "other"—teenage boys, adolescent girls "other" their own—female peers—by reappropriating traditional feminine signifiers as social class indicators. On the basis of clothes, jewelry, and automobiles, upper middle class girls sketch out differences in the professional middle class, variations that disappear on the surface of student narratives committed to the universalism of middle-class consciousness.

A.P.: How do girls from social class backgrounds different from yours appear? In other words, do you see social class differences among the girls in the junior class?

Gayle [PG2]: Things like dressing is obvious. The kind of stuff that they wear.

A.P.: How do other girls dress as different from the way that girls in your peer group dress?

Gayle: Like [we wear] clothes from the GAP. [. . .] The other girls wear not so much clothes from the GAP but like [clothes from] department stores or something, do you know what I mean? Like how you are put together. You can kind of tell [who is from which social class background].

*   *   *

A.P.: Can you tell social class differences in school?

Fiona [PG2]: Uh huh.

A.P.: In what ways do you see differences?

Fiona: Dress [and] people with cars and people who don't have them.

Bella [PG2]: I think that there is going to be less class differences because they took away a lot of the financial aid this year, and as tuition keeps getting higher, less and less people are going to be able to come [to the school]. It's going to be like more wealthy people.

Fiona: I don't think that they can [keep raising tuition] because there aren't that many wealthy people to pay for it. I think that the group of wealthy people is smaller than the rest. Well, in our class, I think it's smaller.

Bella: Yeah, that's true, but, um, the problem is that those people . . .

Fiona: If they can't get away with it, then the school can't function with such a small group of people.

A.P.: Is there ever a time when you notice that social class makes a difference in school for you?

Bella: The only thing is like not having a car [it] is difficult for me, and I envy people who have cars. I look down on people who are so wealthy that their parents give them like a 30,000 dollar car, and they like go and like bang it up, and their parents buy them a new one.

A.P.: Have you ever heard of that happening to any of the students here in school?

Fiona: Yeah, Elizabeth [a senior]. Her parents brought her a Mazda Miata [an expensive sports car]. When she was fifteen, she crashed it. Now she has a red [jeep] Wrangler [a less expensive car].

*   *   *

A.P.: Can you tell social class differences among your friends in the junior class?

Wanda [PG3]: [. . .] I think the biggest difference, the thing that shows me, you know, who has the cash and who doesn't, is jewelry.

A.P.: Jewelry?

Wanda: Yeah.

A.P.: That's interesting. What kind of differences do you see in students' jewelry?

Wanda: Like . . . well, maybe it's like taste too, but the girls that, you know, don't have the cash usually, you know, they'll wear like the same pair of earrings every, you know, day. But people who have it [more money] change up with the outfit and stuff like that. And I mean, you can tell that if they took time to get dressed, then they made sure they had little matching sterling silver amethyst stones in it to match the clothes and stuff like that.

*   *   *

Briana [PG3]: Well, the only difference between me and that table [PG2] is the money. They, I mean, Shelby's [PG2] got, how much money? I mean, I'm not saying that they are all rich, but they definitely have more money than I do.

A.P.: How do you know that?

Wendy [PG3]: Because they tell you. And the cars that they have that are theirs, they're a lot like their parents—a brand new Jeep Cherokee.

A.P.: They tell you about their money? How do they do that?

Briana: I mean, they're not just like—hey, you know what? I got all this money. Some [of them] are like—Shelby will come in [and say]: I'm so mad. I had to drive my father's car, and he used my car. We are like [thinking]—oh, you poor baby.

Wendy: That she had to drive the Porsche instead of the new Cherokee or something like that.

*   *   *

A.P.: Do you see social class differences in school?

Lucy [PG1]: I can because I have been in the situation where girls would sit and tease other girls because of what they are wearing.

A.P.: At your grammar school [Lucy had attended an elite, Catholic, girls' school before beginning high school at Best Academy]?

Lucy: Right. I can tell that Cara and Hannah [PG1] are from a certain class, and Gayle and Sarah [PG2] are from another. It's different. It's not like they are dressed like messed up. You can tell what stores they bought their clothes in.

Casey [PG1]: Do you mean the different quality of dress? I mean, there is a different quality to the way that Gayle and Sarah [PG2] dress. Sarah especially . . . you can tell that her parents are making big bucks.

Brand name clothes from the GAP, sterling amethyst earrings, and a Mazda Miata are named as sorting mechanisms within the professional middle class. Conventional signifiers of femininity are reappropriated as markers of class affiliation that identify certain girls, namely those who member among PG2, as "different" from girls who locate themselves in either PG1 or PG3. Between the lines, we begin to hear an emergent critique of upper middle-class privilege where girls script differences and exclusions between those students who come from families with "more money" and those from less affluent backgrounds. As these girls narrate class-based patterns within peer networks, they shape a critique of the most privileged junior students, the girls of PG2, who have set the terms for consumption through their expensive clothes and chic cars. A number of students are quick to describe this group as "the girls," "the snobs," "the real wealthy people," and "the social climbers." Girls in PG2 are "othered" as "material girls" representing the conspicuous side of privilege who, themselves, become material for girls in PG1 and PG3 to undercut the exclusive and exclusionary elements of the professional middle class.[22]

A.P.: And how about the table where the girls belonging to PG2 sit? How would you describe them?

Dina [PG1]: High fashion, only shop at [places like] DKNY [Donna Karan New York] and Calvin Klein. And don't get me wrong, Amira. I like those people, and I am into fashion too, but they are people who present themselves, not all of the time, but sometimes, in a way like other people are dirt beneath their feet. They are very wealthy, and they have a tendency to walk all over people even if [though] they don't realize that they are doing it.

*   *   *

A.P.: If you were to describe the different cliques in general in the junior class, how would you describe them?

Wendy [PG3]: Okay, pretty much the way that people see it is, the one group with, um, it's been like this since freshman year, is the one group [. . .] they consider, they're like the really smart people that do really good in all their classes and stuff. And then the other group [. . .] those are the real wealthy people, and they have the parents who are the doctors and everything like that. They're the ones that take, we consider, take a lot for granted. And there's our group, where most of us are on financial aid and, you know, we work hard but not as hard as the first group does, but not as little as the wealthier people do, you know, it seems.

*   *   *

A.P.: Could you talk to me about what you see as the different cliques in the junior class?

Lucy [PG1]: There's one clique, um, where everyone is rich or shall we say affluent. Um, they all go to bars. They all hang out in the same places. Most of them have pretty good grades. I mean, you know, they're not really, you know, stupid people. They'll, they just like to, you know, party . . . have a good time.

                    *   *   *

A.P.: Do you see any differences among the junior girls?

Randi [PG1]: Yeah, you know, we have always like categorized our class. There is the ritzy, snobbish group.

A.P.: Who are they?

Randi: Oh, I don't want to name names. I think you could figure it out. There is the ritzy, snobbish group. I mean, that is what they are called. They sit on the left hand side in the middle of the lunch room, [and are] not necessarily altogether juniors [students from other grades tend to sit with them].

A.P.: Why do you describe them as ritzy and snobbish?

Randi: Well, they do have a lot of money. And they don't necessarily want to speak to you unless you've got something to give them. Like say if you've got food that they want or money or something to that effect. I have had lots of people approach me who never even talked to me before, and they were like, can I have this and this and this.

A.P.: From the group of girls that we are talking about?

Randi: Some from that group, and some students from the other classes [grades].

Members of PG1 and PG3, mixed-class peer groups of girls from family backgrounds that cut across the professional middle class and include the blue-collar working-class, are critical of PG2 whose members, they charge, lack social consciousness and parade a felt sense of entitlement purely motivated by self-interest. While Best Academy has historically enrolled relatively less privileged students—students from blue-collar working-class and lower white-collar middle-class families, these students have consistently been in the minority. Given the traditional class base at Best Academy, it is likely that students outside the dominant class culture would be "othered" by the cultural dominant, a protective hedge against having to see, name, and then deconstruct their own location of privilege. Identity and difference exist in dialectical relationship to each other (Sarup, 1996). What we find, instead, are strong instances of othering by students less relatively privileged than their compeers, as girls in PG1 and PG3 scaffold hierarchies through exclusions and negations that delegitimate institutionalized forms of power and privilege.

Asked to describe what it is that separates peer networks in the junior class, the girls in PG1 and PG3 present a range of responses that cast students in PG2, for the most part, in a less than positive light. Dina observes that this group has a distinct "tendency to walk all over people," and, according to Randi, demonstrates a certain self-interestedness in their decision not "to speak to you unless you've got something to give them." Wendy [PG3] outlines differences between groups in terms of a work ethic. "Working hard" is a characteristic that she attaches strategically to the girls in PG1 and her peers in PG3 in contrast to those in PG2 who she "others" as the group who "take a lot for granted" and do not work "as hard as the first group [PG1]." She foreshadows a consistent theme in other student narratives that draw connections between pro-academic identities and class culture. From Wendy's perspective, there is a decided connection between social class and positive school engagement. Carrying this theme further, Mrs. Lewis, a teacher, observes that the students in PG1 and PG3 tend to be more serious in their approach and commitment to school work and concludes that this is a class phenomenon.

> Mrs. Lewis: The junior class is one of the better classes, maybe the best class in the school as far as ability. I see the junior class as two separate classes. You have one group of students who are very interested and very ambitious and, for the most part as they describe to me, are the poor kids. That is how they identify themselves—poor kids.
>
> A.P.: What do they mean to say by calling themselves poor?
>
> Mrs. Lewis: The way it came up was . . . the girls, half of the AP [Advanced Placement], the AP is first period, half of the AP kids went, because they are in advanced biology, Mrs. May, a biology teacher, took them over to Queen of Peace to do something, so we had only five in the class. So we were doing [talking about] General Grant and his scandals [in history class] and all this kind of thing, we were going through the economic picture, and they don't understand hard money, soft money, so we spent a lot of time on money circulation and how that was good for debtors and talked about this. Well, one thing led to another, and the conversation came up to did I know anything about financial aid in the school. And I said no, I didn't have a thing to do with it. Well, you must know something about it, and I said—no, I don't. Well [they said], do you know if they are going to give the same financial aid, and I said—no . . . look, I mean it when I say I don't know anything about it except that I know the school is very generous with it and that you have to fill out a form and mail it in and process it and all the rest of

it. So, I said, obviously this is of concern to you, so maybe you should have your parents come and find out, if it's so much on your mind.

A.P.: Meaning their worries about having enough funding to be able to continue to attend Best Academy?

Mrs. Lewis: Right, so if this is so much on your mind that when talking about General Grant and his economic policy this pops out of your head, you should probably put your mind at ease and find out something more about it. [They said]—at ease, what, are you crazy, lady? And I said, I didn't want to get into it. Then one of them said to me something about—well, how are they going to decide who gets it. I said—number one, I have no idea. [They said]— well, do you think that [who is] working real hard [would be a factor in their decision]? And I said, one year, I was asked by the [former] headmaster what I thought [about] whether these people were working to their potential. [. . .] Well, she [one of the students] said, well, what would you say about us? And I said—different things for different people. "Us" doesn't exist in this school. [They responded, saying things like] don't you think we're working real hard, we work real hard, how many hours do you think we should spend on homework at night? I would say use your free periods in school, use your double lunch when you can and three . . . three and a half hours a night. I said, I think that would really polish off the job well. Well, they laughed. They said that's not nearly enough. And I said, well, could you explain to me why some people are just standing around . . . sitting around eating bagels every day [during those few minutes prior to the start of the school day and during free periods in the cafeteria], and other people are concerned about getting a good report for next year. And this is the junior class. And out of their mouths came—well, if you're poor, you can stand around and eat bagels. No, [it's] the other way around . . . if you're rich, you can stand around and eat bagels. If you're poor, you have to keep working.

Familiar with this Advanced Placement History class, I was well aware that the group of students having this conversation with Mrs. Lewis were from PG1 and PG3 and cut across a wide range of class backgrounds. Unlike the girls in PG2, most of these girls are among the first in their family to attend Best Academy, and two-thirds of them are first experiencing private education as high school students. As indicated earlier, they receive substantial grants-in-aid and scholarship monies relative to the students in PG2, most of whom are near to or full tuition payers. Mrs. Lewis' narrative scripts a defining moment for relatively less privileged students who suspect that access to a private education and equal opportunity to compete does not guarantee that they will be able to see their experience in the private school through to graduation. Unlike their peers in PG1 and PG3, whose relative privilege they perceive as affording them a greater measure of security, they see themselves as not having the financial backing to turn to for "back up" if they do not perform on a consistent level.

While it is not current school policy to retain students who fail to satisfy academic requirements and meet high standards of performance, there is still a rooted perception that students on the brink of failing can buy themselves back into school and that school officials have, at least in the past, supported this practice behind closed doors.[23] As a college preparatory high school, Best Academy admits female students with demonstrated academic records and potential for future school success. While the school has been consistent in aggressively recruiting talented students, it also has a history of attracting students who bring with them strong financial backing. Mrs. Nicholson did indicate that students, in the past, were not always admitted to the school on the basis of academic competency alone. She notes that she has "already made a step in the direction of changing those [our policies on financial aid] to make sure that they are all need-based." As a private school dependent on external funds for its survival, Best Academy is invested in attracting and recruiting the daughters of families with the potential to provide financial support for the school long after their child has graduated. According to Mrs. Nicholson, attracting students with the financial backing to afford a private education no longer drives recruitment initiatives with the force it did in past years, restoring more "meritocratic" practice in the private school.

Students recognize that Best Academy retains a strong commitment to equality of educational opportunity and that the school has worked hard to provide students from less privileged socio-economic backgrounds access to a private education through generous grants. Still, students, mainly from PG1 and PG3, point to a number of contradictions between recruitment efforts geared toward diversifying the student population and an institutional culture founded on the maintenance of class privilege. When asked to reflect on the impact of class background on peer relationships, they point out that class does not influence their interactions with other students, framing their responses in terms of an ideology of equality of educational opportunity that the school administration appears to support through liberal financial aid packages to students. In conversation, Diana reminds me that "a lot of people [students at Best Academy] are on financial aid," which suggests to her that "it's like it's not saying that you have to be rich to go here because if you have the talent and the brains and the effort to want to try to do it, you have a chance to go here." On the other hand, she does not trust that the school will back all of its students and see them all through successfully until graduation. A conversation with Ruth [PG1] adds further support to the felt sense that students who come into school from resource rich backgrounds with financial backing retain the greatest purchasing power in private education.

The tuition keeps going up, so it's really hard to pay for it. And I know other people can't pay for it, but like they work really hard, and they get good grades, and they're good students [reference is mainly to some of the girls in PG1 and PG3], and they still can't come because they can't afford it. But then other students who like slack off, cause problems, fail courses, can come just because they are rich. And they don't ever have to worry about anything like that. [. . .] but it is kind of aggravating when you see some people like crying, like Randi [PG1] and I cry all the time because we know we don't have the money to come to school anymore [might not have sufficient funds to pay tuition for their senior year].

Despite documented restructuring of financial aid policies on the part of the new administration, a profound distrust and anxiety threads through the narratives of girls from PG1 and PG3 who seriously question emergent inequities in the policies and practices of the private school. Cameron McCarthy (1994) suggests that there is a growing sense among the white middle class that their class and race privilege is under attack by an urban underclass. The middle-class response has been to "other" economically and racially underprivileged groups in a strategic move to position itself as the real victim. This emergent "discourse of resentment" wrapped tightly around white middle class identity is useful for decoding the inversions that some junior students draw on and appropriate to their advantage. As Mrs. Lewis details in her account of a conversation in her history class, students from across professional middle-class backgrounds perceive themselves as victims who, unlike those who are "rich" and able to "stand around and eat bagels," "have to keep working." They do not trust that they will be rewarded fairly as part and parcel of the prevailing ideology of equal opportunity for each and every student to develop her potential. What these students speak to is a loss of faith in liberal narratives of equality and individualism that have textured American schooling since the dawn of the Republic (Spring, 1996). Far from convinced that schools embody the fairest possible meritocratic arrangements, these students step into a discourse of "inegalitarian stratification" which marks schools as sites that serve mainly to protect the children of more affluent parents (Oakes, 1986).[24] Scripting this "discourse of resentment," they position themselves as middle-class victims, forced to compete that much harder than their peers for the same educational credentials and rewards. Their concerns are arguably linked to the "fall from grace" that has brought the upward social mobility of the middle class to a halt over the past two and a half decades, and reflect their fears that they will have little to brace their "fall" should they slip up and into the cracks despite what appears to be an open contest system available to all students in school. In the final analysis, real capital carries the greatest weight, providing more affluent students protections that tip the balance of class power and privilege in their favor and help to shepherd them through the private school experience.

Girls from PG1 and PG3 narrate that their peers in PG2 are blind to their own privilege and the ways in which they benefit from it. Wendy points out that she and her peers in PG3 play many roles at home that include taking care of their siblings and that these additional responsibilities teach them to value money more. Relative privilege has meant that the girls in PG2 can "view things totally differently." Through technologies of othering, girls in PG1 and PG3 create hierarchies that deny the competencies of those from the most advantaged sectors of the professional middle class. Actively inverting class status by showing themselves to be *more responsible*, they are able to reclaim for themselves a sense of power that has felt lost on them as students at Best Academy. As they "other," they shape a "discourse of resentment" that fractures professional middle-class consciousness even further than it already is.

Members of PG2, on the other hand, openly admit to the advantages that they enjoy because of their class background and curiously own up to the exclusions and hierarchies organizing class relations in the private, independent high school.

A.P.: What do you think it is that makes you such close friends with the girls in your peer group [PG2]?

Donna [PG2]: I think it's because we all have the same views. There is that group like I just mentioned, and then there is like two other people. I think that everyone related because like the other groups, like Lisa, drink and smoke and stuff too, but they all live in the suburbs. I am sure if they lived in the city, I bet you I would be close to them. We have the same ideals and morals, and like the way of thinking in school and stuff. But then you get like Cara and Hannah, and they are very concerned about their grades, like more than they need to be. They are into boys and stuff, but I doubt that you would see them really in a bar. Like they are very into excelling and everything. And they are also, none of them really have money. I think they are here on scholarships and stuff. They know that they have to work, so that is their main priority. A lot of my friends all have money. They pay full tuition, and it's like screw it [the schoolwork]. We've gotten everything that we ever wanted. I think they have to work for everything they have to get so that is why they are like [so conscientious].

A.P.: When do you think that money makes a difference? Can you think of any experiences that you have had here in school where money has made a difference?

Donna: I know where it makes a difference. It makes a big difference because a lot of the girls are on scholarships and stuff. And like whenever they raise tuition or something, some of the girls are like—oh, no, what am I going to do. We [my peer group] don't have to worry about it, like—oh, I had better start getting good grades. We are like—oh, well, if I don't get good grades, I don't have to worry about getting kicked out. I don't have to worry about getting kicked out because I don't think they would ever kick me out because I pay full tuition. Or like Shelby. She does not do well in school and like they wanted to kick her out many times, but they would never. I mean, there are only like five girls in my class that pay full tuition, and that would be like losing a big part of their [the school's] revenue. That's how money makes a difference.

*   *   *

A.P.: You think that you are sheltered in this school?

Fiona [PG2]: Uh huh.

A.P.: What kinds of things are you sheltered from?

Fiona: Poor people, I think. Even though we are not, like not everyone is . . . there are people who are even below middle class in our school, but like people don't show it.

Bella: They are not . . . they are there to work and to get through school and do really well.

A.P.: People who you would describe as being from lower middle class and working-class backgrounds?

Bella: Right. They want to like better themselves, so I am sure that they are not going to get caught in a situation like getting pregnant or just getting caught in a situation that would let their lower class [status] show because they are trying to like better themselves, do you know what I mean?

*   *   *

Glenda [PG1]: And also another problem I think is that a lot of people don't understand how much commitment, that if you are really serious about performing [participating in performing arts], how much commitment it takes. I think that's a problem. Actually, I see it pretty much in almost all of the areas in this school, in sports a lot too. A lot of people aren't really committed, fully committed to what they are doing.

A.P.: Why do you think that is?

Glenda: I don't know. Maybe it is just the way that they have been brought up. A lot of the girls are from families that are wealthier. They don't, you know, [they say], well—I don't really have to do this because my mom and my dad will back me up. My mom and my dad will make excuses if I don't do something.

A.P.: Do you ever hear people talking that way in school, leading you to believe this?

Glenda: Sometimes they are like, oh well, you know, if they kiss up to you, I am going to have my mom talk to them. Or my dad called and said that I can't make practice. I think that a lot of times, I think that people need to be more committed to whatever they are doing because if you are really serious about something, you shouldn't just go into it halfheartedly. I mean, that's how I feel about it. And so that's the reason that I have the problem with this school because a lot of the people have like no working discipline.

In these narratives, students from PG2 "out" themselves as they claim the benefits of privilege. Out of her concern to guard her own class-based interests, Donna might have easily skirted an answer to my question. Instead, she spoke directly to the protection that class privilege affords through the example of her peer group [PG2] who, she claims, can depend on real capital to keep them from being pushed out of school.[25] She argues that the school needs to keep these students on board as a source of necessary revenue, "outing" herself, her peer group and the school in the process. That their families have the financial means to bargain to keep their daughters in school is an important dividing line between peer subcultures. While girls in PG2 separate themselves from girls in PG3 and PG1, they consistently "other" PG1, linking affluence, class status, and school engagement together. Donna links these dimensions together as well, observing that the girls in PG1, "none of [whom] really have money," are "very into excelling," adding that "they have to work for everything they have to get so that is why they are like [so conscientious]." Glenda, whose father is a medical doctor and whose mother is a high school French teacher, lives in a predominantly white, upper middle-class, suburban area and has only been educated in private schools. Glenda is a pointed example of a student who is able to float in and out of peer groups, straddling horizontal divisions within class cultures. Unlike Donna, she does not tie herself either to a particular peer group or girls "from families that are wealthier." Despite the fact that she describes herself as upper middle class from a relatively privileged background, she scripts herself as *different from others* as a matter of her "working discipline." Like Donna, who earlier "outed" the upper middle class, Glenda indicts her peers for their anti-school attitudes. There are students, she indicates, that "aren't really committed, fully committed to what they are doing," and attributes this to parents who will "back them up." Again, student narratives provide useful insight into an emerging sense among more affluent students that they do not need to apply themselves to school culture and responsibilities around schoolwork to the extent that others feel that they need to because of resources and institutional arrangements in place that will likely "back them up." As she draws attention to the shapes that pro- and anti-school identities take among students in the private school, Glenda cautions those on the outside against broad strokes that paint a seamless picture of class identity production on the inside. While she highlights the wide range of attitudes toward school that occupy professional middle-class youth at this moment, she brings into sharp relief the growing sense of alienation running through segments of the professional middle class as identities are newly reconfigured.

Class Culture as Borderwork

In her study of gender identity production among boys and girls in two elementary schools, Barrie Thorne (1993) appropriates the term "borderwork" as an analytical framework for understanding the ways in which contact between boys and girls marks and underscores gender borders that have traditionally separated these two groups.[26] What her work importantly suggests is that groups different along certain dimensions, like gender, can cross borders through social interactions yet still retain a sense of their difference. As Thorne points out, "although contact sometimes undermines and reduces an active sense of difference, groups may also interact with one another in ways that strengthen their borders" (p. 65). Thorne's insight is useful to analysis of class relations at Best Academy where class identities are simultaneously marked and muted in the context of inter- and intra-group peer relations. As she points out, borderwork involves a complex set of social relations that, in the case of identity productions at Best Academy, deepen our understanding of the fluid quality of class culture in private schooling. While the above narratives illustrate horizontal divisions within the professional middle class, there is ample evidence to suggest that class-based differences across segments of the professional middle class do not keep students from crossing borders and floating into peer networks within the same class structure. In their border-work, professional middle-class students mark class differences by staying within the boundaries of distinct peer subcultures at the same time as they cross horizontal divisions and level class differences that define separations between and within peer groups. Complicated forms of borderwork underline the fact that it is possible to speak of class cultures being made up of multiple cultural identities that are not stable and bounded but tried on and thrown off as youth move into and out of different peer networks and relationships daily.

While students slip into and out of different identities, the importance of shared norms, values, and traditions to the development of students' collective identification with the school cannot be emphasized enough. Earlier, I pointed to salient class signifiers that the school braids into daily school routines as material and representational reminders of the common legacy that students inherit during their four years in Best Academy and take with them after they graduate. Across peer groups, girls, individually and collectively, narrate identity productions that reflect the persistent tension between difference and collective identification with the prevailing institutional ethos and culture.

A.P.: [Different] social class backgrounds never make a difference in how you make friends?

Beth [PG3]: No, I don't think so. If it does, they [the students] don't show it. We do have our arguments once and awhile. Everybody's normal.

A.P.: And do your friends [from your immediate peer group/PG3] come from class backgrounds different from yours?

Beth: Yes they do.

A.P.: Does that ever make a difference in your friendships, that is, with whom you choose to become friends?

Beth: Not in the friendships. I don't think so.

A.P.: Does social class ever make a difference for you in school in any way?

Beth: Not in school, because it doesn't, you know. You don't have to show that you have so much in school, because the only thing you come [to do in school] is to study and to talk with the friends that you have in school. So you will see it mainly outside of school where you will go to parties or you go someplace or where you go shopping. They [some of the girls at school] could go shopping each day if they want[ed]. So that's where you could see how different the person is.

*   *   *

A.P.: Why do you think it's possible for you all to get along well with the other girls despite obvious differences in people's social class backgrounds?

Wendy [PG3]: Because, um, see with the whole money situation, with the one group whose parents are lawyers and stuff [PG2], I think it's more of, like money is really important to them. But I think it's more within their group, like whose father makes more money than whose father in their group. But they don't care about us because they don't hang out with us on a daily basis. I think their battle is like, they judge their [own] people. They don't really judge us. They judge people that they see every day and after school and what not [not within their social class]. So I don't think that that really matters much to them. In school, I think it's more of them on like the outside, like publicly they have to [prove themselves] . . . that's what they use as their basis. But, I mean, we all get along. I mean, we have all run into each other at different gatherings, parties and what not. And you see them, you're like, oh, how are you doing and stuff like that. We get along really well which is really weird [. . .].

*   *   *

A.P.: Do you see differences inside the school community?

Gayle [PG2]: Between me and the school community?

A.P.: Yes, between you and the students?

Gayle: I think that the students, I mean, we are all teenage girls, but a lot of people are into their own thing. I think that most of us are pretty similar.

A.P.: In what ways are you similar?

Gayle: Because we are all like teenage girls. We all go to the same school together. We are all learning the same things. Most of the people who go here have money. Well, a lot of the people don't [have money], but I think that the thing that makes us different is the background from which we came, like at home. Like at school, I think that everyone is similar, but if you went to visit everyone else's house, it would be totally different.

                    *   *   *

A.P.: Do you think that social class differences have any influence on the friendships that you form here in school?

Amanda [PG2]: At school, it's just like everyone has got like the same kind of parents, you know what I mean? Not social background, but we are all like in the middle class, I think. Beth, I think she is one person who really doesn't have the money.

Donna [PG2]: I think it does make a difference because it like reflects, because like look, we are all from the city. We are all friends. [Beth and Wanda and Tess], they are all minorities. They all sit together and talk. Like [Ruth and Hannah], they are all working hard because they have to. They are like on scholarships and stuff.

Shelby [PG2]: Yeah, but not like different classes. There are like variations in the classes, like the middle class is hanging out with the upper class, do you know what I mean?

Gayle [PG2]: I don't think there is that much of a difference between the middle class and the upper class. I think we are all upper class or upper middle class. There is not much of a difference.

                    *   *   *

A.P.: Do you remember an experience in school where class issues were brought up and made a difference for you in school?

Fiona [PG2]: No. Do you think so?

Bella [PG2]: No, not really.

Fiona: We are in a school where everyone is basically of a certain class or class distinctions. They don't really show up that much, and I know that that is sort of contradicting about what we said before about the cars [students coming from more affluent backgrounds often distinguishing themselves by the cars they drive, and in some instances, personally own], and stuff, but I don't think that they [class distinctions] are that relevant, but maybe in a public school where there is such a wide group of people and maybe where a girl comes in pregnant or something like that, then it shows up.

As Best Academy students draw boundary lines separating peer cultures, they also cross borders within and between peer networks. The double-edged nature of adolescent girls' borderwork captures the complex character of class identity production in both vertical and horizontal directions. For Beth, a student from a blue-collar working-class, immigrant, Hispanic family who attends Best Academy on full scholarship, the fact that she is not from a characteristically professional middle-class family neither blocks her from full participation and acceptance within and outside her peer group nor interferes with her felt sense that she belongs at Best Academy. Beth is upfront about class differences between herself and some of her more affluent peers but feels that they are only visible outside school. Class borders are an altogether different matter in school where, she observes, "you don't have to show that you have so much in school, because the only thing you come [to do in school] is to study and to talk with the friends that you have in school." For Beth, class distinctions fade until they are nearly invisible. Wendy, a white girl from a lower white-collar middle-class family, also sees class differences between herself and other more affluent students like her peers in PG2. Like Beth, she feels that class differences do not keep girls from being able to "get along really well" both inside and outside school. As she points out, class conflicts tend to be contained within a single peer group and typically do not involve girls from other peer networks, observing that other girls, like her peers in PG2, tend to "judge people that they see every day and after school and what not [not within their social class]." Fiona adds that "certain class or class distinctions . . . don't really show up that much" and goes on to say that class differences might be visible "where a girl comes in pregnant or something like that." In sum, class conflicts are projected outside school, showing up in a wide range of neighborhoods, homes, and friends. Despite visible class signifiers that mark class borders within the professional middle class, class differences are, once again, contained and virtually muted inside Best Academy. As Gayle reminds us, "everyone is similar, but if you went to visit everyone else's house, it would be totally different."

Faculty and administration describe the class culture at Best Academy as less classist than some have found to be the case at other local private schools. Just as the class base separates private and public schools, so, too, there are variations in class cultures among private institutions. For some faculty, it is the relative absence of classism that sidelines Best Academy from the

traditional preparatory high school and makes it a more inviting place to work
for teachers from a variety of class backgrounds and experiences. Questioning
Ms. Rogers about her experience as a teacher at Hartford School, a reputed,
private, co-educational high school in the area, she notes:

> I like working at Best Academy a hundredfold better. As a student, I
> probably would have done terribly at Hartford School. At Best Academy, I
> probably would have done very well as a person. It's just different styles of
> education, styles of social behavior. I mean, it's interesting when you men-
> tioned different elements of education in class because I have always said
> that the things that made the difference between coming to Best Academy
> and Hartford School was that there was a very big feeling of classism at
> Hartford School. And basically, you can survive [there], I think, as a student,
> if you are intellectually brilliant, if you are athletically superior, or if you
> have a social connection. If you don't have one of those three things, you
> could get lost. And after seeing some of the parents, I think some of the
> middle-class parents send their kids there to make connections which to me
> is like selling your kid, to get your kid into this environment so that they
> will be rubbing shoulders with the right people when they get older. [. . .]
> The faculty, the middle school faculty was fine. I enjoyed working with
> them, but I thought there were a fair number of the faculty who still believed
> it should be a boy's school and viewed themselves—they had a tendency to
> hire their own graduates and people, so there is a real kind of snobbism there
> that I found intolerable. [. . .] I mean, there was a real distinction between
> "we" and "them" which Best Academy has never impressed me that way.

According to Ms. Rogers, Best Academy's *uncharacteristic* class culture is
unlike that in other private schools, at least in the local area. The current of
"snobbism" she remembers from the time she taught at Hartford School is not
part of her experience as a teacher at Best Academy where established
boundaries between "we" and "them" seem absent from school culture at large.
A conversation with one Best Academy junior confirmed the difference
between class culture at Best Academy and Eastmeadow School, another local
private school, where, she observes, "there was a total separation" of students
on the basis of class status. Unlike Hartford and Eastmeadow Schools, Best
Academy manages to create and sustain a bounded, inclusive community.

   Classism comes into sharp relief, though, during those moments that
students negotiate border crossings in a bid to manage class differences.
Wendy narrates the risk she takes in choosing to introduce some of her friends
from considerably more affluent backgrounds to her blue-collar working-class
family and community. This is a critical moment of identity production for her
as she develops a deeper understanding of who she is in opposition to who she
is not as she moves to cross class borders.

Wendy [PG3]: [. . .] But still, the amount of work that they do here has helped, you know, from what they're [friends who have graduated from Best Academy and gone on to college] telling me and from what other girls who have graduated told me, that it does pay off, which I'm going to be grateful for. And then it goes back to the friends thing again. I mean, I've learned that there's people who aren't just, because I always thought, before I got to high school, that all my friends, even beginning freshmen year, would just be the people that live in my neighborhood, that I see on a daily basis. Those were the only [people who were] my friends. But now I realize that I can have friends who just aren't like me. I can have friends whose parents own these big companies, whose parents aren't like my parents, you know. I can have friends from all over the place. And I think that's, and I think that, which that's what they miss. I mean, more important to me than really school, is my friends. It really is.

A.P.: Do you think going to Best Academy has allowed you to have different friends from what you would have had if you had made the decision to go to high school in Bayview [a working-class neighborhood]?

Wendy: Right.

A.P.: How does that make you feel?

Wendy: It makes me glad. Because at first, I said I didn't want to leave. I wanted to go to school with my friends. But I'm glad because if I would have gone to Bayview, that's it. I would have been friends with the people that I'm friends with, you know, now besides the girls from here. But it's like, I came here, I met Susan, I met Briana, I met Diana. I got, you know, especially Susan, the best friend that you know you could ever have. She's great.

A.P.: And yet you are both so different, from such different class backgrounds?

Wendy: Right. And I would have missed out not meeting her, you know. And that's why I'm really glad that I ended up coming here because she's the greatest friend. And I would . . . if I didn't come here, I would never have met her. And I would just have been having the same friends. Not that there's anything wrong with them because I adore my friends from home, you know, just as much as I do her, but I've like widened my horizons, and I wouldn't have had any new experiences. If I would have stayed, it would have been just like grammar school because the whole group of us would have been moving together, and we all would have been going to school together and seeing each other. So I've experienced things.

A.P.: Do you think you give anything to these girls who come from backgrounds so different from yours?

Wendy: Um, pretty much the same thing that they give me.

A.P.: Which is what?

Wendy: Like new, new experiences. Like if we go out, like their idea of what they want to do when they go out and my idea or when we go, and I meet friends of theirs that they grew up with and when they were little. And they meet friends [that I had] when I was little. You know, just the differences in people. And I think that's just new experiences like socially, like new friends and stuff like that. Not really, they haven't really, I haven't given them, or they haven't given me any things like academically [speaking]. Because we're all learning it all together. But I think it's a lot of having like, socially wise, like our social levels. Now they have, a couple of them have the experience of Bayview. When they heard Bayview, they were like—oh my goodness. But they went [to my party], they experienced it. They know it's not as bad as people think it is. So they have the experience of my society and my way of life, and I have the experience of theirs, you know.

Sharing and exchange of class cultures becomes a test of Wendy's ability to become a border crosser. With confidence, she states that "I can have friends whose parents own these big companies, whose parents aren't like my parents." Forging new friendships with girls who are more privileged than she provides her with an experience she might otherwise not have had and believes that her friends also benefit from learning about her working-class family and friends. As Wendy comes into contact with new and different class cultures, she discoveres the benefits of border crossing. In effect, Wendy and her peers learn to become multicultural, that is "culturally competent actors in multiple cultural contexts" (Wellman, 1996, p. 37). Borderwork within and across class cultures opens up new possibilities for who she and her peers can become. Interestingly absent from her narrative is any mention of the symbolic and cultural capital potentially gained through connections with privileged girls. When asked whether, given the opportunity, she would move into the upper middle-class neighborhood surrounding the school, she responds:

Wendy [PG3]: No. These houses are too big for me. Too big, too expensive. I mean, I like where I live now. I'm having problems with people at home. It's like, in my neighborhood, where I'm just getting fed up with them [people] for different reasons. Because a lot of them tend to make remarks about my new boyfriend [Wendy's boyfriend is Asian-American]. Because he's not from the neighborhood. He's from out at my aunt's house. She lives in Newton. It's like an hour away. And he's from out there, and they tend to make remarks about it because they're so jealous, you know. But, so we've been having problems there. But no, if I wanted to move out of Bayview, I would want to move out to my aunt's house. She lives in a trailer, you know, in a mobile home.

A.P.: Would you like to live in a trailer home?

Wendy: Yeah. It'd be perfectly fine with me. Not these big houses like this [in the neighborhood immediate to the school]. It's too much, too much for me.

Wendy struggles to carve out a safe space for the elaboration of a class identity in the borderlands—that space between her class location as a daughter of blue-collar working-class parents and the institutionalized class privilege of Best Academy—without having to compromise and ultimately reject her class background and experiences. Navigating the borders between "us" and "them," students like Wendy typically "work" class differences to their advantage.

A.P.: If you were to locate yourself in a social class, where would you place yourself?

Wila [PG3]: You mean like money?

A.P.: Yes, your lifestyle and financial status.

Wila: Average.

A.P.: Do you mean to say middle class?

Wila: Yeah, but maybe a little below middle.

A.P.: Why would you say that you are a little below middle class?

Wila: Well, my mother has to work and go to school. That is kind of hard. We don't always have money for what we want. We charge a lot of things.

A.P.: Do you like the lifestyle that you lead?

Wila: Uh huh.

A.P.: Did you ever want it to be something different than what it is?

Wila: Sometimes you wish you had money, a lot of money, but it might change you too.

A.P.: How might it change you?

Wila: It might change my mother or something. I don't know. You take it for granted.

*   *   *

A.P.: Do you find yourself interacting with girls from different social class backgrounds here in school?

Hannah [PG1]: Yeah.

A.P.: And how does that make you feel?

Hannah: Fine.

A.P.: Do you ever feel different or strange?

Hannah: No, it's not . . . I know, like freshman year, I guess Nina went over to someone's house and like said—whoa, you have such a big house—and all of this stuff. But I don't really do that. I'm like—oh, your house is cool. But it's not like I wish I could live here, why don't I live here, my house sucks. I mean, I like where I live.

*   *   *

A.P.: You told me that the differences in social class backgrounds of your friends don't have much of an impact on your friendships but that sometimes when things come up like skiing and you don't have the money to go, you get a little upset. Talk to me more about this.

Randi [PG1]: Yeah, every once in a while. I have things that they don't have like the dance [dancing lessons]. But I think it evens out eventually. And for the people who have all of the money in the world, they don't have very much that's worth anything to them. It's handed to them. They don't think anything of it. And when it's not there, then they are going to wonder.

*   *   *

A.P.: Would you like to have more money?

Ruth [PG1]: Yeah.

A.P.: What would you do if you had more money?

Ruth: My mother and I were just talking about this because we went to the mall to go look for prom dresses. My mom was like—we need to go on a shopping spree. And I was like—well, fine, let's go. And she's like—I wonder how much money we need to go [on a shopping spree]? I am like—we need an infinite amount. I would just love the feeling of going to the store and buying anything I want.

A.P.: Can some of the girls in school do that?

Ruth: I think so. [. . .] A lot of them have great clothes. But I can't afford clothes like that.

A.P.: Do you ever feel different because you don't have clothes like what you have just described?

Ruth: Oh yeah.

A.P.: Does it make you feel uncomfortable?

Ruth: It used to, but now I say—hey, if I don't have it, I don't have it.

A.P.: It used to bother you then?

Ruth: In eighth grade and then freshmen year. After that, I said, I don't care. I mean, I have friends, and they said the same thing.

Identity production processes articulated in terms of simultaneous acts of accommodation and resistance do not convey the complex meanings that girls construct for themselves on a daily basis in the private school (Anyon, 1984). Their narratives fundamentally challenge any suggestion of the linear reproduction of class identities in this institutional setting. Wila, Hannah, Randi, and Ruth, from families whose parents' occupations fall into the lowest tier of the professional middle class in terms of professional status and projected income, do not reject their class backgrounds altogether as a strategy for *getting over* the class culture of the private school. Despite emergent moments where girls desire the distinctions that upper middle-class privilege affords, they summarily agree that a change in lifestyle might "change you." They choose to work class borders, moving away from seeing themselves as the "other," and, instead, point out how being less privileged actually positions them as more responsible than their more affluent peers. Together, their narratives suggest that professional middle-class girls and those outside the middling classes manage class differences through exclusions as well as through border crossings within and across class cultures that find girls negotiating class in highly complicated and unexpected ways.

Teasing out varieties of identity production inside the professional middle class, I have argued that Best Academy students are actively engaged in reconstituting class identities. They do not simply reflect the prevailing class culture of the school in the ways that they see themselves in relation to one another, in the practices that they take up as they struggle individually and collectively to "become somebody." Best Academy students shape objective and subjective understandings of class within and across peer networks, negotiating class cultures within the unstable and shifting space of the borderlands. Student narratives highlight class differences through technologies of "othering" that allow girls from less privileged backgrounds within the professional middle class to *reposition themselves*. Such inversions paint a dimensionalized picture of the identity work that girls within the professional middle class engage in a school climate that by all appearances fosters a shared collective identity. As privilege is decentered, class identity production surfaces as a highly differentiated process that reminds us that identities are constructed across multiple discourses and practices that *have not* escaped the private school. As Best Academy students shape complicated processes of identity production in the borderlands, they poke at the longstanding assumption of the relatively seamless culture of the private school. While student voices roundly point out that "class distinctions [they] don't really show up as much," they gather together many experiences that suggest quite the opposite set of dynamics.

Chapter 4

Race Identities in the Borderlands

In chapter 3, I explored the emergence of class identities as they are shaped in relation to institutionalized discourses of class privilege. Social practices played out within and across peer cultures focus attention on the dialectical relationship between identity and difference, self and other. Privilege in the private school is not only embodied in discourses of social class but also extends to the organization of social relations of race which, like class discourses, are relatively invisible in an institutional site of dominance. Chapter 4 redirects cultural analysis in a similar way, raising questions about the embodiment of race privilege in a school whose student body is approximately eighty-five percent white with a majority white faculty. The production of a discourse of the western, white "self" has historically depended on the production of a discourse of the non-western, non-white "other" (Weis, Proweller, and Centrie, 1997), meaning that race difference is a matter of exclusionary practices that arise out of the cultural center. While we have considered the co-construction of racial identities, focusing the lens on the racialization of the non-white "other" (Weis, 1990), social scientists have indiscriminately sidestepped examination of whiteness as a site where racialized constructions of self are forged from/within a standpoint of cultural dominance (Frankenberg, 1993; Thompson and Tyagi, 1996; Fine, Weis, Powell, and Wong, 1997). The discourse of whiteness as identity and social practice has remained unnoticed and unexamined as a location of power and privilege. In this chapter, I offer a countermove to discussions that have typically taken up the issue of racial identity production through the narrated experiences of youth of color alone. Instead, I force whiteness to the surface and de-center it as an integral element of private school culture and a structuring dimension in the lives of white, adolescent girls. The voices of students of color will be folded into this discussion since they are an essential part of understanding the relational production of identity, but they will not be used to color in the white experience.[1] That task will fall to white girls who historically have been able to choose not to speak to issues of racial identity as it inflects their lives. Students of color, on the other hand, have typically not had this privilege, forced on a daily basis to mediate and negotiate racial contradictions that have been cleverly obscured through their institutionalization. Their narratives cannot continue to substitute for the confessional tales of those at/in the cultural center who need to take responsibility for *whiting in* identity productions and social relations of inequality that have been consistently and effectively *whited out* (Gallagher, 1994; Fine, 1997).

Scripting White Privilege

For nearly two decades, research on identity production in school contexts both in the United States and across international borders has focused inquiry on expressive forms of racial identity formation among youth of color. Recent ethnographic work has unearthed a repertoire of strategies that African-American youth draw on to find their way with, through and over liberal, middle class standards of communication, interaction, and self-presentation (Ogbu, 1988; 1991; Stanlaw and Peshkin, 1988; Weis, 1991; Grant, 1992; Delpit, 1993; Shujaa, 1994; Hemmings, 1995) complimented by emergent scholarship dedicated to examination of the voices and experiences of underrepresented groups that have been consistently marginalized and silenced by existing institutional arrangements (Phelan and Davidson, 1993; Weis and Fine, 1993; Davidson, 1996; Weis and Fine, 1996; Valdes, 1996; Carger, 1996; Lee, 1996; Seller and Weis, 1997). While race discourse and analysis has called attention to the relationship between school structures and semi-autonomous identity production among youth in educational contexts, it has not moved to deconstruct those embodied codes that inscribe and contribute to normalizing social relations of power and institutionalized forms of privilege.

Discourse on race has broadened in the past five years to include examination of whiteness as a fractured and continuously shifting racial border (Thompson and Tyagi, 1996) and exploration of how it is that whiteness accrues and hides its own power and privilege (McIntosh, 1992; Chalmers, 1997; Giroux, 1997). By turning the ethnographic lens back on the cultural center, social critique of whiteness has forced what has been generally implied in the study of race to the surface as a separate social and political category of analysis (Hurtado and Stewart, 1997). In her pioneering work on the social construction of whiteness, Ruth Frankenberg (1993) points out that whiteness, least recognized as a structurual dimension of race, has been diffused and displaced through a set of unmarked discursive practices and coded racial signifiers that prevent us from seeing the cultural center.[2] Where it enters contemporary race discourse, the construction of a white "self" strategically depends on the counterproduction of a discourse of blackness where representations of whiteness exist in relation to an "other," usually denoted through a language of binary oppositions that assigns positive attributes to being white (Mohanty, 1988; Yudice, 1993). Expanding on this important point, Frankenberg (1993) rightly observes that "to be white within this universe of discourse is thus to not be a number of other things: *not* Jamaican, *not* a person of color (p. 70)," meaning that whiteness is discursively constituted through the language of "otherness."

White students at Best Academy are implicated in constructions of racial identity as they position others at the borders of whiteness. Their narratives *do not*, but also more importantly *cannot* escape turning to the experience of the "other" as a point of entry into race discourse, the point being that whiteness as racialized identity tends not to be engaged through self-introspection.[3]

A.P.: What racial group do you locate yourself in?

Dina: White.

A.P.: What does it mean to you to be a young, white female in Best Academy? Is it a particular kind of experience that you can describe for me?

Dina: I guess you would have to say that it would be different from being a black female here at school. I mean, a black female would be able to answer that.

A.P.: What is the experience like for you as a young, white female at Best Academy?

Dina: Well, the white people are the majority at Best Academy. I don't know. It never really bothered me, and it never really occurred to me until seriously, this year, [when the school put on a series of morning presentations on Martin Luther King during Black History Month].

*   *   *

A.P.: What racial group would you put yourself in?

Sarah: White.

A.P.: White, right. What is the experience of being a white woman like here at Best Academy? Can you describe this?

Sarah: Um, well, this school, I mean, doesn't, I mean, we have black people, we have like all different kinds of people in this school. So like today for announcements, or in Morning Meeting, doing like Black Americans and people like that who influenced everyone. So, I mean, maybe in English classes, it's nice to have maybe like a black person, or maybe another kind of, like a Puerto Rican or some other kind of racial group like in your class, so they can voice their opinions too on how they look at things. So, I mean, it doesn't bother me. I like it. I don't know.

*   *   *

A.P.: What racial group do you see yourself apart of?

Victoria: Caucasian.

A.P.: What has the experience of being white been like for you here at Best Academy?

Victoria: It's the majority.

A.P.: What does that mean? What does it mean to be white in this school?

Victoria: I want to say normal, but it's not like African-Americans are abnormal. It's just the majority.

*   *   *

A.P.: Do you ever think about what it means to be white?

Nina: I never thought about it.

A.P.: Uh hum.

Nina: Because, probably we're the majority and, you know, we never really think . . . I mean, I'm sure the minorities think about it because maybe they think they're prejudiced [discriminated] against. But usually the people who are prejudiced [feel that they have been discriminated against by whites], were prejudiced by the whites. And since we are the whites, we don't think about it [being white] at all.

Representation of whiteness is confounded by the fact that white people subsist in a condition of raceless subjectivity (McLaren, 1991) where the invisibility of whiteness as race obscures the extent to which it organizes social relationships and identity productions. Analyzing mainstream filmmaking in the United States and Great Britain, Richard Dyer (1988) captures the essential paradox of white identity, that it is everywhere and nowhere to be seen at one and the same time.

> The colourless multi-colouredness of whiteness secures white power by making it hard, especially for white people and their media, to 'see' whiteness. This, of course, also makes it hard to analyse. It is the way that black people are marked as black (are not just 'people') in representation that has made it relatively easy to analyse their representation, whereas white people—not there as a category and everywhere everything as fact— are difficult, if not impossible, to analyse *qua* white (p. 46).

As they script them-(selves) as white, we begin to hear white students construct racial identities through an explicit language of otherness. Snared in the fundamental paradox of white identity, these girls necessarily have to shift their focus away from the cultural center onto the experiences of their African-American and Latina peers in order to be able to begin to see themselves as white. Because of the difficulties that surround representation of whiteness for whites, students, like Dina, project what it means to be white onto the backs of the "other," insisting that being white "would be different from being a black female here at school," and that "a black female would be able to answer that [question]." Ironically, I had asked Dina to consider what it means to her specifically to describe herself racially as white. Casting the spotlight in another direction on students of color keeps her from having to discuss white identity altogether. Being white is somehow different, but she is unable to articulate that difference from the interior of her own cognition as a white youth. Like Dina, Sarah draws on a language of "otherness" in her construction of a racialized identity, framing a response to my question in terms of the experience of the "other" rather than her own. In some instances, students would substitute ethnicity, religion and culture in place of explicit discussion of being raced as white.

A.P.: Let's talk about race. In what racial group would you locate yourself?

Dina: I basically consider myself Irish. I consider myself white, but like my friends, like Lucy, when she thinks of me, and we have had this conversation before, she doesn't think of me as white. She thinks of me as Irish, and I think that's really weird. I look Irish, I think Irish, I talk Irish . . . everything about me is Irish which is really cool. I like that. I am not sure if you meant black or white.

*   *   *

A.P.: What racial group do you locate yourself in?

Gayle: Jewish.

A.P.: And you are white? You had told me [earlier] that you are white.

Gayle: Yeah.

A.P : How do you see the experience of being white in this school? What is it like to be white in this school?

Gayle: I don't really know if there is so much of a difference. I mean, I fit in more.

Dina is white and is the daughter of American-born parents. While she self-identifies as white, this follows the first leg of her response to my question. Focusing on ethnicity, she denies the particularity of whiteness by skirting the question of race. Substituting her Irish background, her observation—"I consider myself white"—is nearly lost as whiteness is filtered through the category of ethnicity.[4]

Looking at many of the responses that Best Academy girls offer, it is apparent that white youth are not certain how to answer my query since they have generally given little thought to a discourse that is obscured through its own invisibility. For many of the white students participating in this study, reflecting on their racial identity as white was undoubtedly uncomfortable, for many the first time that they had ever been asked to consider the ways in which race privilege creates possibilities and structures limits into their lives differently than it does for non-whites. Their struggle to narrate racialized identities importantly reflects the persistence of color evasiveness in public talk about race where the effort is, either consciously or unconsciously, not to see race and not to acknowledge race as a marker of difference (Sleeter, 1993; Omi and Winant, 1994; Gallagher, 1994).[5]

In her interviews with white women, Frankenberg (1993) not only found color evasiveness to be a recurrent theme in their talk about race but also discovered a double-edged quality to this effect. While her informants acknowledged the existence of unequal institutional and structural arrangements in American society, they also went to great lengths to avoid seeing race difference, concerned that the act of seeing and drawing attention to race necessarily implicated them in the production of racism. The race narratives of white students at Best Academy embed this tension in deep worries that their talk about race will be misconstrued by other white students and their peers of color as racist. As long as whiteness is not forefronted in discussions of race, it remains naturalized and unproblematized. By probing what it means to be white, I denaturalized and problematized this category for a group of youth whose attemps at delinking white identity from racism clearly reflects what McLaren (1997) has recently described as "a refusal to acknowlege how white people are implicated in certain social relations of privilege and relations of domination and subordination" (p. 24). As they detached talk about race from racism, the respondents in Frankenberg's study drew clear lines of separation in their narratives between those who are racist and, therefore, "bad" whites, and those who are not racist, or, rather, "good" whites. Along similar lines, the practice of color evasiveness has a double-edged effect to it for white students who do not wish to appear unwitting defendants of race privilege, simply put, racist, as they recognize and speak to issues of race difference in social relations and institutional arrangements in Best Academy.

A.P.: Now how about race . . . what racial group do you locate yourself in?

Cara: Well, I'm a WASP.

A.P.: You're a WASP [laughter]. What has the experience of being a white, Anglo-Saxon Protestant been like for you inside Best Academy?

Cara: To me, it's never made a difference. But isn't that just because I am white? I mean, because I am a woman, it makes it a little different. So I get that kind of, if you want, discrimination. But I'm white, I'm Protestant. I mean, it doesn't . . . it has never effected me. I have friends who are Catholic, who are Black, who are Asian. I have a few . . . I mean, it doesn't come into play until we get into these whole racial discussions where I have to sit down and think—God, am I really racist? You know what I mean? It doesn't figure in.

A.P.: Do you think issues of race are discussed adequately in school?

Cara: Too much.

A.P.: Too much?

Cara: Well, in one sense too much, and in one [another] sense, not enough. I mean, how could you ever talk about, enough about something where whole races are being discriminated against because of color. But when you, yourself, are happy with the way you're dealing with it, and you have friends from different races, close friends, why should you have to sit there and defend yourself to people who, you know, are KKK members or, or are completely, you know, go back to your roots—Africa, and that everybody should be black or they should die. I mean, you get two sides of it, and why should . . . I don't want to be trapped into saying well, you know, I have black friends, so of course, I'm not racist. And I don't know . . . weird things like that. So I don't like to think about it.

*   *   *

A.P.: What does it mean to you to be a young, white woman at Best Academy?

Fiona: I don't really see a distinction. I mean . . .

A.P.: Between what?

Fiona: If I . . . I don't know. Most of the people who go here are white. So it's like I feel a part of the majority. But I don't really think about the fact that I'm white. A lot of the things that we have talked about like in English and in history, about slavery and racism, I think that that brings out the fact that I'm white. But not in my opinions, I'm not white in my opinions in terms of how I see those things. Um, but I don't think I'm black. I mean, I just don't think that I'm like, um, I don't, I guess it's not like my opinions are because of my skin color or anything—an issue of racism. I mean, I don't think I'm a racist person at all. Um, I don't really think that I think about the fact that I'm white really, you know, when I'm in school.

Just as I introduce conversation about racial identification, Cara defensively shuts it down, claiming that "it [race] has never made a difference." She speculates that maybe she has not been conscious of her racial identity because of her own location of privilege and then goes on to use the Ku Klux Klan as an example of how whiteness is highly marked as "bad," positioning herself in opposition as the "good" white who has "friends from different races, close friends." At the moment that Cara first *sees* race, she becomes uneasy with the possibility that she, herself, might be racist on some level. Fiona shares this undercurrent of apprehension in her efforts to delink the color of her skin from her opinions on race. Perhaps the juxta-position of "I don't think I'm a racist person" closely followed by her statement that "I don't really think that I think about the fact that I'm white" most clearly illustrates the persistent dissonance between the dis-course of whiteness and racism that whites find easier to ignore and forget than to face in a culture that has worked at keeping the codes of race privilege hidden and firmly in place.

During my time on site at the school, I observed Best Academy faculty peppering the junior curriculum with special topics units on race and ethnicity, setting aside time, usually in English, foreign language, and history classes for studying the literature, languages, and histories of people of color, but this was not consistent and uniform practice across the curriculum. While some faculty worry that incorporating the experiences of underrepresented groups into a history class, for example, will cut up the "pie that is American history," others describe a deep sense of obligation to move beyond the comfort zone to discuss the contributions of women and people of color in their classes. Throughout the year, Mr. Fischer, for example, infused his curriculum with discussions of the contributions of women writers and poets of color, lacing class conversations with instruction on the historical foundations of social inequalities, helping students to see where and why imbalances in social relations of race, ethnicity, class, gender, and sexuality remain constant phenomena in American culture

> [. . .] I'm not going to retreat from [text and class discussion of] homo-sexuality. I am not going to retreat from sexuality. I'm not going to retreat from talking about racism which in a way is difficult, being a white male talking to white girls with maybe one African-American girl in the class talking about racism. You can sort of feel like—am I looking at her [a student of color] too much, or things like that. In a way, it's very self-conscious, but I think it needs to be talked about, and they need to know that, yes, you should talk about it, and it's something that you can talk about, and I feel pretty strongly about that.

Mr. Fischer's statement reflects well on other faculty who fully support curriculum that calls attention to voices of difference, not hesitating to add these discourses to teaching and learning in their classrooms.

Mrs. Berson[6]: I really believe that one of my jobs as a teacher is to try to broaden the kids' minds and try to make them think about the things that obviously, that I think are important, and then I hope that they do. Uhm, and I guess I would say, unquestionably, I'm the person in this school who cares, by far the most, about that. Mr. Fischer does too. He's pretty new, but I did it by myself for a long time, and, uh, I certainly had complete approval of the former head. Nobody ever told me what to teach. But, I think it's extremely important to try to broaden their minds through the literature. I teach a lot of black literature. I teach a lot of women's literature. I had a student who was Native American a few years ago, and I had the class read a book by a Native American author, and she just came back and told me that it changed her life, that it was the thing that made her start pursuing her own heritage. She was only half Native American, and she had been living in her other half. And then I had a girl from India, and I just ran into her recently, and some of her friends who remembered how we sat on the floor, and she brought out some of her costumes and jewels from India. I mean, I try to capitalize on the kinds of students we have, being able to identify what we read but also having the other students try to understand what the experience is of somebody who is a minority.

Outside the classroom, cultural enrichment during specially scheduled Activities Periods or regular Morning Meeting assemblies devoted attention to the voices and experiences of underrepresented groups. Again, efforts at integrating the curriculum more broadly were not seen being played out across content areas, but only selectively in certain classes. Where and when race, ethnicity, social class, and gender were entered into the curriculum, they were typically treated as additive points of information rather than integral to curricular design and instruction.

In the face of this curricular orientation, it was not altogether surprising to hear from Best Academy students that they perceived efforts by the school administration and faculty to integrate girls of color into school activities as self-serving strategies. Taken one step further, it is possible to draw connections between their observations and core elements of white liberalism whose commitment to liberty, equality, and fraternity importantly factor into the organization of institutional life in the private school. While liberal thinking presupposes a fundamental humanness, it also calls for acceptance of racial differences, therein laying the foundations for the persistent tension in American race consciousness between seeing racial differences and the desire to see society in terms of a discourse of universal sameness that unites rather than divides individuals on moral ground (Goldberg, 1993). Chandra Mohanty (1990) has argued powerfully that race management, described in parallel terms as the domestication or mismanagement of race, particularly as it is played out in the context of higher education, seeks to recognize diversity and difference but that a discourse of pluralism can and often does fall short of a critique of the forms that the institutionalization of race privilege has and continues to take in educational settings. Although sidestepping discussion and analysis of conflict in race discourse creates the conditions for achieving diversity through harmony, conditions that school officials look to create, it can have the ironic and opposite effect of securing and recentering race privilege. Along these lines, Goldberg (1993) has suggested that,

> liberals are moved to overcome the racial differences they tolerate and have been instrumental in fabricating by diluting them, by bleaching them out through assimilation or integration. The liberal would assume away the differences in otherness, maintaining thereby the dominance of a presumed sameness, the universally imposed similarity in identity. The paradox is perpetrated: the commitment to tolerance turns on modernity's natural inclination to intolerance; acceptance of otherness presupposes as it at once necessitates delegitimization of the other (p. 7).

As white liberals support recognition of difference in organized institutions and social relations, their calls are, in effect, instrumental in propping up the codes and practices of race privilege. What is all too commonly the case is that acceptance and tolerance of diversity underlying decolonizing pedagogical practices in classrooms leave out critique of the historical and material bases of power, in short, reproducing assymetrical relations of power. Student narratives fill in the outlines of race management by implicating the school administration in these kinds of subtle practices. Dina and Marlene are among those students who indict school officials for supporting what they perceive as nothing less than token celebrations of race that have the opposite effect of alienating and silencing students of color in the classroom.

A.P.: What has the experience been like for you as a white person in a predominantly white high school like Best Academy?

Dina: Well, the white people are the majority at Best Academy. I don't know. It never really bothered me, and it never really occurred to me until seriously this year. Did you see the Martin Luther King Chapels? Mrs. Harrington put like a week of that stuff on [presentation at Morning Meeting during Black History month]. It made me think that they [the school administration are only doing this to satisfy the African-American students]. It just seemed so fake. It just seemed so fake because the people who did it were white. They were the ones who organized it. That is so wrong. We all should learn about that. It really seemed to me that they [the school administration] only did that thing just to satisfy them [the minority students].

*   *   *

A.P.: How do you think the experience of being non-white is for students at Best Academy?

Marlene: Oh, I think it's really hard because, I mean, I don't know. I probably just know from being friends with Lucy [an African-American student] because she gets so frustrated because of like the things that people say sometimes. I don't know. Oh yeah, like in English class, she always wants to talk about the African-American point of view on this or that. And everybody sort of rolls their eyes like [as if to say]—here she goes again.

While they do not know for sure the motivations behind these events, Dina and Marlene can only speculate that school officials scheduled these events as a show of respect for and tolerance of non-white students. Philosophically, Best Academy is committed to a climate of acceptance and tolerance of differences, a stand that runs through its mission statement and is clearly highlighted in a section that reads: "because as citizens, we live in a community which is increasingly global, young people have an obligation to understand those from different backgrounds." In conversations with some teachers, they would describe an official school culture that is relatively free of racial conflict. While teachers peppered descriptions of racial harmony with some tense moments they remembered between students in past years, these appear to be isolated exceptions to the rule. Teachers report that they generally neither *see* nor *hear* racism in school. The point is that there is little *overt* evidence of racism, which should not preclude the possibility of forms and practices of institutionalized racism that are typically hard to see and hear. We need to examine the basis for their conclusions in terms of the subtleties of race management operating in a largely white, historically elite, private school.

Ms. Nelson: [. . .] Also this school is incredibly open about differences between cultures and races and religions. And they are very cognizant around holiday time about making sure that there are equal differences on different viewpoints. The whole *Glorious People*[7] aspect [event], that was a really, really good thing to have happened, the fact that we [as a school] can celebrate the fact that as a black culture, we were repressed and had awful times due to a white culture, but I am not going to blame my white friends for that [kind of view]. There were a couple of grumblings like if I was a white student, and I did something like that, I would be considered racist. You are going to have comments like that.

A.P.: Did you, in fact, hear white students make comments along those lines?

Ms. Nelson: I heard it secondhand and heard about it in English class or a history class. But that ability to see that a minority has to talk about their past and that ability to see that it is okay to celebrate the fact that students are black without saying to them—I'm black, and I'm oppressed, and it's your fault because you are white. I don't see that here. I don't ever see people, in reference to any black student, like [saying] the black girl in the junior class. I don't ever hear that kind of representation in a negative context.

*   *   *

Ms. Donohue: It's not across the board, um, we had a very militant two-sister family in the school at one point, and they made some race problems. I mean militant and claiming racial inequalities and what not that were not in fact happening. They were getting a rush out of it is what was happening. They were enjoying being the leaders of this little group. But apart from that, that brief period, um, I don't think there is any, there is racial stuff going on. There certainly isn't in the classroom. In terms of who works with whom, um, or it doesn't happen in my room, and I would pick up on that as a bi-racial family. I am real sensitive to issues of color and automatic perceptions of people because of their color—my son is dark-skinned. And I would pick it up . . . that is not like the clothes thing which I wouldn't notice. And the girls sometimes will make the same kind of reference to race in a lighthearted way. They will make reference to, well, that's all Italian lovers, or, you know, that there is some kind of racial or ethnic things and usually it's the girl in question who starts the teasing. There is some of that, but it's real light banter, and there is not an undercurrent of anything nasty going on underneath it.

*   *   *

Mr. Vogel: As far as racism, I don't think it exists [in the school]. I don't hear comments in that respect. There's not a tremendous amount of black students here, but the ones that are here, and you saw *Glorious People*. It was marvelous and very well received. I think all the students were impressed by how well they did, and there wasn't anybody who said, it was a black thing, kind of deal.

Teachers candidly admit that there have been racial tensions between students in past years but that this is the exception to what is a generally harmonious and unified culture and climate. Because they don't *see* or *hear* racism, they reach the conclusion that it is not a problem in school. Not seeing and/or hearing racism is a foil for race management just as recognition of diversity can stand in for race domestication.

The practice of race management filters down into student culture showing up, for example, when students roll their eyes when a peer of color brings up race in class "again." Such quiet expressions speak loudly of the contradictions that surround white, liberal commitments to unite rather than divide and exclude people on the basis of differences which has the opposite outcome of delegitimizing the "other" as differences are *whited out*. Some students, however, begin to pierce and poke at the public, polite and, above all, silent language of race that has been so thoroughly embodied in Best Academy. As girls break out of the complacency of omission and silencing around race discourse, they uncover ways in which class culture overlays the production of an invisible discourse of whiteness. The tension between silence and voice floats through a descriptive analysis of one troubling discussion in an English class. Over several weeks, students were asked to read and discuss the text, Malcolm X, as part of a unit on the literary contributions of African-American writers and poets built into the junior English curriculum. This assignment provided students with the opportunity to examine race relations as they stood more than two decades ago but also brought them face to face with the tensions and conflicts that define contemporary race relations in the United States. Mr. Fischer's willingness to have these discussions with his students helped design a safe space for students to engage typically tense issues. Safe spaces can create opportunitites for what has remained private information to become public knowledge, and , in the process, set the stage for a backlash against white, middle-class norms of politeness and propriety. Breaking their silence and coming to voice, white students were, in effect, challenging white, middle-class prescriptions for a public, polite, and proper discourse of race. One controversial discussion pivoting around silence and voice would significantly shape the nature of race relations among the junior students for the remainder of the school year.[8] Glenda, a white, upper middle-class student, found herself at the center of contentious debate during a class session. Her decision to overstep white, liberal principles of tolerance and acceptance of the "other" would be a significant turning point in her racialization as a *white*, adolescent female. Responding to my question whether being white had ever made a difference for her as a student in Best Academy, she began to describe this incident in detail as it had taken place in her English class, centering around her and her classmate Wanda, an African-American student.

> Glenda: Well, we read a book, Malcolm X. We had a discussion about it in class one time, and I think I got myself into a bit of trouble, but I didn't mean to.
>
> A.P.: What happened? What did you say in class?
>
> Glenda: We were talking about Malcolm X and his ideas and his early philosophy, what he believed when he thought kill all of the whites [because] they are bad. And Wanda is in my class, and she really likes Malcolm X and believes in his philosophy. I don't know about the early part [of his life]. It seems like she sees him as a positive role model, I think, and leader in black history. And I said something to the effect that I didn't agree with his early philosophies because I thought it was threatening to me, you know, someone who [says he] wants to kill all of the whites. It makes me feel threatened because it is taking away all of my security.

A.P.: He was too militant a leader for you?

Glenda: Yeah. And it bothered me. And I didn't mean that in a racial [racist] way at all, but it came across that way. And I said that Malcolm X, I understand that he had a lot of hate in him because he was raised in a very poor family where the father left, and he was sent to different foster homes. So he had a lot of hate that had built up in him over the years, and so that's why he had so many negative feelings. And I said that I would never really be able to understand his position because I have never had an experience like that. I am from a middle-class, white background, and it would be stupid for me to think that I could ever really feel or understand what he was saying because I can't. It is just something that I can't [understand].

A.P.: What was her reaction?

Glenda: Well, she got very offended, and she thought that I was being somewhat racist because I was saying that his ideas were wrong or whatever, and, you know, that I was racist because I couldn't see his point of view. But it's not that I can't see it. It's just that I can't really understand it. I would be a hypocrite if I was saying that I could really understand it because I have never lived in those conditions.

A.P.: So how did you respond when she sort of accused you of being racist?

Glenda: She didn't say that she thought that I was racist, but she just got really offended. And then we talked about the fact that he felt that blacks who, when they made a lot of money or had a good job or whatever, and they moved into like a white, suburban neighborhood, that they were selling out because they were moving out of their black neighborhoods or whatever. I felt that it wasn't selling out, I felt that it was just . . . if they felt that it was something that they wanted to do, that they had worked hard to raise the money, that they should be able to do it. And if they were sharing some of their time and their talent with people who were less fortunate, that I really didn't feel that they were sellouts. And she disagreed with it very strongly. She felt that your roots are there, and that is where you should be. And see, I said again, I guess I really can't understand that because it is not something that I have ever been in the position of having really personally to deal with. But, I mean, I was very honest about the way that I felt. And I think that it would be better than just saying—oh yes, I have great sympathy for his feelings, I know how he feels. Because I don't [know how he feels].

A.P.: Did other students share your feelings?

Glenda: I don't know if they did. I don't think they would have come right out and said it.

A.P.: Why do you think that is the case?

Glenda: Well, first of all, they didn't want to offend Wanda. Wanda was really upset about the whole discussion. A lot of people had a lot of really strong feelings about everything. I think that it is a very touchy subject, and if you say something that is even slightly opinionated one way or the other, you will get branded as a racist, you know. And that might have been the case, that people did brand me a racist that day. But I had discussed it with my parents because it did somewhat upset me, and they felt that really I was being very honest with my feelings and that if I felt that I couldn't sympathize with him, then I was right in saying so because it would be better than just pretending that I am something that I am not. And that's how I feel about it too.

A.P.: It's interesting that you were afraid of being branded a racist. You were really concerned about being . . .

Glenda: Politically correct?

A.P.: Yeah. You felt constrained to express . . .

Glenda: How I really feel. I think most whites do have somewhat of that kind of thought in the back of their minds. I think it's probably just because of the whole historical experience that's been in this country. But that's just how I felt, and I didn't think that saying something else would be appropriate.

A.P.: Do you think that white students feel that they have to be careful about what they choose to say here at school?

Glenda: I think they are, just because they don't want to offend anyone.

Glenda's testimony illustrates the internal struggles that white students engage around choosing to speak publicly as whites in discussions about race. Speaking from her privileged standpoint as a white, Glenda moves out from under the complacency that easily settles in for those in structural locations of privilege to shape an opinion of Malcolm X and his platform as a black historical figure. In an ironic twist, race privilege becomes conscious at the moment that white power is challenged. This is arguably true for Glenda who, like many of her white peers, has never actively considered what it means to be white and the ways in which being white bounds her life on a daily basis. Reading *Malcolm X* in English class was a significant turning point for her, awakening her consciousness as a white girl at the moment she felt the security in being white threatened.

In the above narrative, Glenda speaks as an outsider to the black historical experience, making clear in her commentary that "it's not that I can't see it, it's just that I can't really understand it." As a white outsider to the black experience, the race discourse that she takes up potentially places her in the unsavory position of being labeled a racist since, in her mind, *seeing* race is equated with *being* racist. While Wanda does not explicitly call Glenda a racist in reaction to her critique, Glenda feels as though both white and non-white students in the class saw her in this context as "somewhat racist," and observes that "if you say something that is even slightly opinionated one way or the other, you will get branded as a racist, you know." What becomes clear in her analysis is that seeing and speaking publicly to race difference in a predominantly white institutional setting is "bad" practice. Donna, a white classmate present that day, offers her impression of the class:

> After class, I talked to Glenda and Wanda. Glenda was like—is Wanda mad at me? I like respect Glenda in a sense. I think half of the girls thought that [they shared Glenda's position on Malcolm X's race politics], but they just didn't have the guts to say it. But I think that was good. I think half of the people are fake about it. I mean, like some of the things that she was saying. I mean, I didn't think [they were] true [as well]. But it did scare me, some of the things that I was reading about Malcolm X, but I have just been brought up *never to say that* [my emphasis]. I would never say that like being naive. Just from being with blacks and like going to school, I would never say—I can't believe that, even if I thought that. I like respect Glenda for being able to just say that and not be afraid. But like she has never been to a public school. If she said that in a public school, she would probably be beaten up in the bathroom.

Donna's perspective on class that day sheds light on white practices of color evasiveness. In her ending statement that she had been "brought up never to say that," Donna ties the polite, public script of race to middle-class standards of best practice. Class codes overlay a discourse of whiteness to produce and legitimate silence and omission. Practices that risk breaking upper middle-class codes of acceptable discourse turn into "bad" practices that expose what appear to be foolproof conditions of white liberalism. Those who "don't have the guts to say it," as Donna points out, are "good" whites. In another analytical twist, Donna suggests that the private school, unlike the public school, is more likely to be a safe space for "outing whiteness" since middle-class standards for appropriate behavior provide a protective hedge against potentially violent repercussions among students. Testimonials by other white students in a focus group conversation suggest that Glenda and Donna are not alone in their class analysis of the way that race discourse is manufactured in the private school.

> Yvonne: When I had to teach *The Ways of White Folk* [as part of an honors project], I was like—shit! I was so scared that I was going to say something when Wanda was in the room.

A.P.: Do you, as white folks, ever feel tired of having to be careful, as you have suggested to me, about what you say when people of color are within hearing distance?

Briana: Kind of because when you think about it, I mean, I am like for everyone having their own rights, but I mean, it's just, they, they have their own organizations and everything. But if they want to have people's rights as we do, if we had something like that, do you know what a stink they would make about it. I know that I am like saying *them* as opposed to *us*, but I mean if we had like the all-white pageant, why do they need Ms. Black America.

Yvonne: It's like politically correct. They are striving to be politically correct. The best thing that they can do for their race is to just be open about it. Like I remember walking from the bus and talking about this person, and I was careful not to say that he was black. What's wrong with saying that he is black? It's part of his qualities. And Tess is like—well, what color is he? And I was like—excuse me? And a thought ran through my mind [like] what a stupid thing to say. He's black. But then telling a black person that makes you feel so weird. The best thing that you could do would be to just say it.

Briana: I agree.

Diana: They really have to stop setting standards like that. Like I know that my friend from [Oak Dale], on her college application for her race, she would put "other" because her parents were like Hungarian, and so she put that down [on her application] so she would get accepted. She did not put white. She basically is white, but her parents are foreign so she put that so she would get accepted. Just because they have a better shot because of their color, I mean, sure the people on the board may not accept someone because they are black, but I think that in the same way, if two qualified candidates are sitting there in front of them with like the exact same personality, they'll choose the minority.

A.P.: How do you think the experience of being white is different from being black here at Best Academy?

Diana: You are just like, you are just there.

Yvonne: You are just normal. You are not the exception, you are the rule.

Diana: The teachers are more, they are just the way they always are and talk like their personality. But as soon as they put a minority in the classroom, it changes their attitude so they don't offend them.

Yvonne: It may not change their attitude, but they are very careful about what they say.

In this focus group interview, white students express a collective concern that they might say something that they are not supposed to say when forefronting race. In a climate that defers to liberal principles, students are more likely than not to be either silent on matters of race or to tread lightly through the discussion in paternalistic terms that have little to do with undermining social relations of inequality and power than they have to do with the maintenance of privilege as institutionalized practice in the private school (Bartolome and Macedo, 1997). But Best Academy students soon discover that these strategies complicate rather than clear lines of communication across communities of difference. In the end, Yvonne decides against censoring herself and takes on a new outlook, thinking that "the best thing that you could do would be to just say it [recognize and communicate that a black person is black]." By engaging race discourse openly and directly, Yvonne, like Glenda, moves out from under the public, polite language of race, breaking away from the double bind of color evasiveness and stepping, instead, into the light of race cognizance (Frankenberg, 1993).

Still students would return to class on other days where polite practice would win out, out of a fear that they would either say or do the wrong thing in discussions of race. After a different discussion in the junior English class during a unit devoted to dicussion of race in American literature, a white student approaches Mr. Fischer, claiming that whites are unfairly portrayed in African-American literary productions. Mr. Fischer and a non-white student standing nearby are particularly surprised by her comment, and he responds by saying, "I don't think that you meant to say what you just said." Rather than help the student to understand the material bases of white representations in the black imagination, Mr. Fischer silences her, arguably because of his own private fear that he would be perceived as a racist by the student standing nearby. Beneath her comments, this student is struggling with feelings of white guilt that tend to surface at those moments when whiteness moves to the center of critique and is threatened with being exposed (Keating, 1995; McIntosh, 1992; Griffin, 1995; McLaren, 1997). Mr. Fischer might have worked through her fears as a white person feeling under attack, but he chose, instead, to avoid facing the discourse of whiteness head on, *whiting out* race and defending race privilege by omission.

Scripting White Privilege Through Other[s] Eyes

The narratives presented up to this point have outlined in broad strokes white girls' struggles to articulate a race consciousness at the center. When pushed to consider what has been a virtually invisible dimension of their identity, they begin to understand that race privilege makes it possible for the discourse of whiteness to remain invisible to them. Historically, people of color have not had this same privilege. Invisibility has not been their choice. Unlike their white peers, girls of African-American, Latino, and Native-

American descent have grown up looking at themselves through the institutions of white, western culture. Racial identity productions among non-white students are fundamentally different as a function of how they have been historically located vis-a-vis the cultural dominant. Positioned at the borders of whiteness, African-Americans, in particular, negotiate dual identities, one being a private identity, that is, how they see themselves, and the other, a public identity, how others see them. Echoing W.E.B. DuBois' (1961) scripting of the refracted double-consciousness of race, the African-American has grown up "looking at one's self through the eyes of the other world," coded white (p. 3).[9] African-American, Latina, and Native-American students in the junior class wish to be visibly integrated (Stanlaw and Peshkin, 1988), wanting to feel that they belong to school culture at the same moment as they wish to be seen by others as they wish to see themselves—as girls of color in their multiple and different colors. In other words, students of color straddle the conditions of visibility and invisibility. African-American students are the most vocal and explicit in their double-edged desire not to be othered, yet also do not want to be folded into a broad identity that denies and delegitimates fundamental differences. They float this tension between inclusion and exclusion throughout their narratives.

A.P.: How would you describe who you are as a person?

Lucy: [. . .] As a person, though, I think the biggest thing that describes me, at least from society and then comes from like me, is that I'm a black person. I'm everything, in every connotation, every true connotation that comes with a black person, I give out, because that's what I am.

A.P.: Like what?

Lucy: I have, I have totally, I believe, a very different outlook on life than most people my age, meaning most Caucasian people my age. I believe that anything that I get in life I struggle for because no matter what anyone says, there's still a lot of prejudice in the world—against women and against minorities. So if you're a minority woman, you're in trouble [. . . laughter . . .]. I mean, you're going to have a lot of difficulties. So a lot of prejudice, a lot of just things that people just believe to be true that aren't, that it seems like, on a daily basis, I have to fight against.

A.P.: Inside or outside of school?

Lucy: In school . . . everywhere.

*   *   *

A.P.: How would you like to be seen by the students in school?

Casey: I would like to be seen as African-American, who I am. It really, it kind of bothers me when people want to use, being we should all, we should all forget about color and not see people as for this and that, as an excuse to put down racial movements. I don't like that because there is such a lack of history in this country.

A.P.: In other words, you are saying that it is important to identify and emphasize differences?

Casey: Uh hum. But people shouldn't be judged by that, though, which everyone does. I do [it]. People do it. And I think that before you can really say that well, okay, I am not this, I am just going to be this blob, you have to know who you are first. Without knowing who you are, to claim that you are just this person, kind of denounces your history. [. . .] So I like to be identified for what I am. I like to be identified as a black female.

*   *   *

Wanda: I feel like I live in one world with two sides to it.

A.P.: That's interesting. So what are the two sides of this one world you are talking about?

Wanda: Here in America.

A.P.: Here in America. So that's the one world that you live in?

Wanda: Mhm.

A.P.: And what are the two sides that you feel you live in here in America?

Wanda: The noticed and the unnoticed.

As hooks (1990) powerfully observes, black females negotiate race subjectivities between the margin and the center, in struggle between "us" and "them." For Lucy, Casey and Wanda, this means that they cannot escape having to juggle dual conditions of invisibility and visibility in relation to white, liberal, middle-class norms that decide the institutional culture at Best Academy. In Casey's plea that she "would like to be seen as African-American, who I am," we begin to understand in concrete terms how race fractures identity productions among non-white students differently than it does among white students. In earlier narratives, white students described their impressions of efforts by school officials to integrate students of color into school life as disingenuous attempts that primarily served the interests of school officials to build and sustain a public reputation. While schools each have their own distinct cultural orientations, they are generally schematically organized around a culture of power based in the distribution of white, liberal, middle-class standards of communication and presentation of self, and the ability to succeed in school depends on acquiring and assimilating these codes into daily interactions and routines (Delpit, 1993). Students of color are angry over the ways in which the school administration and faculty draw on model black youth as examples of students whose academic success has been achieved because they have managed to acquire white, liberal, middle-class codes and apply them in school.

> Wanda: [. . .] I think that, like . . . I benefit the school cuz when a black girl comes through the school, a shadower [student visitor] might say, oh, wow, they have black people here. She must like it. She's been here three years. Well, I think in that way, I benefit the school [. . .].

>   *   *   *

> A.P.: Does race ever make a difference for you in school?

> Lucy: Yes. [With the] type of events that they have. For instance, if there is ever like an open house or something like that, they always call me. Of course, if there is ever a graduation dinner, they call Casey. One of us has to serve.

> Casey: As the token black, [as though they (school officials) are saying] we do allow blacks in our school. At this luncheon for alumnae that I just went to on Friday, we were sitting there. She [Mrs. Nicholson] was talking about the events that were going on at Best Academy, and she just had to get up there and make her point. She was like—and all of our African-American students were just involved in this play [Glorious People] written and performed by one of our black students, and all of the students were in it, and blah, blah, blah . . . we are so proud. [And she was] just looking at me like . . .

> Lucy: Don't make me throw up!

> A.P.: What were you thinking as Mrs. Nicholson said that?

> Casey: Her whole tone of voice was trying to prove to them [alumnae], you know, that yes, we do let our black students do things like—[I was thinking] gee wiz. I was the only black student that had been asked to go to this luncheon. It was a luncheon for alumnae. Friday was senior skip day, so they had to ask the juniors to do it instead.

As a tuition driven institution, the private high school relies heavily on its reputation as a means of drawing in financial support from the outside, and the administration works diligently throughout the year to maintain a distinct public image toward this end. In an ironic twist, the attention focused on students of color leaves some of them feeling more visible, *because of* rather than *in spite of* race difference. Under the guise of paternalistic acceptance and tolerance, the public, polite language of race has the unexpected outcome of doubly refracting these students as "other." Seeing through liberal attention to difference and diversity, Wanda feels that her peers tolerate her more than they respect her. A history of persistent domination of the other has arguably sharpened her vision along with that of other students of color who see race management operating beneath the public discourse of race in private education.[10]

A.P.: What kinds of things do you wish for?

Wanda: Um, racial respect instead of racial tolerance.

A.P.: How do you define the difference between these two conditions?

Wanda: Well, well, another classmate might, you know, tolerate me being, you know, in school or whatever. But they don't respect my presence here.

A.P.: They [the students] don't respect your presence here at school?

Wanda: Yeah [they don't].

A.P.: You mean to say that they are simply obligated to respect your presence at school?

Wanda: Yeah. Like I'm probably at this school because of some quota that they've [the school] had to fill or whatever, but not because, you know, I'm a black girl or whatever [the implication being that Wanda was not accepted to the school purely on the basis of merit].

Later on in our conversation, Wanda added in response to my asking whether she sees herself playing an important role in the school:

No. I think that, like . . . I benefit the school 'cuz when a black girl comes through the school, a shadower might say—Oh, wow, they have black people here. She must like it; she's been here three years. Well, I think in that way, I benefit the school, but [I have] no role.

When I ask Tess, an African-American student whose academic success in a local Prep Program facilitated her enrollment in a private high school, to describe the ways in which she feels herself to have changed during her first three years at Best Academy, she volunteers:

I think it [the school] has made me know who I am and know my culture better because there are so many people that are different here than me. And like there are so many of them. It makes me want to look more into my background and see who I am, you know, so I can stay within myself.

Paradoxically, Tess' identity is cultivated and her visibility as an African-American sharpened as a student here. Attending a predominantly white institution has positively contributed to her emerging sense of self, helping her, as she put it, to "look more into my background and see who I am, you know, so I can stay within myself." Beth, a Puerto Rican student who befriended Tess during the Prep Program and achieved at a high enough level to gain admission to Best Academy as well, similarly observes that her ethnic identity has been strengthened as a result of being the only Hispanic girl in the junior class. There is very little about the culture of the private school that would resonate with Beth's background, but it has the ironic outcome of intensifying her ethnic identification as Hispanic in a positive sense despite that fact that the school does nothing specifically to legitimate and validate her voice.

A.P.: You say that racially you identify as a Hispanic.

Beth: And I always will.

A.P.: Do you think the experience of being Hispanic is different from the experience of being white or African-American?

Beth: Yeah, I think every racial group is different because they are. They shouldn't be classified as different, you know what I mean? They shouldn't be put in a certain place because they are different. We have different backgrounds, different traditions. That's no reason to be pointed out. 'Cause I know that I have way different traditions than other people here, different backgrounds, different way of being raised and stuff like that.

A.P.: Suppose another Hispanic friend of yours was thinking about coming to school here at Best Academy, and she asked you how it feels to be Hispanic and go to school here, what would you tell her?

Beth: Well, people here [at Best Academy] don't make you feel different, you know. But you know that you are different because you are like the only person that is Hispanic here. But you don't see people like pointing [you] out because you are different. So, I would say that knowing that you are Hispanic is just enough. Don't change because, you know, maybe by coming here, you like figure out that you have to change because you are the only one, and you don't want to be the only one. But I would tell her, just don't change. Be yourself. [. . .]

A.P.: Do you think you make a contribution to this school?

Beth: Well, my three years here, I've noticed that I am the only Hispanic here. I think that's what my contribution is going to be—the only Hispanic that is going to graduate that I have known of for the last three years.

A.P.: How does that make you feel?

Beth: Me, personally, it makes me feel good. It makes me feel that I accomplished something, you know. There's been times that I think I can't handle this, [that] I have to drop out and stuff. People sit me down and make me think and make me realize that this is going to be something good for our race because it is something big that a Hispanic could do—graduate from such a big, popular school like this one.

Outside of private parochial and some types of independent schooling, minorities have been significantly underrepresented in private education.[11] Against this backdrop, Beth and Tess' acceptance to Best Academy represent important turning points in their individual and collective histories. Admission to Best Academy also recognizes the potential for their success, which pokes at the historical underachievement and consistent failure of minority school children that has been attributed to cultural deficiencies among ethnic and racial minorities in the documented history of American education (Ogbu, 1987; Carger, 1996; Valdes, 1996). As Beth proudly states, "[P]eople sit me down and make me think and make me realize that this is going to be something good for our race because it is something big that a Hispanic could do—graduate from such a big, popular school like this one." Tess and Beth each manifest a public racial and ethnic identity that is two-sided—a pro-school and an oppositional identity (Davidson, 1996) forged in resistance to subtle pressures for students of color to adopt the norms, values, and dispositions of white, middle-class culture that bound the experience of private schooling. Rather than fade into the white background, their presence becomes even stronger as they phase into the foreground as girls strongly identified with their African-American and Latina heritage respectively.

Working Race in the Border Zones

In recent years, discourses of identity formation have recognized multiple cultural identities that individuals try out and exchange for others as they interface with other cultures they find themselves participating in. Identity production in the borderlands underscores the fact that identities are neither stable nor unitary but, rather, fluctuating and plural in relation to the multiple contexts and conditions that individuals unavoidably have to navigate. As I indicated earlier, linear descriptions of identity development among youth of color have captured strategies that they draw on in accommodation of and/or resistance to the intentional world (Schweder, 1991) of the white, middle-class school whose institutional practices have consistently devalued, marginalized, and silenced the voices and experiences of underrepresented groups. These accounts overwhelmingly suggest the development of oppositional identities among this group of youth as their way of getting through and over the culture of power in place in mainsteam schooling. I argue, however, that identity production is not as linear as earlier studies have suggested and that we need to begin to look more closely and probe more deeply the varieties of identities that students of color slip into and out of without having to abandon the racial and ethnic signifiers that they first brought with them into Best Academy. Changing and reinventing who they are, students of color choose not to throw off their racialized selves strictly through the development and incorporation of oppositional identities. Instead, these students work the borders of race in sophisticated ways, slipping into identities that hold out new modes of self-definition in the borderlands. Those who have been historically othered have been the centerpiece of discussions of borderwork. That focus needs to be adjusted in order to decenter white privilege. Speaking out of his own experience in the Academy as both a graduate student and later as a professor, David Wellman (1996) recounts significant points where he felt himself very much the outsider to academic culture despite the fact that multiple dimensions of his identity fit the academic profile. Comparing himself with his colleagues of color, he sketches penetrating differences between the borderwork that he engages as a white, male, heterosexual and the delicate border crossings that his colleagues of color risk daily in higher education. He writes,

> The borders I live on are porous. My crossings are opportunities as well as options. I can choose to live on borders, or avoid them. That choice is privilege, even when experienced as pain. My colleagues of color don't choose border identities. They cannot refuse them either. And they can't move between them as easily as do I. The elements of choice and privilege in my life mean I cannot be otherized in the same way as people of color (p. 38).

There is no question that race introduces different possibilities depending on where one is relationally located and positioned with respect to the cultural dominant, and Wellman draws clear comparisons between what is and is not possible for him as opposed to his colleagues of color. While he has the option of living on the borders or skirting them altogether in his practice as an academic, he still cannot escape the contradictions that the border zones of his own lived experience as a white, male, heterosexual present for him as they interface with the conditions for membership and inclusion set by the Academy.

Best Academy officials are invested in creating an inclusive school culture for learning and interacting. Earlier, teachers described their attempts to bring the voices of underrepresented groups to the center of class discussion, drawing on transformative pedagogies that partially reflect liberal commitments to unite rather than divide people across differences. While the white, liberal classroom moves beyond social and cultural differences to focus on the common strands that link individuals together, it can have the damaging effect of positioning students of color as sources of authentic experience (hooks, 1994). Transformative pedagogies whose goal is to create a common context and comfort zone for learning can have the opposite effect of reifying these voices in dynamics that "vacillate between a high level of tension and an overwhelming desire to create harmony, acceptance of 'difference' and cordial relations in the classroom" (Mohanty, 1990, p. 195). Pedagogies that focus the lens of cultural experience and interpretation on the "native informant" may give voice, agency and visibility to students of color, but they roundly fail to destabilize race privilege. Race continues to be studied from the standpoint of the "other," unwittingly recentering and obscuring the discourse of whiteness.

> A.P.: What is your experience of being an African-American here in school? In your mind, how is it the same or different from being a white student at Best Academy?
>
> Wanda: Well, um, I think the black students, because there's so few of us, and when you are in this school, you're expected to, whenever there's like a black topic, you're expected to, you know, be able to jump on it, be like, well, this happened here, and I feel this. You're expected to know everything about the black race because you're black and stuff like that.
>
> A.P.: How do you feel about that? How do you feel in your classes when these kinds of situations come up?
>
> Wanda: Well, I don't like it. And, you know, I let the teachers know that I don't. But I'm, I pretty much just . . . I know something, I say it, but if I don't, I just let it pass. But I let them know that just because I'm black, doesn't necessarily mean that I have an opinion about everything relating to something black.
>
> A.P.: Do you get angry? Or do you feel that you have a responsibility to educate others?
>
> Wanda: No. I don't feel that I have a responsibility at all.
>
> A.P.: To white culture, to inform others who are white?
>
> Wanda: Mhm [no, I don't feel as though I have that responsibility].
>
> $*$ $*$ $*$
>
> A.P.: And how about the backgrounds of the girls in the junior class—in what ways are the girls different from you and how do you respond to this?
>
> Tess: Like Lisa [. . .], I think Lisa, she has been mostly . . . she hasn't been anywhere because really, she is not aware of other people's cultures, anything but their own. I guess they haven't experienced it or haven't been out of their neighborhood.
>
> A.P.: How does that make you feel as a student in a predominantly white high school?
>
> Tess: It makes me want to inform them more of my culture and say, hey, you know, this is what happens. But I never get harsh with them because I know

that it is not their fault that they don't know, and they are trying to learn. But I just try to inform them. [. . .].

A.P.: Are the students at school open to hearing what you have to say?

Tess: Yeah. Like Lisa, she doesn't know anything. She asks me like . . . she doesn't think that there are like people in Africa with clothes and regular stuff. She thought that it was like antelopes running around and zebras. I am like—Lisa, it's just like here. I just tell her that it is like a regular community, not that different.

A.P.: Did any student ever ask you anything that got you mad?

Tess: Wanda gets mad, but I just figure, it's like Lisa, where she lives at, like Mandy and them [referring to the other girls in her peer group [PG3] who tend to live in predominantly white towns and villages on the outskirts of the city], like they say that before they came to Best Academy, they had seen like two or three black people. It's not their fault where they live. Maybe the school [they attended prior to matriculating at Best Academy] just didn't teach them, or their parents didn't know about it. It's not really their fault. But now they are trying to learn, [and] it's better.

A.P.: Do questions ever come up in your classes about your culture and your background and how do you respond when you find yourself facing those situations in school?

Tess: Yeah, like if we are having a discussion, maybe Shelby or somebody will say—well, so what is it like being black and stuff? Mr. Fischer will tell them not to say that, but it doesn't really bother me. One time it bothered me because everybody was just talking, and as soon as someone turned around and said [to me]—what is it like for you or if they are having a discussion, and I am just quiet, I can see Mr. Fischer looking at me, and then all of a sudden, he will say—well, Tess, what do you think?

A.P.: As if to imply that you are the representative black person in your class and necessarily have something to say on this matter?

Tess: Yeah. I don't like that.

A.P.: How does that make you feel on those occasions where you somehow fall into the position of being the representative African-American in class?

Tess: That is one reason why I don't answer as much because I don't like the way that Mr. Fischer just calls out at me. I don't really like that.

A.P.: Do you tell him you don't like it when he does that?

Tess: No [I don't tell him].

In predominantly white classrooms, African-American youth are inescapably positioned as expert witnesses to life on the "other" side. We hear this in the admittedly naive questions that their white peers field them. Wanda recounts a time when Lisa, a Native-American student and close friend of hers, asks her through half-embarrassed chuckles if black people ski. Apparently, she had never seen African-Americans on the ski slopes that she has travelled down. With patience and good humor, Wanda smiled and candidly answered: "Yes, Lisa, black people ski in the winter." Had Wanda been asked this question by another peer with whom she was not as close, she might have come back with a more emotionally charged response. Because Wanda and Lisa are part of the same peer group, Lisa's question is seen as well-intentioned. The point here is that Wanda and Tess are both positioned as resources on matters of race, roles that are assumed and prescribed for them. Thrust into the intentional world of the private school as it has been defined, African-American students respond by working the borders of race culture in multiple ways. Their classrooms present a double burden for these students who oftentimes find themselves split between volunteering or withholding information in resistance to how they have been positioned as tokens. In some instances, students of color willingly silence themselves despite learning environments that appear to legitimate the "other." Guarding the borders of race culture, some of these students refuse information in counter-response to having been located as experts. In this regard, during several in-class observations, I saw these students invert and reappropriate a public, polite language of race by refusing to cross color lines through cultural trading. Pedagogies that invite students of color into mainstream discourse by situating them as experts unwittingly legitimate silencing of their voices in the classroom. Snared in the double-bind of whiteness (Ellsworth, 1997), teachers' attempts at creating more inclusive, multicultural classrooms can, in fact, work in oppositional ways to delegitimate the "other."

There are times, though, when students cannot overlook black stereotypes chiseled into the white imagination and strategically work against white, middle-class prescriptions for politeness and silence around race. For example, overhearing talk about drug dealers in her gym class, Wanda had her response ready, observing that "it was like instinct upon me to, to, you know, say—not all people who wear beepers are drug dealers." Wanda pierces representations of blackness cradled in the white imagination in colors of darkness and strains of danger that shape images of black drug dealers. Her deliberate intention is to undercut mis-representations of blackness through counter-oppositional strategies in a bid to *manage race on her own terms* inside white, professional middle-class school culture. At other times, students go the route of self-silencing, because they either wish to redirect race discourse in the classroom or are less than optimistic in thinking that anything they might say could impact on and transform white students' thinking and behavior. When I asked Casey to explain why it was that she had decided not to respond to a student who failed to understand Malcolm X's philosophical position on race relations in the United States, she answered in a tone of reconciled contentment—"I felt like I was beating a dead horse."

African-American students express that they feel most comfortable with their black peers with whom they are able, as they narrate, to be "true to themselves." Within their own peer networks, I would often catch them drawing on the language and discourse styles of Black English, marking off a kinship system that separated them from their white peers.[13] Tess, Wanda, Lucy, and Casey were "loud Black girls" (Fordham, 1993), "acting out" in open study hall through rough play that allowed them to find a "homeplace" (hooks, 1991) in a school culture they have to negotiate daily to make their own. Each of these girls had a variety of friendships in school that crossed race and ethnic lines, and the peer groups in which they located themselves, PG1 and PG3, were racially mixed. As I mention above, they slip back and forth between voice and silence, depending on how "real" they feel their engagement with white peers and teachers to be. What appears to trouble them most, however, are practices of cultural borrowing among white students and the motivations behind their actions. Girls of color see white girls obligatorily trying on and appropriating such known cultural signifiers as clothes, language, and mannerisms as bridges to race cultures not their own.

Tess: Um, I think the [white] girls have, a lot of them have looked into maybe like, like me and Wanda have certain styles of dress and music, and the way we talk and everything. They started to do it. Me and Wanda, I notice that we use words like—ah, man, "that ain't nothing," "that's fat," "that's dukey." And Lisa will say, what's that, what's that? And then we tell them, and then if you notice, like if you see them walking down the hall saying, ah, "that's sweet" or "that's fat," they mostly got all of those words from me and Wanda [we use them when we are] joking around. Or they would be like walking funny. A lot of words, they will ask us what they mean, and then they will start using them. They come to us and say, show us this dance move or have you seen anything new on TV. Like in freshman year, they wasn't all into Rap or like into their Nike sneakers, but I think it's changed just by listening to us and seeing what we do and liking it.

A.P.: That's a pretty powerful role.

Tess: I like it.

A.P.: Does Wanda feel the same way?

Tess: I don't think so. She is not like that. She is one of the persons that says—look at the person trying to copy off of us. She is one of those persons. I am like, if they are trying to copy off of me, that means that I am the leader, and they are the followers. If they want to do it, just let them do it.

A.P.: Do you ever get any sense that some of the white girls try to act black?

Tess: Yeah. I know Shelby. She will act a different way in front of me and Wanda like saying—did you go see CB4, it's like a movie, and there are a whole bunch of black people in it. [Shelby will then say] did you see the new Air Jordan [sneakers], and then [she will say things like] "that's fat," "that's dukey" and "that's sweet." When I get in front of my family, I talk the same way in front of them, using those same words. And then I went to her house one day . . . it's a whole different thing, a whole different talk. She didn't use any words like "fat" or "sweet." It was just like—daddy, did my brother come home yet? She was talking real nice to their maid and everything, and she didn't really have her baggy jeans on. She just had her skirt and her shoes. It was just a whole different outlook on her like this in-school thing that she was doing.

A.P.: What was your reaction when you saw that this girl sort of lives two different lives?

Tess: Her and Wanda got into an argument. She said that Wanda was fake because we might talk a certain way with her and then get in front of the teachers here at school and talk another way. There is a certain way that you have to talk to people like teachers and important people. You can't always talk, you can't use words like "fat" and "nasty" and stuff. You have to talk a certain way. And Wanda was trying to tell her that. But she was telling Wanda that she was phony, and that's when I got [stepped] in.

A.P.: That who was phony?

Tess: Yeah, Wanda. Because we would talk a certain way. And if you go in front of an English teacher or somebody, she has to use different words and maybe a different vocabulary because that is the way that you are supposed to talk in front of a teacher. And she was calling Wanda phony, and that's when me and Wanda jumped in [and said]—well, wait a minute, you are the phony one. You are the ones using the words like we are using in front of us, dressing like we are dressing, and then when we go over your house one day, you are with a different vocabulary, different talk, trying to suck up to your family and stuff, because when I am around my friends or my family, I talk the same way [that I do among my friends in school]. Except like if I am going for an interview or something, you have to change the way that you talk.

*   *   *

A.P.: Do you ever feel that some of the white girls in school try to act black? Do you know what I mean by that?

Casey: I know what you mean. Are they the people that we sit with at lunch? No. But like Gayle and Amanda [the girls from the peer group who are from predominantly upper middle-class homes and private school backgrounds] and all of them. They drive me nuts just because they sit there and just try to act so down, just try to be so down as in being hip to black culture.

A.P.: What do they do that gives you the impression that they are trying to act hip to black culture?

Casey: [They] just try to, you know, learn all of the lyrics to the [Rap] songs, walk a certain way, and talk a certain way.

Lucy: They think they talk the way that black people talk.

Casey: I mean, this is going to sound really awful, but it's like if you get a bunch of black people together and have a bunch of white kids try to act like that, it's like a joke. I mean, nine times out of ten, you'll see the black people going—look at them, look at that. It will become the hot topic, and that will be the new discussion, you know. It almost becomes like a joke.

It is possible that white students see black cultural forms as novel and their reappropriation a means of skirting white, middle-class codes for polite, acceptable behavior. It is arguable, though, that practices of cultural appropriation among white students are apt illustrations of what Stephen Haymes (1995) has identified as the signification of black culture in the discourse of mainstream white culture:

> The mostly white dominated culture industry has made its fortunes by providing whites with access to "life," by exploiting black music, dance, art, fashion, sports, and linguistic codes. Recognizing white culture's exotic interest in black cultural practices, the culture industry has played a pivotal role in the commodification of black culture, in order to expand its mainstream, white consumer market—except that what has been commodified has not been black culture per se but the sexualized exotic and primitivistic images and representations it evokes in the imagination of whites. Henceforth, stereotypical black images and signs are inscribed in and on mainstream American white popular music, dance, television, styles, fashions, advertising, and magazines. Through the luxury consumer market, mainstream whites can purchase a style of life in which black cultural productions are the signifier that permits them to imaginarily indulge in the exotic and sensual (p. 119).

African-American students in Best Academy point out that white girls are, in part, drawn to friendships with them on the basis of powerful images of consumer culture wrapped around black people and black culture. Tess notes, "they [white students] come to us and say, show us this dance move or have you seen anything new on TV." White girls, on the other hand, appear to stake out relationships with girls of color, in part, because they understand that it is through black cultural forms and practices that they will be able to participate in the exotic and the sensual, otherwise out of the bounds of white, middle-class social practice. The friendships that white girls seek out and forge with girls of color appear to be motivated partially by desires to purchase cultural forms they have been prevented from participating in. African-American girls come to see themselves as cultural providers for white girls who recognize and own up to the absence of culture in their own lives. Because Tess and Wanda engage similar practices in their own border work, they do agree to excuse the "copying" or commodification of black cultural forms among their white peers, but continue to question in their own minds counterfeit motivations white students might have for crossing race borders.

While white students engage border crossings of their own through the commodification of black cultural forms described above, they also patrol the borders of whiteness as a protective hedge around race privilege. This strategy emerges in critiques of their non-white peers who subvert constructions of race set in American culture by "acting white" (Hebdige, 1979; Jones, 1988; Wellman, 1996).

> Gayle: [. . .] I mean, some of the black girls are like, I wouldn't fit in because I wouldn't want to be here. 'Cause you have to like act white, do you know what I mean? They are like acting white. They are like whiter than I am.
>
> A.P.: Do they act white?
>
> Gayle: It seems like it.
>
> A.P.: In what ways do you see that?
>
> Gayle: I mean, I listen to more black music than they probably do. You know what I mean? Or like I talk more slang or whatever. Like Lucy, I think she is whiter than I am. I mean, she went to St. Sophia's for middle school.
>
> A.P.: Can you give me a few examples of this in your interactions with some of your non-white friends?
>
> Gayle: Like well, Lucy . . . were you here for the morning announcements? Well, she made an announcement . . . she's like, I'm flustered. It's just like who would use that word? I don't even think that a waspy grandmother would use it. Do you know what I mean? It's just so weird.
>
> *   *   *
>
> Victoria: Yeah, there are cliques of black people. They go in cliques. And then when they talk to each other about something, they get really excited about something, you know, [they talk] in the black lingo.
>
> A.P.: How do you feel as a white person when you hear that?
>
> Victoria: Uch, it annoys me because they shouldn't, they don't have to talk like that. They know how to talk normal. Like Lucy, who is this intellectual person, will use Black English.
>
> *   *   *

A.P.: Do you think some of the black students here in school try to act white?

Shelby: Uh huh.

A.P.: In what way do you see them doing that? What gives you that impression?

Shelby: Like when they're talking to us, they'll talk with, um, our kind of language.

A.P.: Sort of what is commonly understood as white English?

Shelby: Yeah. And when they talk to each other, it's like they talk in their black language.

A.P.: How do you feel about that?

Shelby: I don't like it. Because I said, like [with] Wanda, you know, always makes fun of the way we talk. And I'm like, Wanda, I can understand everything you say, you know. Why can't you just talk to me? And she's like, because you're not from the same background. And I'm like, I understand what you're saying, you know. Because I did go, I did hang out with a lot of black kids growing up and things like that. And it's just . . . I think it's sad that they think that they have to accommodate for us, and I don't like it at all.

White students are openly critical of African-American girls who appear to be pretenders to white culture, acting more white than white students, an inversion of the critique that girls of color lodge against their white peers who cross borders when they try to "act black." White girls become uneasy and quickly move to guard their privileged standpoint when border crossers threaten to disrupt and subvert established racial categories. Stepping outside of acceptable middle-class standards for practice, they become less than polite as they draw on a visibly *public* language of naming race and race difference, arguably facilitated by the fact that they are telling their stories in *private*. Consider that Gayle is harshly critical of Lucy's tendency to act "too white" while Victoria rejects attempts by girls of color to cross white borders by appropriating a vocabulary beyond what a "waspy grandmother" would say. Shelby observes African-American girls trying to "act white" as they move from one cultural zone to another, finding it difficult to marshal understanding around why it is that girls of color feel the need to "accommodate [themselves] for us." Caught inside of her own contradiction, she rejects "their black language" at the same time as she would like African-American girls to be themselves in school. White girls weave in and out of a critique that either charges African-American girls with being too black or less than black. Gayle faults Lucy for using English that is "whiter" than what a waspy grandmother would say, yet Victoria takes issue with Lucy's use of "black lingo" which somehow suggests that she is less than "normal." Either way, girls of color are inescapably deficient, positioned in relation to a white standard —not black enough, too black, less than white—reflecting the constructed superiority of whites over blacks that persists in the white imagination.

The practice of color evasiveness allows faculty and students to retain their belief in democratic ideals of equality of educational opportunity inscribed in the tradition of common schooling in the United States. When asked whether she sees differences between students in her teaching, Mrs. Harrington insists that there is no relationship between student achievement and race and/or ethnicity.

> I don't really see a lot [of differences between students in terms of cultural or racial backgrounds], and I don't connect backgrounds. And I really couldn't tell you who, in my class, is from an upper middle-class [family] or from the city as opposed to the suburbs. I really couldn't tell you because I don't know. I never really [noticed]. And I notice some differences in the way they dress and that kind of thing. I could probably relate that to differences in them as individuals, but basically I try to notice learning differences, learning differences in math. And everyone of them is different. [. . .] I notice differences in them, but I don't really tie it to anything else—learning differences and that kind of thing.

While she states that she "notice[s] differences in them as individuals," she adds that she doesn't "tie it to anything else." "Color blindness" preserves the liberal commitment to uniting persons rather than dividing and separating them across particular social and cultural differences. If she were to draw any connections, she runs the risk of undermining the liberal investment in equality that presupposes equal and open opportunity in American education. Draping her classroom in principles of equality, tolerance, and diversity, Mrs. Berson finds ways to create a culture of inclusion by capitalizing on the "exotic" experiences of "others." Her earlier comment to me, that "anything that I can do to make them [white students] try to understand what it is like for other people is all the good," is wrapped tightly in the liberal commitment to unite all people on common moral ground.

Liberal ideals captured in teacher narratives are present as well in student narratives that stand firmly on democratic visions for the advancement of individualism and the provision and exercise of equality of educational opportunity. As they see it, all students, in spite of their differences, are equally valued and treated the same at Best Academy:

> Bella: I don't think there is really a focus on race [at Best Academy]. I mean, there are very few black people at this school. But I don't believe that it is

because they're black. I believe that, well, it's possible that the interest doesn't lie here since if a black person comes to this school and says—hey, wait a second, there is something wrong here, there is only like five black people in the whole school, what's going on? That might scare black people away. Like, I don't think that you should make sacrifices and try to get black people to come—just because they are black—to make the school look better. I think that the best students and the most interested students should be the ones that get to come here. And I don't think that race has anything to do with the way that they run the school.

*   *   *

A.P.: How would you describe the experience of being a white girl here at Best Academy?

Diana: Um, no I think it's the same for everybody . . . [laughter].

A.P.: Do you think that it is in any way different for those girls who are not white?

Diana: Not at all. Because we all get taught the same and treated the same. And everyone treats each other the same. So it's all equalled out.

*   *   *

A.P.: What is the experience of being a white girl at Best Academy? Can you describe what the experience of being white has meant for you here at school?

Sarah: Um, well, this school, I mean, doesn't, I mean, we have black people. We have like all different kinds of people in this school. So like today for announcements or in Morning Meeting, doing like Black Americans [reference is to a series of student presentations staged in recognition of Black History month] and people like that who influenced everyone. So, I mean, everyone's basically looked at the same, you know.

A.P.: Do you think the experience of being white here at Best Academy is different in any way from that of a student from a different ethnic or racial background?

Briana: I don't think it's different at all. I don't think that it matters.

Wendy: Definitely not in our school.

Briana: I don't think so. I mean, out in the workplace, definitely. Or when you apply to colleges, definitely. But not in this school.

Wendy: Even in the public schools, like the City Public Schools, there's not that many black people out in the suburban schools. Well, in public school, there's a lot of white people [that] don't like the black people. But here it's just like no one cares. There's no difference within anybody's eyes.

*   *   *

A.P.: Do you think the experience of being a white person at Best Academy is in any way different from the experience of being a minority here at school?

Wila: I think it probably is, but I don't know. It is kind of hard to tell because you [I] have never been in that position. But I don't think you are treated any differently.

Lisa, of Native-American descent, shares similar impressions of the containment of race differences in school.

A.P.: And what racial group would you locate yourself in?

Lisa: American-Indian.

A.P.: What is the experience like for you as an American-Indian at Best Academy?

Lisa: In Best Academy, nothing. I am no different from any other person. I am no different from the black people here. I am no different than the white people here. I am no different from the Hispanic people here. I am just a different bloodline.

Best Academy manages to contain and level race differences, leading white and non-white girls alike to believe that they are treated as equals despite the fact that race borders have constructed the limitations and possibilities of their lives in altogether different ways. The power of white, liberalism resides in its ability to persuade those at the cultural margins that they are part of a broader, universal identity or humanness that ignores differences. In the process, differences are effectively *whited out* and those in the cultural center secure the invisibility of their own privilege.

Class fractures identity production at the borders of race, suggesting that race and class identities are co-produced. Although not a strongly emergent theme in white student narratives, an understandable outcome given the powerful hold the myth of classlessness and meritocratic ideals have on American class and racial consciousness, a white student, in one example, did cite class as a contributing factor to the containment of differences in school. Speaking to the role that class plays in creating a cohesive school culture, Yvonne observes that "there are African-Americans here, but I still think that they are, you know, upper class and have, you know, kind of been suburbanized, and so even if it is a different racial background, it's like a toned down cultural, a different cultural background." In other words, a shared class culture facilitates leveling of race differences. That is, racialized identities born of varied and multiple border experiences are filtered through a common class culture. Despite the fact that girls enter Best Academy with unequal social and cultural resources, the school works to develop in each of them individual competencies that will benefit them later in the form of educational and occupational attainments suited to the social and professional standards of upper middle-class membership. Again, this is only introduced incidentally, but is instructive for understanding the possibilites that arise at the intersections of border zones like race and class.

This discussion has reframed a predominantly white institution as a borderland culture where white girls give voice to an emerging consciousness of what it means to be white. The discourse of whiteness moves from relative invisibility to an increasingly visible dimension as they straddle the race borders of their own lives and negotiate the codes of the institutional culture that they participate in. What their narratives reveal to those of us on the outside looking in are those institutional arrangements in private schooling that secure the invisibility of whiteness and prop up discourses of power and privilege. Through their observations and their own practices, they illustrate how silencing, either by politely naming or failing to take up the discourse of whiteness as racial identity, reinforces social relations of privilege despite educational platforms that speak to creating more inclusive, multicultural instructional contexts. As they wade through the polite language of race that they have been educated in, white students begin to see and name the contradictions in white, liberal commitments to the construction of broad identities that transcend cultural particularities. Their border work disturbs conventional liberal signifers of rationalism, universalism, equality and harmony.

White students' identity work dredges up the persistent tension in American race consciousness between seeing race differences and the structural bases of social relations of inequality and the desire to see and organize social arrangements in terms of a liberal discourse of universal sameness. The deep emotional investment that white Americans have in the myth of 'sameness' (hooks, 1992) allows whiteness to continue to accrue its own power. On closer look, though, white students, joined by their non-white peers, are breaking through the institutionalization of privilege through complicated border work shaping new identities at/in the cultural center. Turning a predominantly white institutional space, mistakenly understood as being relatively static, into a charged border zone, they are working in productive and transformative ways, crossing color lines and filling in white spaces with living colors.

Chapter 5

On the Horizon/At the Frontier: Girls' Projections for the Future

Since the post-war period, women have made steady social, economic, and professional gains, surfacing early in the 1970s as a visible presence in the American labor force. National statistics on women and work bear out the feminization of the work force where, as of 1992, more than half of the 100 million women in the United States were either employed or seeking work outside the home, and this percentage continues to increase.[1] Labor-force participation has provided women with economic resources, lessening their financial dependence on men while helping them to carve out space to define themselves differently, not simply in relation to their spouses and families. The global economic revolution decisively reshaped women's relationships to family and work, giving rise to the dual-career family. The dual-income model suggests that for women in elite professions, their husbands share equally in housework and child care responsibilities.[2] As the economy presses down on families, creating a greater need for women's labor-force participation, merging career and family become tremendous challenges for women, in particular, where the traditional division of labor in the home has not changed significantly to accommodate their broadened participation in work outside the home.

In the late 1970s, education researchers first began to look at gender inequalities in mixed-sex public schools. Research findings leave no doubt as to the highly contested nature of educational debate around the provision of single-sex schooling but generally reach agreement on the academic and social benefits of single-sex education for girls (Riordan, 1990; OERI, 1993; AAUW, 1993).[3] In a school context dedicated to girls' intellectual and interpersonal growth, female students are presented with a range of possibilities for the future that follow from the supportive foundation that administration, faculty, and female peers provide on a daily basis. Drawing on poststructuralist frameworks that center children's active agency in identity production, feminist

133

researchers have exploded modernist assumptions that girls passively bear the imprint of school culture (Jones, 1993).[4] While students at Best Academy are certainly prepared for and socialized into certain roles shaped at the intersections of class, race, and gender, their narratives and behaviors demonstrate that they are subjects actively involved in repositioning themselves in complex and contradictory ways with and against prevailing social norms. The ways in which girls in the single-sex school define themselves as girls, the meanings and practices that they draw on and carve out for themselves as they *do gender*, are limited by dominant notions of femininity as much as girls participate in the production of new discourses of femininity fashioned out of those that have been made available to them in school and society.[5] Far from being the inert products of socialization, they are active participants in the production of femininity, creating and reinventing themselves along the way.

In chapter 5, I examine the production of gendered constructions of work outside the home, marriage, and family, looking closely at the ways in which professional middle-class girls are both positioned by and actively reposition themselves within and against available discourses of femininity. Best Academy stands on a platform of "full equality for women—equality in job opportunities, equality in pay, equality in political life, equality in decision-making, equality in every major and minor aspect of life" (Best Academy Admissions Information, 1992), goals closely reflecting the commitment of feminism and the feminist movement to changing women's position in a structually unequal society (Delmar, 1994). By encouraging academic achievement, the single-sex school fosters positive connections between school performance and gender. Doing well in school is a key part of doing gender in an all-girls' school, where achievement has the opposite effect of strengthening rather than diminishing and compromising one's sense of self as female. The immediate effects of positive school engagement spill over into elevated academic and professional aspirations for the future. As women began to enter the public sphere in greater numbers and to benefit from the resources that economic independence from men and autonomy in decision-making have afforded them, qualitatively new visions of family and work have emerged. Where women's identities had previously taken shape in relation to the economic and sexual desires of men, they now take shape as a matter of women's desires, agency, and empowerment (Mann, 1994).

Consciousness-raising and collective mobilization around feminist principles in the 1960s made it possible for women to consider seriously conjoining career and family. Taking the school's lead in guiding girls down professional paths, Best Academy students, not surprisingly, have decided to pursue careers first, planning marriage and family for a later time in their lives. In narrating their future careers, girls develop an understanding that marriage and family will impact inescapably on their future careers and that a contingency approach, whereby one fits work around family responsibilities, might be the best strategy short of abandoning their professional aspirations altogether (Almquist, Angrist, and Mickelsen, 1980). From what they have seen of their mothers' struggles to balance family and work, they gather early on that these two roles are not complementary as has traditionally been the case for men and that family responsibilites can interrupt women's labor-force participation. Some hold out for a future where it will be possible to have it all, and others have little confidence that they will be able to pull off being wife, mother, and working professional at one and the same time. Folding school and more far-reaching messages that prescribe what girls should aspire to be into their identity work, Best Academy students are both positioned by and multiply reposition themselves in discourses of femininity that have been made available to them, wading through the complications that choices, as they have been presented to girls in the private girls' school, have paradoxically mapped out and opened up for them. The responses that Best Academy students provide to my questions about their future projections will shed light on the possibilities that might exist for changing traditional gender roles as well as reasons for the persistence of patterns of gender inequality *because of* and *in spite of* the platform of single-sex education for girls. Do professional middle-class girls support traditional patterns through the choices they are making for their futures? Are these girls demanding equality? How might the women's movement have influenced the approaches they have taken to adulthood? And finally, what role has the girls' school played in their decision-making? These questions and others arise out of girls' responses as they project who and what they want to become on the horizon of young adulthood, on the frontiers of womanhood in the decade of the 1990s. Negotiating their own promise and promises for the future, Best Academy students help move our understanding of how girls actively en-[gender] themselves in a single-sex school further along.

On Career

Research examining the intersections of gender with class have documented a range of expressive identities among working-class adolescent females. Angela McRobbie (1982) found that working-class adolescent girls tend to elaborate subjectivities through a constructed ideology of domesticity that privileges private roles of home and family while relegating work identities to secondary status. In opposition to school sanctioned attitudes and behaviors for girls, working-class girls forge a distinctly feminine, anti-school culture intended to disrupt official definitions of femininity. Where girls are expected to be orderly, considerate, hardworking, feminine and passive, these working-class girls self-style their 'femaleness' through an emphasized femininity (Connell, 1987). In visible and vocal expressions of resistance to official school culture, they accept traditional feminine roles within the working-class prescribed inside and operating outside the school. Throwing off school definitions of what it is to be female, they become overly preoccupied with fashion, dating, and boyfriends. Positioning themselves within the gendered discourses of femininity available to them in working-class culture, these girls, in effect, reproduce women's second-class status at home and at work. In Jane Gaskell's (1992) study of the school to work transition among working-class girls in three Canadian secondary schools, she finds that while working-class women tend to value paid labor outside the home over domestic labor inside the home, they do not see themselves assuming a main breadwinning role for their families. For reasons that include women earning approximately sixty percent of what men earn in Canada [the country in which Gaskell's school-based study was undertaken] and their experiences of patriarchy in their own families, these girls hold on to the belief that paid work outside the home is not as important as work inside the home, in effect, reproducing patriarchal structures as they have defined the traditional division of labor in the private domain. While they value paid work for the emotional and economic autonomy it affords, the fact that women can expect to earn less than a man limits their being able to be the primary breadwinner for their families. Not unlike the responses of working-class girls in McRobbie's (1982) study, working-class girls making the transition to work only partially undercut the ideology of domesticity supporting women's secondary status at home and in the work place. Gaskell's data points out that women's choices, that is, whether to stay at home or seek work outside the home, are not arbitrary, but, more often than not, grow out of and in response to existing structures like patriarchy, the economy, and child care that delimit opportunities for working-class women, in particular. There is no question that constructed identities need to be located within and against the situated realities and boundaries of women's lives and that social class defines women's experiences differently.

Drawing parallel conclusions in her ethnographic study of girls' identity formation in a cooperative education program, Linda Valli (1988) discovers that school forms and practices inside a business curriculum actually discourage girls from pursuing alternative studies in high school that would prepare them for jobs outside of service sector employment. Folding in messages from the school and the broader society around appropriate social roles for women, working-class students overwhelmingly choose not to project futures that include college and training for the professions. As Valli concludes, "even though many of them were clearly capable of college success, their working-class backgrounds exerted a strong influence on their life plans" (p. 101). A later study of identity production among working-class youth in a de-industrializing, urban context tells a radically different story as it pinpoints the emergence of a "moment of critique" in female identity forms where girls do not construct their identities exclusively around an ideology of romance, but, rather, envision their futures in the public domain of waged labor, aware "that they must settle themselves first (go to school, get a job, and so forth) before entering into family responsibilities" (Weis, 1990, pp. 65–66). Aside from this formative study, ethnographic studies of gender identity construction have found consistently that working-class girls opt for rather than against marriage immediately after graduating from high school because the realities of their lives stop short of other alternatives (Lees, 1986). With Weis' study, we begin to see glimmers of an emergent feminist critique where working-class girls find that it is no longer possible to rely on men to be the main breadwinners in the family. At a time when insecurities in the labor force leave women little to depend on, they look to themselves as the resources for their own and their families' survival. Education and job training are key to working-class women being able to successfully accomplish this.

Educational and occupational avenues closed to their mothers and grandmothers before them are within reach of this generation of female youth, and Best Academy's mission statement is oriented toward helping its students reach their personal and professional goals. In a speech before Best Academy students and faculty, an alumna honored for her achievements as head coach at Stanford University, contrasts current opportunities available to young women with the professional limitations she remembers having faced only twenty years earlier and encourages girls in the school audience that day to envision open futures for themselves in both public and private sectors.

> My choices were quite limited; yours aren't. Women can do anything— astronauts, Supreme Court Justices, governors, movie producers, etc. You will see a female president in your lifetime. Maybe there is a scientist in this room who will find the cure for cancer or AIDS. I am hopeful that there are future teachers who will teach values, and parents who will really love and nurture their children.

A poster that reads "great visions often start with new dreams" helps students in Ms. Donohue's classroom imagine the hopeful visions for women that this alumna has projected as possible professional options for the future. Women authors, poets, artists, and performers regularly invited into the school to share their talents remind students of the range of opportunities available to them. Faced with the possibility of a merger with a competitive, local, private boy's high school a little more than two decades ago, Best Academy, at great financial risk, opted to remain single-sex. Mrs. Nicholson traces the decision of the Board of Trustees not to merge to Best Academy's broad commitment to girls' education and the intellectual development of young girls locally. Comparing other girls' schools with which she has had previous professional contact with Best Academy, she describes the longstanding connection the surrounding upper middle-class community has had with the school.

> [Because] I think this school in this community served an absolutely powerful and meaningful role in the lives of women. Women who have left Best Academy historically, I mean we are 142 years old, are powerhouses in the community, in [their] respective fields. They certainly were empowered when they were here, and they all know it. And they all point to Best Academy as the source of that empowerment.
>
> A.P.: What is the philosophy of the school as you understand it to be? I've read the mission statement but am interested in your thoughts on this point.
>
> Mrs. Nicholson: It's not even a mission statement. It is a philosophy statement, and it is certainly to provide young women with an awareness of who they are in society and to provide them with a meaningful educational background that will enable them to be significant contributors. I would add some things to the written philosophy as it stands and simply say that we are not here for academic purposes only. And we are not here to, although we are college preparatory, to provide the steppingstone to college. We are here for a much broader purpose and that is to prepare young women for life and who knows what that life is going to be, given the rapidity of change in our world over the last five years . . . three years. I don't know what that is, so it comes down to making some choices and preparing them for roles which are pretty undefined except that it's clear to me that the obligation to prepare them as human beings is overriding and gigantic. [. . .]

The school mission, according to the Head of School, is broader than simply transferring to students the necessary technical skills to prepare them for future work and adult roles. As Mrs. Nicholson explains, the school's educational goals extend beyond a limited focus on academics to women's "preparation for life" at a time when women's social roles and identities are no longer narrowly and tightly defined. Against the backdrop of global economic restructuring, women's relations with family and work have been re-defined, and Mrs. Nicholson is keenly aware that the single-sex school has an "obligation" to prepare its students to meet the multiple challenges they, as women, are more likely than not to face in the future.

Without a doubt, catering first and foremost to women's intellectual development drives Best Academy's curriculum where nearly one hundred percent of the graduating student body proceeds immediately into higher education after graduating from high school.[6] Among professional middle-class families whose parents generally reflect high levels of education and professional training, there is the persistent expectation that children will take this direct path. Despite hiking tuition rates and confessions of worry on the part of many Best Academy juniors about financing a college education, most students agree that "it's just unspoken that you go to college after high school," that it is "the thing to do," and that "for us [in the private school], not going [to college] would be different."[7]

Women's relations to work and family have changed over the past three decades, a result, in part, of the feminization of the work force, key social movements like feminism, and critical legislation like Title IX, passed in 1972, which prohibited sex discrimination in education and the Women's Educational Equity Act (WEEA) of 1974, which required that states direct attention to eliminating sex bias from vocational education programs and provided funds for the development of sex equity programming (Scott and McCollum, 1993). Changes in the traditional division of labor at home and more equitable compensation for equal work on the job have, though, not followed women's broadened participation in the labor force. Increasing incidence of sexual harassment of girls in schools and women in the work place as well remind us that patriarchal norms of femininity are deep-rooted in American society and culture and that they persist in essentializing females and attributing to them certain behaviors, attitudes, and roles.[8] I am not suggesting that there have not been critical structural and attitudinal changes in this direction. The feminization of the work force, feminist consciousness-raising, and collective mobilization have and continue to make significant dents in social institutions. The spillover effects of these forces over the past thirty years show up in trends in Best Academy students' projections for the future. Mrs. Oliver, the school guidance counselor who oversees the college application and admissions process, points to clear contrasts between the professional aspirations of the current student body and the more marriage-minded students attending the school decades earlier.

> The difference between now and twenty-five years ago is that they [the students] see potential professional possibilities. Whereas before, we didn't really think about going to college in order to prepare for a career or in order to get a job. That really wasn't necessarily the main thing. It's just what you did after high school. So I think that that's really significant, that they have inculcated the value and the goal that they will do something [. . .]

The sense that girls are being prepared for future professional roles is supported widely by the faculty, some of whom offer their reflections on professional directions that they remember being pointed in as Best Academy students years earlier. Narrating their experiences as alumnae of the school, Mrs. Berson and Mrs. Oliver chart the changes that appear to have taken place in students' visions for the future.

> Mrs. Berson: But I, in many ways, I admire them [the students] a great deal because they are so confident, and they really think they can get out in the world and do what they want to do. They can, I think.
>
> A.P.: How do they express that to you?
>
> Mrs. Berson: Sometimes they say it [to me]. Uhm, well, I guess for me, being my age, it's still a thrill here; a student—say she's going to be a doctor or a lawyer, [and] I never said that. None of my classmates did.
>
> A.P.: What did [students in] your class say?
>
> Mrs. Berson: Oh, we were educated to be married and the same in college. I went to Smith College, which you would have thought would have encouraged us to think that we would use our minds after graduation, but, in fact, there was never . . . the whole time I was there, nobody ever talked to me about what I might do after I graduated. And since I got engaged in my junior year, it was all taken care of anyway. And that was, that was the way it was. That was just a huge change, of course. But that was already happening in the 70s, but it certainly is more so now. They're not at all thinking in terms of husbands and families first.
>
> A.P.: For the most part, what kinds of things are they aspiring to do in their futures?
>
> Mrs. Berson: Well, that's an interesting question. [. . .] Students have been, the past few years, have aspired to be professional people. A lot of them [hope to be or are] doctors, lawyers. Many of them [are] teachers. And when they come back and visit, many of them are, indeed, doing all those things [. . .].
>
> $*$ $*$ $*$
>
> A.P.: What kinds of women do you feel that Best Academy is preparing for the future?
>
> Mrs. Oliver: I hope women who have a certain amount of autonomy in their lives. I don't mean to imply that they should not have relationships or connections which may involve some dependence, but autonomy. I mean, we talk in the [career] internship meetings about their career paths, and there is never a question of, well, will I have a career path, but what will that path be, how might I integrate it into other aspects of my life. And when I was here [as a student in the 60s], it was never a question, I mean, [of] you will have a career. Maybe you will, and maybe not, but certainly marriage and children were always the first consideration. So I think that that has changed and rightfully so. I mean, I hate to use the word well-rounded—gag.

But we do make a conscious effort, that we require kids to take art and music, dance, even those "sciencey" kids, that they should have that because that's what a well-educated person [should have]. A well-educated person has some awareness of that, and it goes along with autonomy. But a sense of their own competence, I think, is so important.

As alumnae of Best Academy, both Mrs. Berson and Mrs. Oliver provide the historical backdrop to changes in student goals over the past three decades as they have moved away from a decidedly domestic focus and more toward professional training for careers outside the home. Like many of the female academies founded in the mid-nineteenth century, Best Academy, early on, offered a curriculum that included the natural and social sciences as well as ornamental studies in drawing and music (Solomon, 1985).[9] Training was designed to prepare girls to be the social gatekeepers and caretakers of the upper middle class. Elite status was assured through marriage, and bourgeois girls destined for private schools were essentially prepared for lives of lived dependence on their spouses.[10] As Mrs. Oliver and Mrs. Berson narrate, these trends continued until the early 1970s when students began to project different plans for the future, at the moment when women's relations to family and work began to shift as women became a stronger presence in the work force and feminists began to push the issue of equal pay for equal work.

The effects of global economic transformation have not left professional middle-class girls untouched. In the main, Best Academy students express strong desires for marriage and family, but only at a later time, toward the tail end of their twenties. Best Academy students project careers that fall within the range of occupational categories that span the professional middle class. Their choices, including but certainly not limited to doctors, lawyers, teachers, social workers, physical therapists, and veterinarians, dovetail the official expectations for professionalism that students have assimilated into their own felt perceptions of what the private, all-girls' high school envisions for its female graduates. Best Academy juniors consistently note the value that the school attaches to women's professional development and couch this in terms of school expectations for social and economic success. While research on the career choice patterns of students at secondary levels of schooling is scarce, proponents of single-sex education do stress that a less traditional curriculum and more egalitarian relations between teachers and students are more conducive to students in girls' schools choosing careers that have been historically male dominated (Min, 1991). As students talk about their professional desires for the future, they articulate an emergent conflict between their expectations and those that the private girls' school has for its students, reflecting the ongoing negotiation work required of students living in the middle of shifting and fracturing class cultures and consciousness.

A.P.: What do you think the school would like its graduates to become as far as their professional futures go?

Randi: Doctors, lawyers, professionals. They don't like students going to the local community college or to two-year colleges. They want their students to go to four-year colleges. They like to keep the reputation of their students, to become professionals. They go to graduate and post-graduate school. [. . .]

A.P.: How do you think the school regards a graduate like yourself who would like to pursue a career as a physical therapist?

Randi: Actually, there have been a few other people that have been wanting to do it.

A.P.: Do you think you fulfill Best Academy's future vision for its students?

Randi: I think it is almost there. I think they look for doctors and lawyers and people who are socially, are known in the community. Like oh, yes, like name dropping. If I was a physical therapist, it is not likely that my name would be dropped.

> *   *   *

A.P.: What do you think Best Academy would like you to be?

Briana: Successful and representing it. I don't really get the entire picture that Best Academy, I mean I do, except like individual teachers maybe, but Best Academy as a whole wants me to be productive for the school's sake. Some people, other people . . . I get the impression that they want me to be successful, and they want me to do that for me and for no one else. Like I would think that Mrs. Nicholson would want us to get into the best school as possible because we would represent our school. And, therefore, if we get to good schools, we can get good jobs [and], therefore, donate more money to the school.

A.P.: How do you feel about this?

Briana: I'm sure I am being just a little too dramatic about the whole thing.

Wendy: Like the graduates from here, they get into the good schools. They get good jobs. They will give the money [to the school]. Plus, if other people see that these people are getting into good schools and [getting] good jobs, then more people will come and give all of the money [to the school]. But then there is good people like Ms. Donohue and Mr. Peoples [that say]—do your best for yourself, not for this establishment.

> *   *   *

A.P.: What kind of future do you think the school envisions for its students?

Michelle: I sense the more prestigious professions, like doctor, lawyer, like big ten money things. I thought I would see more of, okay, now go be a teacher, okay now go be a nurse type of woman thing. I don't see that. I think that's more because it's an all-girls' school, and they want you to become . . . because there are no guys to compete against, they want you to become what a guy would have been in a public school, and so I think they want women to have the more male jobs that stereotypically are [for men].[11]

Professional middle class girls have before them a range of professional possibilities supported by the platform of the single-sex girls' school, increased economic opportunities, and transformed work relations. Their choices, as they see it, are somewhat constrained, though, by the self-interests of private school culture. At the same time as they are encouraged, as *individuals*, to choose what they want to do, they feel directed to choose future work roles from within the range of professional possibilities that private training in a girls' school has opened up for them. At the intersections of class and gender, professional choices for the future seem, in part, to be *made for* and *ready made for* Best Academy students. As they see it, career decisions translate into market value for private schools that need to sustain their reputation on the backs of their students at a time when these institutions can no longer afford to depend exclusively on an internal private network of privileged families, but find themselves having to cast their net more widely as a matter of survival.

Stringing their projections for the future together, professional middle-class girls like Bella link desires for a career with economic independence. Researching career, marriage, and family projections among graduating male and female seniors across class strata at the University of California—Berkeley, Anne Machung (1989) found that male undergraduates generally state as their main reason for working monetary gain while females name 'self-fulfillment' and 'independence' as their primary goals. Although Machung focuses her study on college-age youth, her conclusions mirror the narrations of the Best Academy cohort. Only slightly younger than these college seniors, they share a felt sense of instability in an age of economic decline and look beyond marriage to their careers to provide them with resources for their own security. Anticipating such future life events as death and divorce, they recognize what paid work and stable earnings afford, especially in the event of the loss of a spouse or a partner either through death, imminent for everyone, or divorce which is increasingly becoming part of the experiences of youth in contemporary culture as current rates of divorce escalate across the nation. Being educated and trained for a profession is key to economic survival, not only for oneself but also for one's family. The social and economic security that those inside the professional middle class have benefitted from over the past three decades now appears visibly threatened as economic decline pushes forward and moves deeper into the mid-1990s.

On Marriage and Family

A.P.: What do you think the school sees a women's role being?

Bella: I think that they are just focused on the—go to high school, go to college and get a job. They are not really worried about the family life. No, I don't think that they stress that at all. I think that they just want to make sure that you get a job and can support yourself. I think that that's what they stress.

A.P.: And do you believe all of this?

Bella: Well, I think that's important. But you should also have a family. Well, for me, that's what would make me happy. I think it's different for every woman. There are women who would be happier without a family, you know. But I think that isn't myself.

As I mention earlier, marriage is often the only alternative available to working-class girls whose teachers and parents have steered them away from more professional training and careers outside service sector employment. This starkly contrasts with the gendered ideology of the private, independent, all-girls' high school where students assimilate school messages that speak to and validate unlimited avenues available to women, creating the conditions for them to be able to choose whether or not to get married. For professional middle-class girls, marriage is one among several alternatives, but not the only option for women's economic and emotional security. In large measure, the junior girls desire to be married and plan for this in their late twenties and early thirties. At the same time, they partially reject this institution on the grounds that it places too many restrictions on women's independence and freedom. The disabling effects of marriage on women, as they name them, include curbing "freedom," being "tied down," having to "ask permission," and increased "responsibility."[12] Others project a profound cynicism of the institution, not surprising in light of their experiences as children of separation and divorce, because of deep-seated fears that they will repeat, in their own adult lives, the emotional traumas and financial hardships they saw in their own homes.

A.P.: Do you want to get married?

Fiona: I don't know. Um, my parents are divorced, so it's sort of like, put a little damper on that thought. Maybe, I think, I don't want to miss out on that experience. I don't want to get divorced either. So maybe later in life.

A.P.: Do you think a lot of people who get married get divorced?

Fiona: I think so. Especially these days.

A.P.: And that scares you?

Fiona: Yeah. It does. It sort of like, just turns your life upside down. So I think yeah. Um, and I also, I mean, I think, I don't want to miss out on the experience of having children, but it, it totally changes everything that you can do in life. I mean, I wouldn't want to, I would want to be involved with my children, if I have children. And I, I also would want to have a career. So I think that would be a really difficult thing to do. And you wouldn't have as much freedom either. But I think now in my life, I can't even think about being married and having kids because I wouldn't want to give up any freedom that I'm going to have.

*   *   *

A.P.: Why not get married and have a man take care of you?

Sarah: That would be nice. But how realistic is it, you know?

A.P.: But you said that you might like that . . . why is that?

Sarah: I would like that a lot. But there's always some sort of problems and divorces and stuff like that. But if you have your own, like you're stable with a career and you know that you'd be able to live on your own, I mean, it just makes you feel better. And you're achieving something. I mean, I'd love to marry rich and just like leave everyone else [. . .] yeah, leave a job and stuff like that. But then it just kind of makes me nervous. I'd be nervous to see how life is going to last for, if it's going to last like two years, five, ten, fifteen years [the implication that marriage is not an institutional arrangement that these girls can confidently rely on].

*   *   *

Briana: I think once you find the person. I think that people definitely marry for the wrong reasons. Marry for money, marry for power or whatever.

Wendy: That's why I would never get married because I know that I would marry for the wrong reasons.

A.P.: What would you marry for?

Wendy: It wouldn't be money. I could care less about money. But a lot of it is just feeling that you want someone to love you, and if you're married, you think they are going to love you forever. Or like intimidation, if people are pressuring you to get married. Especially when it comes to pressuring you to get married, the thing is . . . like especially when it comes to certain guys, I know I would end up marrying for the wrong reasons. It would turn out bad in the end. It would be a waste of time, a waste of money, a waste of hard feelings.

A.P.: Briana, what would you marry for?

Briana: This sounds corny, probably love, probably like . . . I've seen weddings before, and you will see, it's little things. 'Cause I see my parents, and they are the biggest, corniest people I have ever met in my entire life. But they do the corniest little things for each other. Like when I was at a wedding one time, a family friend got married, and her husband was holding her hand, and her hand was shaking. And he was like petting her hand, and it's just those little things that you can see that somebody really cares. But it's hard to tell in this day and age if somebody really cares or not.

Rising divorce rates in American society in recent decades ratchet up levels of anxiety among middle and upper middle-class women who fear downward social and economic mobility for themselves and their children, either because of a loss of a spouse or a partner. The economic impact of divorce on women is far greater than it is on men since women only retain 29–30 percent of the family income they benefitted from while married after divorce (Newman, 1989). Divorced women experience greater "relative deprivation" the higher up they sit on the class scale, and their per capita income after divorce is far less than that of their husband because of household dependents (Weitzman, 1985). Many of the children of these families carry this fear with them into adolescence, draping their projections for future life passages in rising apprehensions.

Over fifty percent of the junior students are children of divorced homes, forcing the likelihood of their witnessing the financial burdens currently falling to their mothers. The data suggest the reappropriation of their mothers' fears of "falling from grace" in a time where statistics foreground the strong possibility that they will repeat the devastating emotional and financial repercussions of family breakups in their own lifetimes.[13] Since divorce often does precipitate a downward economic spiral, upper middle-class girls find themselves thinking seriously about shoring up economic resources for their own survival. What they vocalize clearly is that class privilege is no longer guaranteed, understanding that their best option for security for *themselves*, and the families that they plan to have in the future, lies in cultivating themselves as the resource for their own economic well-being. Seen from the context of their own lived experiences of family separation and divorce, marriage is an institution that girls have grown to mistrust, casting a long shadow of doubt over the future. Reflecting on her own parents' divorce, Fiona decides that she would like to be married but plans to delay marriage for a "later time in life" because of her own parents who married in their twenties and were later divorced. A career provides some measure of security so that, as Sarah puts it, "you're stable with a career and you know that you'd be able to live on your own," and "it just makes you feel better." Professional middle-class girls worry that their generation will get caught in the downward spiral of divorce in a culture that has not left otherwise sacred rituals untouched. They are clearly anxious about diminished returns on their emotional investments and question whether, once married, they will, in fact, be able to stay married. Hurt by their immediate experiences as children of separation and divorce, they fear potential betrayals inside future relationships, leading Briana to comment that "it's hard to tell in this day and age if somebody really cares or not."

As economic trends raise the current percentage of women in the work force, new social roles and responsibilities can produce a 'schizophrenia' that has the opposite effect of disabling rather than enabling girls, an outcome that Best Academy faculty are deeply worried about in the context of girls' professional development.

> Mrs. Lewis: We don't help them make choices. We don't help them sort it out. I talk about it with the seniors, you know, the schizophrenia in women, you know, to be the perfect career person, the striving for the, to break the glass ceiling. And you go home, and you see an ad on television where you have to be the perfect mother, and you are supposed to be the perfect wife. You know, it's the schizophrenia in the society that says you have to do everything, and you have to do it the best possible way. It is nuts.
>
> A.P.: Do you think this schizophrenia is very much a part of this school as a girls' school?
>
> Mrs. Lewis: I do.

Adolescent girls fold into their consciousness a variety of popular messages from consumer culture that encourage them to want it all, to have it all, to do it all—equally and well. Told repeatedly in printed media and visual images that "they can bring home the bacon and fry it up in a pan," they equate being able to juggle marriage, career, and family with being a woman. Changes in the traditional division of labor in the home have not paralleled women's increasing participation in paid labor. The feminization of the work force has created the double bind for women, forcing them to find ways to merge domestic roles and responsibilities with work outside the home. Change in one direction and not the other has had the effect of creating the "double day" where domestic labor at home is simply tagged onto the time that women spend working outside the home (Ferree, 1984).

In her journalistic analysis of the rise of the 1980s post-feminist generation, Bolotin (1982) finds that women in their late twenties and early thirties express concerns over being able to effectively manage family and career effectively. Increased access and representation of women in the labor force figured among the important political gains of second wave feminism, but, as the women Bolotin interviewed point out, broader work options have created conflicts around women's ability to "have it all."[14] Paid labor has introduced competing roles and responsibilities between work and home that find women, unlike men, for the most part, juggling domains that do not complement each other. As Elizabeth Fox-Genovese (1996) put it in her cogent analysis of the rejection of feminist politics and identification among women of the baby boomer generation,

> But women have not mindlessly been slipping out of an old life and into a new one. They have consciously been trying to combine both. And so we now have the myth of the superwoman who does it all and with ease. Unfortunately, the life of a superwoman is easier to dream than to live. Real women find their lives as mothers clash with their lives as workers. Economic mobility and job schedules make no concessions to nursing, diapers, or colic. Nursing, diapers, and colic make no concessions to production schedules or board meetings. All of which, any working mother could tell us, if only she were being asked. For there are no superwomen, and something has to give. Hence the grim threat of the economic revolution: As workers, women need to be liberated from children; as mothers, they need to be liberated from work. Whatever the consequences of the economic revolution, women's lives lie at the center (pp. 113–114).

Expanded opportunities and roles have introduced new sets of challenges and complications. The question remains, at what cost. In her social-psychological analysis of identity formation among mainly white, middle to upper middle-class adolescent girls at Emma Willard School, Janet Mendelsohn (1990) attributes youthful optimism in students' projections for the future to feminism, class, and race privilege. Some students express doubt about the future, worried that they will fail to reach their goals as well as the expectations that their parents have held up for them. Somewhat apprehensive about being able to manage competing domains of work and family, they still feel, however, that they will be able to meet these challenges head on as their mothers did before them through a combination of drive and hard work.

Best Academy students have similar responses, not only to Emma Willard school girls but also to the generation of women that Bolotin (1982) interviewed, who are nearly 12–15 years older than the students at the center of this study. When I asked students what they saw as their role as a woman in the 1990s, they offer responses that link future roles with school-based expectations and goals, providing the standard comment that "the expectations for a woman, for the females here [is to] graduate, go on to college, and become very successful." Most add to this their plans for marriage and a family but worry that their earned independence will create new conflicts between public and private roles. A fair number of them are confident that it is possible to have it all—career, marriage, and family—and believe that they will be able to manage it, having seen their mothers do this as they were growing up.

Gayle: Well, I see that my mom, she handles it pretty well. She's only part time. I mean, I see a lot of working moms that have families and good marriages. All of the moms that I know work, well kind of. Most of them have a marriage and a family. Like Donna's mom works. She is a nurse, but she also works with Donna's dad.

*   *   *

Bella: Um, I think that women are expected to go to high school, go to college and get a job, and help support the family with the husband and also have children. I think that is like a basic, like the expectation for women. That's perfectly fine with me. I have no problems with that. I mean, that is what I want for myself. I think that would make me happy, 'cause I want to be successful. I don't want to stay home and just raise children all of my life. But I do want to have a baby eventually.

Others are more hesitant, feeling the weight of balancing competing domains of work and family on their shoulders, uneasy about their abilities to cope well, despite experiences of working moms who have been able to pull this off without too many problems, or so it appears on the surface. Deep frustration winds in and out of Glenda's description of what she sees as her role as a young woman in the 1990s.

Well, I think that society wants women . . . well, I don't know if it's society or if it's like how women are seeing society, but they want women to be everything, like you can have a career, but then you also have to be, well, you don't have to be, but then you have to balance the wife and having a family and everything. And I think that society has to change and like realize that men have to have so much of an equal share in the household because women just can't do everything. I mean, I am not saying that women are weak or anything like that. But it is physically impossible to balance all those things and be sane, I think. I think after awhile, if you have like a really intense career, and you have a family, and you have no one to help you, I mean, after awhile, I think I would just get exhausted. But I don't know. There are lots of different roles in society for women.

While careerism, marriage, and motherhood all fall within the boundaries of female desire among professional middle-class girls, future projections are fraught with apprehension as these girls move to reconsider the competing pressures that career can bring to marriage and family and visa versa. Glenda, who expressed a strong interest in becoming a doctor in an earlier conversation, points to the range of social expectations that surround women's roles and recognizes the enormous difficulties she will face in "balancing" desires and responsibilities. She holds men accountable for their share in this balancing act yet questions whether barriers to change inside cultures of masculinity will keep men from taking on equal responsibilities for housework and child care. We get a strong sense from Cara and Gwen, as well, that they would be more willing to agree that it is possible to have it all if they had some confidence that men would take on their fair share at home. As they see it, males and females are still subject to different social norms and their experience of patriarchy as it has traditionally organized gender roles at home makes it hard for them to believe that they will be able to handle both family and work.

A.P.: Do you think that it's possible to have it all—marriage, career, and family?

Cara: I hope so.

A.P.: Do you think women have to sacrifice anything to have it all?

Cara: To have a career and have a child, um, ten years from now, when I, maybe if I get married around twenty-seven or whatever. I hope that it is more equal where it isn't that the woman can have the job and have a kid and make the dinner and feed the kid and everything. And then the husband just comes home from work. I hope it's different from that. I hope I marry someone who will do equal responsibilities with the child or children. So it isn't the wife doing all the housework and all the cooking, even if it's the husband who has a better job making more money or whatever to support the family.

*   *   *

A.P.: And how about family. Do you want to have a family?

Gwen: Yeah, some day.

A.P.: Do you think it's possible to have it all at the same time?

Gwen: Yeah, I think so.

A.P.: Career, marriage, and family?

Gwen: Yeah, I think it's really hard, but I think it's possible.

A.P.: How do you think it could become easier for us as women?

Gwen: Probably if the men had more to do with the family and helping with the kids.

A.P.: How can we [women] change that?

Gwen: I don't know.

A.P.: Does that bother you when you think about that?

Gwen: Yeah, a lot. Because a woman can go and have just as important a job as a man, but be expected to come home and clean and cook and everything.

A.P.: Do you think that mindset still exists?

Gwen: Yeah, I think so.

A.P.: Do you think it will change?

Gwen: Yeah, maybe. I think boys have to be brought up that way, kind of.

Gaskell (1992) points out that working-class girls only partially challenge the ideology of domesticity because they recognize that men are not willing to shoulder an equal part in domestic work. The gap between working-class and professional middle-class girls' narratives curiously narrows here as the latter join the former in their fear that men will not take on childrearing and other family responsibilities. Like working-class girls, professional middle-class adolescents only partially challenge the ideology of domesticity. The effects of second wave feminism based, in part, in growing demands for women to receive equal consideration at home and in the work force, are far from having reversed and dismantled patriarchal structures organizing family life. Attitudinal changes among men have not kept pace with women's social and economic gains in the work place. Instead, double standards remain firmly in place, leaving this generation of female youth wondering whether the hard won gains of second wave feminism are really empty successes afterall. A tone of reconciled contentment bubbles up from the depths of adolescent girls despair over the seeming permanence of gender inequalities, holding out little hope of seeing positive change in the direction of more equitable gender roles in their lifetimes. Girls seem bothered especially by the persistence of double standards in normalized constructions of femininity and masculinity that have been cast widely and rooted deeply in American culture. A glimmer of hope that change will be slow in coming is shrouded in cynicism as girls are quick to add the strong possibility that it is more likely than not that it will not happen at all.[15]

The cost of negotiating all three might, in the end, be too great, where aspiring to "have it all," can require of women substantial sacrifice. Balancing professional gains against personal losses, many Best Academy students choose to privilege the domestic code, projecting, out of desire and necessity, their wish to stay at home to raise their children. Professional middle-class girls wax nostalgic for motherhood, recalling that many of their mothers either stayed home to raise them or worked part-time during their formative years as children. Given the choice and the economic resources to do so, some girls would choose not to "have it all," preferring either full-time motherhood or a part-time career, but not both at the same time.

Marlene: [. . .] there are still a lot of guys who think—oh women should stay at home and take care of the kids. But then there are a lot of guys who are starting to realize—wo, maybe I can stay at home and take care of the kids. But they still have that very macho idea that they can't.

A.P.: How do you feel about that when you hear that?

Marlene: Well, I don't think that there is anything wrong with staying home and taking care of the kids. When I was little, that used to be like my dream, you know, to have the guy go out and bring home all of the money. I just wanted to take care of the kids. It was sort of like the Cinderella/Prince Charming idea. And I mean, I still think if my husband said—oh, you can go out and get a job, or you can stay home and raise the kids, or you can do both, whatever you want—that that would be great because I would probably like to stay home and take care of the kids. But I would also like to have a job too, maybe not all at once.

A.P.: Did your mom stay at home and raise the children?

Marlene: Yeah.

A.P.: Did you like that?

Marlene: Sort of. She had like one job when she was like twenty years old for about a year and that was it. And she has always been at home. I mean, I kind of liked it, but then sometimes, I thought that she was kind of too overprotective because that was all she had to do.

*   *   *

Briana: [. . .] Because once I have a family, that's that. It's not going to be a full-time job, both parents [working] and three kids. That's not what it's going to be. It's going to be . . . I'm going to be home with my kids. That's how I want it. [I would probably like to be home with my kids] up until, cause I saw like what my mother did, and I even see my friends whose mothers work. I used to come home off the bus . . . when they are little, I don't think I would want to leave my kids at home up until they get into either the middle school or the high school, even if I did want to go back to work. Just because I think, you know, parents are needed when kids are young. A lot of trouble can start if you let a small kid, like middle school aged kids . . . they are experimenting with new things when they are that age, and if nobody's there when you get home and nobody's going to be there for two hours, a lot can happen.

*   *   *

A.P.: And would you like to have a family?

Diana: Yeah. I suppose. Once I, you know, have my whole thing [career] settled out, then I'd have a family. I wouldn't want to just have a family and do it all at once. Because something would have to give. And if I had a family, I would want to be very close and not have to be like working all the time and leaving my kids at home and things like that.

*   *   *

A.P.: Would you work while having and raising children?

Wila: If it was necessary. If it wasn't, I would stay home.

A.P.: So you would like to stay home and raise your children if you could?

Wila: I think so. I think I would like to. It bothers me when people are like—oh, you shouldn't put your kid in day care—because I was always in day care and stuff. It didn't bother me. I don't think that I am like a bad person. Sometimes people say stuff like that, and it's annoying. Oh, she should stay home. Some people can't. If I could stay home, I would.

*   *   *

Victoria: I want my husband to be rich.

A.P.: You really want him to be rich, how come?

Victoria: Because I really want to raise the kids, him too, [but] I don't want a baby-sitter doing it.

A.P.: What is the relationship in your mind between being rich and being able to raise your kids? Clarify this for me.

Victoria: Just that I won't have the pressures of having to work, you know, and I will be able to stay home with the kids.

Like Marlene, Briana is nostalgic about her mother who stayed at home to raise her as a child and hopes to be the same kind of visible parent in her young childrens' lives. Imagining imminent difficulties when one tries to balance career and motherhood, she would like to stay home to raise her children, a feeling equally shared by Diana whose mother never worked outside the home. Wila is hopeful that she will marry into money so that she can make the choice to raise her children as a full-time homemaker. Victoria agrees that this would make it easier for a woman to decide to stay at home as her children's primary caretaker. In only one instance, a student frames her desire to stay at home with her children in essentialist terms that reflect persistent patterns of gender inequality based in patriarchal feminine norms.

A.P.: What role, if any, do you think a man should have in helping women balance career, marriage, and family?

Michelle: I think that we should be equal. I am a little old-fashioned in the sense that I do kind of think of the male as the head of the household and the woman takes care of the kids and everything. I don't think of it as being as confined as it used to be. I think it would be very awkward for me if I married someone who stayed home with the kids, and I worked. I don't think that I could handle that not only because of traditional values. I think I

> would be more [do better] with kids than someone that I would marry would
> be. I think that there should still be the traditional mother-father type thing
> too.

Michelle's narrative centers on the traditional domestic code and gives voice
to a felt sense that women are better suited biologically and by social
convention than men to perform well in the private domain. Her narrative is,
though, an exception to the rule among Best Academy students. Narratives
centering home and family identities while relegating salaried labor to the
margins are generally absent among the junior girls who rather curiously fear
that openly privileging the private over the public domain betrays the hard
won gains of second wave feminism. Victoria breaks her silence around this
middle-class taboo.

> [. . .] When I think about women's lib, I don't know. It's not a big thing to me
> as it is to like some other people because I love kids and besides maybe
> getting some degree, I really just want to raise a family, stay home and like do
> certain things for my kids.
>
> A.P.: Do you think if people have kids that they can't be part of the women's
> movement?
>
> Victoria: No, no. Like all of my friends say—oh man, if any guy ever says that
> I should stay at home, and he will support me, man, he is out of there. But, I
> mean, not that I will feel dependent on my husband. But I want to stay home
> with him, and I never say that to my friends.
>
> A.P.: You never say this to your friends? Why?
>
> Victoria: I never input that into that conversation. They make fun of people
> who want to, like Jody, [a senior], I guess, [who wants to stay home and raise
> her kids]. They just mock it.

Acting out traditional gender roles appears to run at cross purposes to school-
based messages oriented around careerism and popular *images* of the independent, working feminist who has no children, nor appears to have any
maternal desires to have and raise children. Victoria is snagged by her own
desires and expectations that she feels she needs to live up to, noting that she
"never input[s] that [a critique of feminism] into that conversation," not
simply because she fears being alienated from her friends, but arguably because
she would appear a traitor to the hard-won gains of middle-class feminism and
women's historical struggles for social, political, and economic emancipation.
Her friends, she claims, "make fun of "people who want to, like Jody, [a senior
who wants to stay home and raise her kids]. Best Academy girls grew up either
part of or observers to latch-key culture, and they do not want this for their

children. Unable to shed the scars of separation and divorce, they want to provide for their families the stability that they were not able to enjoy as children, and they do not want this for their own children. Partial rejection of the domestic code among Best Academy students can be attributed to the structural realities of professional middle-class lives where girls defend traditional choices like motherhood out of their own sense of responsibility to children and families often compromised by the hectic pace and overwhelming demands women face as they try to balance work and family. In an ironic turn, it is also a strong possibility that girls feel forced back on traditional choices like full-time motherood or part-time careers out of their own desperation over the persistence of traditional gender arrangements and patterns of inequality that they do not see changing very quickly in the future. Like working-class girls who continue with traditional choices because it is more realistic to stay at home rather than work outside the home, professional middle-class girls are responding to another set of structural conditions that cast a dark shadow on their visions for the future in spite of the choices that have been made available to them.

At the (Post)-Feminist Frontier

Victoria's narrative keys us into certain aspects of women's experiences, like motherhood, that adolescent girls in the 1990s perceive as being at odds with feminism. Choosing to stay at home and raise one's family, as they see it, does not resonate with feminist theories and principles. Victoria is uneasy with aspects of feminism as are many of her classmates, in spite of the fact that they recognize forms of inequality in their lives between men and women and demand change. Probing attitudes toward feminism among women fresh out of college and new to the work force in the early 1980s, Bolotin (1982) discovered among this group a profound uneasiness around identifying themselves as feminists and an ambivalence toward feminist politics. Speaking out of the politically conservative mood of the Reagan years and the struggles women expect to wage around balancing career and family, the children of the baby boomer generation selectively engage those feminist principles that fit their emerging identities as working professionals and jettison others. The notable absence of a strong feminist identity among this generation of women reflects the extent to which the ideology and culture of post-feminism has defined women's identities and politics. Post-feminist strands heard in adult female narratives in the early 1980s reverberate in Best Academy students' elaborations on feminism and the feminist movement in the early 1990s. While femininity is operating centrally in adolescent girls' narrative constructions of gender, feminism is separated out and relegated to the margins of girl talk. Nearly fifteen years younger than the women Bolotin interviewed, Best Academy girls assimilate, refashion, and strip of any political meaning issues relevant to third wave feminism, what has popularly been dubbed post-feminism (Rosenfelt and Stacey, 1987). What their narratives strikingly reveal is that feminism remains a contested space for professional middle-class adolescent females whose ambivalence seems, at times, to border on antifeminism, when, in fact, they are actively negotiating a feminist identity politics that will fit in with the competing pressures and demands that they are planning for in their adult lives.

One faculty member noted that among Best Academy students in general, very few choose to associate themselves with feminism and the feminist movement.[16] A school admissions officer agreed, observing that the school has "offered women's courses, like women's historical perspectives courses," but that the students "just see it as feminism and they are not interested." What she points to is the equation that adolescent girls appear to make in their minds between gender topics in the formal curriculum and feminism, seeing the two as synonymous with each other. Remembering the responses of a group of freshmen when he asked them if feminism was a bad word, Mr. Fischer recalls his students saying, "I wouldn't call myself a feminist," and that "they thought that a feminist was a bull-dyke who hated men or who hated anybody who wanted to have children and stay at home."

Adolescent girls' ambivalence with feminism wraps around persistent images of feminism in popular culture and the popular imagination, one among them being that a woman who is a feminist or in any way departs from patriarchal norms of femininity through collective female resistance, for example, is a lesbian (Griffin, 1989; Frye, 1992). There is no doubt that feminism has been negatively represented in mass media and that adolescent girls' retreat from feminism is, in part, a defense of compulsory heterosexuality against the perceived threat of lesbianism (Rich, 1981). In no uncertain terms, they describe "sexism [as] a charge trumped up by feminists," who they summatively label "lesbian." Implicit in heterosexual privilege is the assumption that heterosexuality is and should be the dominant sexual choice for women. As Sandra Harding (1994) reminds us in her powerful analysis of the insights that a lesbian standpoint offers for deepening our understanding of social relations, heterosexual privilege casts female heterosexuality as natural and inevitable, and relationships that depart from this norm are seen as deviant, unnatural and, at their worst, pathological.

> From the perspective of heterosexual lives, feminism is "unnatural," against "nature" (read: "patriarchal rule"), just as are homosexuality and any attitude toward sex and gender that male supremacy chooses not to legitimate. Feminists have often been labeled lesbian, since defenders of male supremacy

cannot tell the difference between females wanting fully human rights (rather than only the rights women are permitted to have) and women refusing to devote their lives to men. In a culture where everyone is expected to be enthralled only by men and their achievements, such a confusion is understandable. (p. 352).

Although Mr. Fischer speaks for his freshmen students, his point is that obligatory heterosexuality, in fact, produces a form of mandatory antihomosexuality (Herek and Berrill, 1992). Constructing their femaleness in the climate of the single-sex school in interesting ways calls on girls to emphasize their femininity which they do, not as an expression of anti-school culture, but in order to affirm an education where it is encouraged and certainly possible for femininity and school achievement to complement each other. They are comfortable as the *objects* of the project of women's education, where femininity is validated in context. Undeniable, though, is their emergent uneasiness around women as *subjects* of political and social change. While they identify with some feminist principles, and in that sense are not antifeminist, they do not wish to take up active agency in the movement at all.[17] Folding in images of 1960s radical feminism and hyper-mediated portrayals of feminists as "the bearers of female anger, as female incendiaries" (Delmar, 1994, p. 19), they draw lines around feminist principles and politics that are acceptable to them and reject others that do not mesh well with the way that they do gender inside school.

> Yvonne: [. . .] I think the school should do a little more of like, not like women's lib and burning bras but like the things about the declaration of the feminists [at the Seneca Falls Convention in 1848, reference to a Morning Meeting presentation during Women's History Month]. That was nice.
>
> A.P.: What was that?
>
> Yvonne: That thing that Alice [a sophomore] read [at Morning Meeting]. I think they [the school administration and faculty] should do stuff like that, just like pride in what women have worked for and stuff like that. I just think that since we are a girls' school, we should do stuff . . . like we should make girls' proud of themselves and proud of their history.
>
> A.P.: Do you, Diana, feel the same way as Yvonne, that more needs to be done in school in the way of emphasizing gender issues?
>
> Diana: Yeah, because it absolutely has the chance to have it done. And so it should be done. In public school, you couldn't do that.

Linking women's accomplishments to political actions taken by women to change women's position in society in the past, Yvonne and Diana are careful to bracket the attention that school officials bring to women's history and powerful movements for social change. At the same time as they support efforts to rescript women's structural subordination, they opt for a less aggressive, vocal, and above all depoliticized approach to social transformation. "The school should do a little more," they say, but it should not consist of highlighting "women's lib and burning bras," actions that cross the line of acceptable femininity for these two students as well as for most of their peers (Genovese, 1996).

A.P.: What do you think of when you think of the women's movement?

Dina: I think of feminists, and I can't stand feminists because I think they give women a bad name.

A.P.: Who and what makes a feminist as you see them?

Dina: Feminists are those people who go out and protest on Washington and down on Church Street [in the city], [who say] give us equal rights. We have equal rights, you know, at least in my opinion. We should have a woman president. Why does it matter? Is it going to make so much of a difference? Oh, we have a woman president now. Everything is going to be happiness and sunshine. I don't think so. It really bothers me. I think they come across as violent, and that's not good.

A.P.: Do you see yourself as a feminist?

Dina: No, not at all. I hope not.

*   *   *

A.P.: What does the women's movement mean to you?

Lisa: I think it's really important that women can have equal rights, but I think now, not this year, but lately, in the recent past years, that they have gone just too far. I've heard that they want to change, in all of the books, dictionaries, the spelling of woman to "womyn" so that it doesn't have the word "man" in it. That's just stupid. My father is a lawyer, and they have like all of the law books and everything. The women's movement is not trying to pass wherever it says—the person convicted, he may have rights or whatever—they want to pass it so that it has [reads] "he" or"she." That's stupid. That's a waste of money. It's not needed just to have the word "she," and when it's implied, it's the whole human population—he and she.

A.P.: Why do you think the women's movement would want to make these kinds of changes? Do you have any idea?

Lisa: I have no idea. They are insecure. I have no idea. But it frustrates me 'cause they are just unneeded things.

A.P.: Do you see yourself as feminist?

Lisa: I hope not.

A.P.: How would you define feminism?

Lisa: The people that are going overboard with the spelling of woman, that kind of thing. Like feminist to me means that I am a woman, I am better than everybody else, I have more power than you, I am a bitch. That's pretty much what I see as a feminist.

A.P.: So you don't see yourself as a feminist?

Lisa: No.

*   *   *

Donna: [. . .] like the feminist movement and stuff. Some women said—I am not taking this anymore, and then it like builds up. I think the school is very feminist, but I think it's like mild. They don't teach us to be like—shave your head and run out with Nazi boots on.

A.P.: What is a feminist to you?

Donna: A feminist is someone who gets mad if a guy tries to open a door for her. It's like Ms. Magazine and stuff. That's good. I wouldn't mind getting the magazine either, but very feminist [women] take things like to extremes. Like I don't think it's bad if a guy opens a car door for you. I wouldn't like punch him out and say you chauvinist pig. But I think that a feminist would, like a major feminist. I think we are all feminists at this school in a sense.

A.P.: What kind of feminist would you describe yourself as?

Donna: I don't think that I am a major feminist because I like guys. I don't mind if they open the car door, just as far as like dating and stuff. You kind of have to. No guy wants to go out with a girl who doesn't shave her legs and stuff like that.

A.P.: Do you mean to say that feminists are independent women?

Donna: Yeah. You can't picture like a feminist like dependent on a guy. I can't see a feminist who has like ten kids and like stays home and washes dishes.

*   *   *

A.P.: What do you think feminism is? Do you have any thoughts on that?

Michelle: I think it's basically what they call it when you are trying to get equality and what people's attitudes and relationships between people are if they want to be equal with people. I think right now it seems like feminists— to be feminist—you've got to be overly feminist.

A.P.: Which means what?

Michelle: Totally outgoing, totally like—I hate men. In that case, it's kind of stupid. When I hear of feminism, I think of the very extreme. I don't think of the middle ground. So I think there should be another word for the extreme, but I don't think there is, and that's what I think of its being—feminaziist.

A.P.: Do you see yourself as a feminist?

Michelle: I think of myself as [belonging] to a middle group. I don't feel limited by men. I mean, I would not do something because there were only guys here. But I wouldn't like refuse to do something because there were only guys there.

*   *   *

A.P.: What does the feminist movement mean to you?

Diana: It's just something, I think it's a . . . it's sort of an intangible word. I mean, you can't sit there and definitely define it. To each person, it's really different. So I guess in my way, it would be, I just [guess], strength, I guess. Strength.

A.P.: Do you see yourself as a feminist?

Diana: Um, in a way, I guess, because I, I'm all for like women being equal, but I'm not like a . . . [laughs] . . . I'm not like a, I don't know, I don't know how to say it. Um, like someone that always runs around saying everything you [men] do is sexist, and all men are pigs and all that sort of stuff. I'm not like that.

Seeping through this body of student narratives is an emergent post-feminism that casts a long and wide shadow of suspicion, doubt, and anger on feminist identity politics. Shrouded by negative representations of feminism in the mass media, the perceived threat of lesbianism to obligatory heterosexuality, male intimidation and collective expressions of female resistance, adolescent girls conclude that feminism is a radical, violent, separatist movement that does not resonate with norms, attitudes, and behaviors that professional middle-class families and schools have prescribed for these girls. Just as race is constructed through a public language of politeness, so is feminist solidarity acceptable through polite forms of identity and activism. Just as class norms arbitrate the management or, rather, mismanagement of race, so, too, do they decidedly inform post-feminist ideologies practiced by adolescent girls in the single-sex high school. When I ask Dina and Lisa individually to comment on whether they would describe themselves as feminists, they quickly disassociate themselves from its politics. For Dina, feminists "come across as violent, and that's not good." What she is, in effect, saying by stating that "I can't stand feminists because I think they give women a bad name," is that they somehow compromise naturalized femininity. As Lisa sees it, being a feminist gives the impression that women are "more powerful" and that they are "bitches" because of their power. Willing to see herself on some level a feminist, Donna concedes that she is not a "major feminist because I like guys," the implication being that feminists are man-haters, but opts, instead, to describe herself as a "mild" feminist. Similarly, Michelle takes the middle road, rejecting what she sees as "extreme" forms of feminism in favor of the "middle ground," more private and less openly political demonstrations of feminist solidarity. While these girls recognize and validate the political gains of first and second wave feminism and the work that has begun into the third feminist wave, they remain within the safe borders of an apoliticized feminism. In a striking reversal, they lodge their own subtle backlash against feminism which is, for them, the new opposition (Faludi, 1991). Donna's feminist limits are set when she says that she is "all for like women being equal, but . . . " Folding in virulent commentary sported by such popular radio hosts as Rush Limbaugh who has consistently spoken against "femi-Nazi feminists," she is not about more than a politically moderate and polite brand of feminist identity politics.[18]

Obligatory heterosexuality has conventionally assumed dependence on a man for a women's sense of power and value, locating women in service to men's needs and desires (Scott, 1994). The feminization of the work force has released women, to a large degree, from having to depend on a man. Best Academy students are reaping the benefits of structural change, yet their hopes are curiously frustrated by what they describe as the persistence of double standards. When I pressed students to consider how they might be able to play a role in changing women's position in society, they would defer to individual rather than collective solutions to gendered inequalities both at home and in the work place, as Randi suggests below.

> A.P.: Do you feel that there are ways that young women like yourself could work to see the roles that men and women play in society somehow changed and would you be interested in working towards that?
>
> Randi: I think it has to be on a personal basis before anything else can happen because, I don't know. It's not the type of thing that can be, like, now you are going to be more open. It's got to be worked out by the individual.

In a focus group interview, similar frustrations became apparent.

> A.P.: Do you think that the feminist movement could play a role in bringing about these kinds of changes?
>
> Yvonne: Guys will be like, oh, you bitch [feminist].
>
> Diana: I am like, excuse me, just because I can sit there and communicate for myself, doesn't mean that I am some go girl lesbian because I actually sit

there and don't submit to your manliness.

Yvonne: We were talking about this in English class. If a woman's [car] breaks down on the side of the road, she is supposed to sit there and hail for help. If she fixes that tire, oh my god, [she is viewed as a] dyke. Stuff like that just irritates me.

A.P.: So how do you think you can play a role in changing that?

Yvonne: It's never going to change.

Lisa: I would have no clue where to start. It's like the violence thing. I would have no clue where even to start.

Yvonne: You can put your own two cents in, you know, do what you can with each guy that you encounter. But it's never going to change.

Frustrated by incremental changes in existing patriarchal structures as they see it in their own experiences at home and in their male friendships and relationships, professional middle-class girls demonstrate an overwhelming reconciliation around the possibility of a radical structural overhaul in existing social relations of gender. While they support many of the issues that have been advanced in feminist politics up into the third feminist wave, they are ambivalent about the likelihood of change, seeming to operate both within and against a post-feminist critique.[19] Returning to the question of what Best Academy girls' projections for the future teach us about the role the single-sex school plays in fostering gender identities and possibilities for social transformation spearheaded by the professional middle-class, it is increasingly evident that the culture of the private girls' school, both as girls are positioned by the school and as they position themselves, supports a tamed and depoliticized feminism. Single-sex schooling, no doubt, opens up choices for young women, so that marriage, as is the case in large measure for working-class girls, is not the only available alternative after graduation from high school. Girls want desperately to be able to support themselves economically, and the school provides them with the tools to achieve success in their future adult roles at home and in the work place. While the conflict between being a female and achieving at high levels is resolved early on in a school climate supportive of girls' intellectual development, tensions between femininity and feminism, fueled by broader structures outside school, are substituted in its place. Within and against an emergent post-feminist ideology and culture, adolescent girls establish the outer limits of their own feminism which, generally speaking, is not challenged by school officials and the prevailing school culture.

Adolescent girls are designing their identities at the intersections of school and society, positioned by and actively repositioning themselves within and against discourses of femininity made available to them. They earnestly want to see existing double standards reversed in the direction of greater equity between men and women in public and private domains. Active questioning weaves in and out of narratives that challenge the naturalness of arrangements constructed around housework, salaried labor, motherhood, and parenthood. Wanting to strike a careful balance between career and family, they are frustrated by existing patriarchal norms that unproductively stand in their way. In spite of this, many project that they would like to stay home to raise their children given the economic resources to do so. It is possible that home and a restored focus on family life represents a site where they can recast a faulty sense of security and meaning that they expect might be lost on them as women if they should choose to devote themselves exclusively to a career. In choosing to pursue a career, their greatest fear perhaps is that their choice will have won them no more than empty success, and projections for the future become a metaphor for their struggle to reclaim desires, agency, and empowerment that work has compromised and forced underground.

Chapter 6

Schooling Our Daughters

As market driven institutions increasingly dependent on independent funding sources for their continued survival, the private school cannot afford to be unresponsive to parents' interests, needs, and tastes vis-a-vis their children's education. Part of deepening our understanding of professional middle-class girls' identity productions depends on gathering information on parents' attitudes toward and influence on private school structures and arrangements. That there has been a decided tendency among educational researchers to "study down" rather than "study up" accounts for a number of studies of the values, attitudes, and involvement of poor and working-class, white and non-white parents in school (Connell, 1982; Obgu, 1987; Brantlinger, 1987, 1989; Weis, 1991; Carger, 1996) in contrast to the relative dearth of data gathered around the perspectives and dispositions of middle and upper middle-class parents toward school (Sieber, 1982; Lareau, 1987; 1989; David, 1993).[1] Early on, Herbert Bowles and Samuel Gintis (1977) argued for a correspondence between parents' class status and work experiences based in the social division of labor, class culture, and employment opportunities. What is being suggested here is that families play a strong role in the reproduction of class consciousness in their children, and that parents transmit to their children norms and values that will prepare them for class-appropriate work roles. Interviewing the working-class parents of Freeway High School students, Lois Weis (1990) found that these parents attached important value to schooling and the high school diploma, holding education up as an enabling structure that would help their children negotiate unstable and unpredictable market conditions. Large-scale plant closings and corporate mergers in the wake of deindustrialization have effectively fractured the working class by cutting off opportunities for young, working-class men to find work but also to retain jobs inside those factories that once employed their fathers and brothers. Downward economic slides forecast highly unstable futures for this generation of working-class youth. In a late capitalist, post-Fordist economy, parents recognize that the educational and occupational attainments and job security that were available to them and their families only two decades earlier are no longer guaranteed for this generation and their families yet to come. Working-class parents know this and respond to these conditions by reframing the school as a place where their sons can acquire the skills they need to enable them to compete in other employment markets outside the local region and for jobs that require more specialized training. Working-class parents in Australian state schools similarly report that the school is, for them, a "way of putting a floor beneath their kid's future economic circumstances," in their bid to block their children's descent further into the economic hardships that they struggled within and against (Connell, 1982). There is strong evidence of rather fractured relationships between working-class families and schools, feeling themselves "frozen out" of school involvement (Connell, 1982) by school officials who perceive that these families do not value education because of their own educational deficits. Despite a history of widening mistrust between working-class parents and school officals based in fractured class relations within the working class, Freeway parents still turn to the school in their search for ways to best outfit their children for economic survival. For working-class parents, both in the United States and abroad, the school is one of the last bastions of hope in the struggle against a limited labor market.

Middle and upper middle-class parents historically have had strong involvement in and powerful influence over their children's education (Brantlinger, Majd-Jabbari, and Guskin, 1996). Where attitudes and values parallel those found in school, parents are confident that the school will develop the competencies and cultural capital that students first receive in their families and translate it into future educational and occupational attainments (Bourdieu and Passeron, 1977). As an agency of sorting and selection, the private school plays a significant role in reproducing class stratification. By reinforcing dominant norms, values, and attitudes that circulate between the upper middle-class home and the private school, Best Academy serves class-specific interests in intergenerational status mobility by helping to secure a child's place in the status continuum.

Unlike the documented reproduction of working-class culture, the reproduction of middle and upper middle-class consciousness plays itself out in parents' desires for their children's educational achievements and occupational attainments to exceed their own. Deindustrialization has cast a long and dark shadow over the life chances of working-class youth, and parents are encouraging their children to educate themselves for other employment markets as a matter of their own survival. While the working class are arguably more vulnerable than other class strata to economic shifts, downward structural movement has had broad effects, touching the middle and upper middle-classes as well. Upper middle-class families are now more than ever positioning themselves as downwardly mobile, a condition they anticipate being lived out in the next generation and worry that their children will not be able to exercise control over the conditions of their own lives in the face of a diversifying, restructuring global economy (Ehrenreich, 1989; Newman, 1989; Reich, 1992).[2] These parents recognize that the assumptions of class privilege, the likelihood of their child being accepted at a competitive college and one of their choice, and the ability to pay escalating tuition costs that are increasingly outpacing the cost of living and far outweigh the current availability of student loans, for example, are no longer guaranteed for their children. Working-class parents of Freeway High and working-class state schools in Australia are fighting for their children's social mobility, just as they "feel the floor slipping beneath their feet." Professional middle-class parents, in not too distant terms, are also caught in a similar struggle. The fight they are waging is around holding onto class privilege as they fight the "fall from grace," whose effects will impact their consciousness, their place in the status continuum, and the sense of possibility for their children's future in currently unstable times.

Many difficulties surround studying family dynamics since they are generally played out in intimate ways in the private domain, away from the public eye.[3] Gaining access to parents is further complicated by the tendency for parents of secondary school-aged children to work outside the home.[4] Unlike students who live closely with an ethnographer during field work, parents typically do not have the same opportunity to develop a trusting bond with the field researcher. Parents of Best Academy students also faced a difficult year of administrative transition which layered onto growing suspicions that they already had about me since they had not had the distinct advantage that their children had of gradually getting to know me over time in context. For these reasons, I only hear, in this chapter, from close to half of the parents of junior students, amounting to twenty-two parents from across the professional middle class, asking questions that solicit their perspectives on school choice, single-sex education, and ideal aspirations in the midst of inclining fears as resources are being squeezed and with that, the prospects for their children's future cut short.[5] Hopes and expectations for their children's future remain high, but they are inescapably cloaked in rising apprehensions that these youth will lose hold of the social and economic gains that their parents, themselves, have worked hard to sustain and build on. In the name of their children, parents are working against growing odds that favor the middle-class fall from grace. Upper middle-class parents' voices strikingly parallel working class and lower class parent narratives at this moment. While high income and low income parents hold similar ideals for their children (Laosa, 1982), the question remains why parents from clearly different class locations suddenly sound very much alike. This chapter will explore this emergent paradox as parents unravel their aspirations for this generation against the backdrop of mounting insecurities.

Private Schooling as Opportunity Structure

As discussed in chapter 3, school officals cite definite changes in the clientele typically served in Best Academy, and single out a group of parents who they describe as newcomers to the private school experience. Parents new to the culture of private education are represented here, but they are certainly not in the majority. Still, the number of parents fresh to this context are evident enough for administrators and faculty to form opinions on the cohort of parents that they are now dealing with. School officials wrestle with what they describe as a pervasive "consumer mentality" among parents who have decided to purchase a private education but do not have a complete understanding of what it is that they have invested in for their child. Transforming what school officials describe as a "public school mentality" into a "private school mentality" is only one of a larger set of issues defining the scope of transitioning going on in the Independent School Movement at this moment.

A.P.: How do you feel the independent school movement has changed?

Mrs. Nicholson: I think we have certainly the population. We have . . . there is an uninformed, truly uninformed perception of elitism, but it is so uninformed, but in the old days, that was valid. That was a valid comment about most independent schools. We certainly are having to do more with fewer resources and be more accountable. All of us. But the Independent School Movement has long been a leader in education, and I think we are the key to educational reform to be honest with you. The public school system is not going to make it.

A.P.: In terms of reform?

Mrs. Nicholson: It's too big; it's too cumbersome. I mean, I'm a Chubb and Moe[6] advocate when it comes to markets and so forth, um, despite the fact that most people, most consumers of the public schools are happy with the education their children are receiving. They are the most uninformed consumers I can imagine. And that's something else we're dealing with in this city—uninformed consumers. If St. Sophia's is three thousand dollars less, and the education is just as good—I hear it all the time. The education isn't just as good. It's very different. And I'll give you a very good example of that. This summer, there was a student who was part of our summer theater program who I really wanted [to recruit]. She was talented and delicious, and we would have been a great school for her. And her father called me in New York [the summer prior to the time that Mrs. Nicholson began her new

position as Head of School] and said—we are not going to send her because
. . . why should I . . . [and he was] very middle class, plenty of money to do
this [to be able to send his daughter to a school like Best Academy]. St.
Sophia's is three thousand dollars less. And I said, I'll come, when I come to
[this region], and talk to you about why St. Sophia's is three thousand dollars
less and what the benefits of our education are. I said, I'm not going to talk
about St. Sophia's, I'm only going to talk about Best Academy, and you can
make those comparisons. So he came, and we met. It was a summer day, and
I pulled—there was just so many faculty here, and I pulled all of the teachers
that this girl would have [as her teachers] together who happened to be
department heads by accident. We all sat in the library with these parents,
and I said, tell us what it is that we can speak to that appeals to you so much
about St. Sophia's. Well, he said, we went to visit, and there were television
sets in every room and in the corridors. And the girls were watching
Channel One, and they were simply mesmerized. That this faculty did not
jump out of their chairs and throttle the man is to their credit. [. . .] Gradually
each person [faculty member] spoke about how we deal, what the
philosophical roots are of our being are, [but it] didn't make any difference.
He saw technology, modern equipment, technology combined with passivity
and thought it was great. [. . .].

Wrapped in the rhetoric and debate of school choice, a movement that gained
momentum during the conservative high tide of the Reagan and Bush
presidencies, Mrs. Nicholson draws on the language of the proponents of
radical market-based school choice plans that argue for parents having greater
freedom to choose the schools their children will attend.[7] Basing her response
on a market metaphor, she, in effect, argues that providing parents with the
highest quality educational goods and services in a market setting allows
consumers, in this scenario, parents, to comparison shop. Given this, they will
be able to make the most informed decision possible about how best to
allocate their resources to educate their child. Thinking that an open market
creates the conditions for more informed consumers, Mrs. Nicholson quickly
discovers, through the example of this one parent, that it is wrong to expect
this. The lure of technology was great for this parent, and the fact that St.
Sophia's had worked Channel One into the school curriculum, added an aura
of specialness that justified, on a small but not insignificant level, sending his
child to private school.[8] Motivated by what she calls the "consumerist
approach," parents seek a "quick fix" that will give their children "an edge" in
a tightening educational and occupational marketplace.

A.P.: And the level of parental involvement at Best Academy, what is that like?

Mrs. Nicholson: Dual-working families, for the most part. It is a consumer
mentality that says, I'm paying for the most part. It is a thousand dollars a

year. I want X in exchange for my Y. It's negative, it's you owe me. There's
not that old-fashioned trust and investment and sort of sense that "I've
turned a daughter over to you, let's work together."

A.P.: At what point in time did you notice this shift in parental attitude?

Mrs. Nicholson: I don't know. Probably . . . when did I first see it? I was doing
admissions [employed at another prestigious private school in the Northeast]
when I saw it. Probably in the last decade, and it's coincident with the . . . it's
just about right—the rise of Wall Street in the 80s, the quick economic fix
that many, many families had. And they were able to turn to the independent schools which they did recognize in their sort of untutored way as
having an edge and besides, it was socially the way to go. And they could buy
an education, and they bought it. But with it, came an entire attitude
different from what any of us in schools have seen before, and I call it the
consumerist approach.

For the professional middle-class parent, a private education sets their child on
a course different from the public school where students have a greater likelihood of being accepted at a more competitive college where there is more
chance of making contacts with families who share similar class status, values,
and sensibilities (Cookson, 1994). This kind of educational and occupational
edge inclines professional middle-class parents to choose private education for
their children, with the expectation that established networks will help
protect their children against the effects of a restructuring economy that has
forecast low returns on college education in a narrowing job market.[9] Mrs.
Nicholson is not altogether surprised by parents' pragmatic belief that the
private school owes them something in return for their investment. With
hiking tuition rates that refuse to keep pace with the cost of living, parents
understandably want to have their voices heard and authority respected in the
educational marketplace. One teacher describes private school parents as
individuals who "feel as if they own you, and they demand more control of
what goes on [. . .] than public school parents who haven't paid [for their
children's education]." When I asked another teacher to elaborate on his
impressions of how his teaching experience has changed during the many
years that he has taught at Best Academy, he explains that "the family has
changed, the idea of parenting has changed, and the idea that the school will
somehow, some way pick up all of these things that have been left that parents
used to do is part of the change, and we find that here." Parents demand
greater control over their children's educational experience at the same time
as they have, on many levels, handed their parenting responsibilities over to
the school. School officials find hard evidence of an [ap]parent[10] shift away
from parents who, at one time, did not hesitate at all in giving the private
school their grant of approval. They chose a private school because they had

confidence in school officials and believed that the school would follow through on its end of the bargain to educate their children. Rather than parents and school officials working together on their children's behalf, Mrs. Nicholson and school faculty see a growing divide in school-parent relations, a moment that signals a profound shift in the attitudes, needs, and preferences of parents of private, independent school goers.[11]

While school officials find themselves facing a parent population that they perceive to be increasingly uninformed about the institutional form and practices in private schooling, it appears that this is not entirely the case, that parents of Best Academy students are more in command and understanding of the educational marketplace than school officials presuppose, and that parents seek private schooling for their chidlren largely out of very clear, class-specific motivations. As they see it, the private school is an open opportunity structure where, provided one gains access, they have equal opportunity to compete, to be fairly rewarded for individual effort through grades, and finally through the credential, a high school diploma from a reputable private high school. To maximize their daughter's life chances, professional middle-class parents look to the private school to set intergenerational status mobility in motion. Given the wide ranging characteristics of the professional middle class, it is not altogether surprising to hear from a number of parents an emergent sense of confidence in the academic and social advantages that going to a private, as opposed to a public school, can bring to their daughters.

> Mrs. Gold: I think the parents of the girls at Best Academy want their daughters to do well in whatever they want to do after they're out of high school and college. And that's why they're sending them there is because they feel they'll be best prepared for whatever comes, be it parenthood, be it a career. They just want them to be able to survive in society and have that little edge that you've got to have these days because there is just so much competitiveness. And you've got to be that, have that little something extra to be noticed. [. . .] And so we can get these girls as rounded as possible to be able to deal with whatever might come up. It's a plus in their favor. And I think they really do try to strive for that at Best Academy.

> *　　　*　　　*

> A.P.: If you could do it again, would you send your daughter to Best Academy?

> Mr. and Mrs. Snyder: Yeah.

> Mr. Snyder: Best investment that we have made, no question about it. All the suffering and pain that we went through is clearly worth it. There are advantages coming out of there. There are trustees. She is going to be a graduate of Best Academy. She is going to have thirty-seven girls [her class] that she is going to know for the rest of her life. Some of them are going to

be very, very important people. She has now an advantage that she would never have at West High, and they will know each other for the rest of their life. And she has more than thirty-seven because any graduate of the school as with the Citadel, as with Vassar College, if you are in town, and there is a Vassar Club, you are welcome. You immediately have a social circle. You don't have that from the local university. [. . .] That is a tangible benefit that you now have that nobody else has. And let's face it, the way things are acquired in our society, it doesn't matter what you know, it matters who you know. Eighty percent of all jobs are filled based on referral from someone else, not from your resume.

*   *   *

A.P.: What do you think graduating from Best Academy will mean for your daughter?

Mrs. Carpenter: Oh, I think it's money in the bank in some ways.

A.P.: In which ways?

Mrs. Carpenter: In just having this diploma from this school, just really, a real accomplishment.

A.P.: Do you think it promises anything for the future?

Mrs. Carpenter: It should. It should promise that anybody coming out of here with the kind of standards they have here, they don't seem to keep anybody who's really doing poorly. I mean, we've watched people fall by the wayside every year, not just because of personalities or whatever. Anybody below C level work is, doesn't seem to be staying on. And so I would think more people coming out of here, a poor student coming out of here is really an excellent student. So you would think that would do well for any of them in terms of where they apply to college. That should help them. And a good strong base for whatever they want to do, wherever they go from here. I would think coming out of here with this piece of paper would be very important, just like coming out of Harvard or coming out of Vassar or whatever.

*   *   *

A.P.: In what ways do you think your daughter's life will be the same or different from yours?

Mrs. Andrews: Oh, it is already different.

A.P.: How would you like it to be different?

Mrs. Andrews: More different? One thing is a choice of schools. I went to crummy schools [colleges], and I would like her to have the right schools to make the right connections and the right opportunities. I didn't have too many opportunities. So I think considering where we came from, my husband and I did okay, but we are hoping that the girls [two daughters] get a little farther than we did in terms of personal growth and economics too.

A.P.: Do you think Best Academy affords your daughter a stepping stone of opportunity for the future?

Mrs. Andrews: Most definitely.

A.P.: You do? In what way?

Mrs. Andrews: It's that networking thing. We wanted Hartford School for our other daughter [a prospective freshman] too, and the reason for it was networking. You meet a lot of people who stay friends for a very long time and end up doing business twenty years down the road.

A.P.: Do you think your daughter will be upwardly mobile?

Mrs. Andrews: I suppose. She is well coordinated, she is smart, she is beautiful, she is a nice person, so she has got sort of a nice package. So I would think if she uses it well, that is what she has to learn—how to use all these gifts—she will be upwardly mobile. And if she makes the right decisions, I keep telling her that one decision, one mistake can really affect your future.

A.P.: And would you say that the school has influenced the probability, as you put it, of her being upwardly mobile because of such things as networking that you point to?

Mrs. Andrews: It's the whole package. It's the reputation, the physical plant. It's everything. Look around, and it creates a little mindset. This is where I belong, that kind of feeling, and she will be upwardly mobile I would think.

*   *   *

A.P.: If you were to tell me what it means for your daughter to be a graduate of Best Academy, what would you say?

Mrs. Moore: Best Academy carries with it a certain reputation, that you feel, hopefully, will give her some assistance perhaps, you know, at least for getting into college. I don't know how much influence it would have in future years as far as careers, you know, to say what high school you went to. The longer down the line, certain things tend to lose their importance. Right now, what high school you went to has an effect, hopefully, on getting into a good college. Then if you go to a good college, that is what hopefully leads to good career choices and opportunities. I mean, sometimes you might wish that that wasn't so. But you got to be realistic when you look at the world too. And there are a lot people out there that that is exactly what they are looking at. When they get these kids' college applications, they are looking at what high schools they went to. And if it has, if it carries with it a good reputation, then your chances are better. That is just black and white, practical, you know. Whether it should be like that or not is another question. But it affects it. So I guess that is one of the things that you look for. [. . .] I just see for my daughter more opportunities in her future coming from Best Academy. I'm not saying compared to her brother [who attends a public school] because I think he will create his opportunities also.

A.P.: But as far as what her education here has meant for her?

Mrs. Moore: I would hope that her education would create a better future, a productive, creative future for her.

Parents choosing the private school cloak this institution in an aura of special-ness, believing that their investment will show significant returns across educational, occupational, and social arenas. More than hinting at a felt sense of "the floor slipping from beneath their feet," these parents fix their sights on the private school as an institution that can help them secure the social and economic gains for their children that they have managed for their families up to this point in time. Their hope is that graduating from a reputable private school will give their children an advantage that many of them do not have from their own backgrounds. A diploma from Best Academy is a credential that gives its graduates "that little edge that you've got to have these days because there is just so much competitiveness." The "edge" that Mrs. Gold speaks to is fleshed out in further depth and detail by other parents like Mr. and Mrs. Snyder who run down a litany of benefits that students attending a private school are bound to receive. Because of advantages like those above that follow from private training, Mr. Snyder is confident that his daughter will gain on many levels that go far beyond issues of school success. Building a network of friends that his daughter will have for life is a point of entry into a "social club" and further connections down the line. Together these parents weave a tight class analysis of private education, attributing to Best Academy a principal hand in developing and transforming resources and competencies into capital that will allow their daughters to exert greater influence over the educational and occupational marketplace. As one parent plainly puts it, a diploma from Best Academy is "money in the bank."

Earlier, I document a diversifying student body in transition to a broader representation of class cultures at Best Academy. Changes along these lines index broader shifts in the independent school movement as a whole. A number of Best Academy parents have been socially mobile, having moved out of a lower income bracket and standard of living into one higher than what they experienced as children. For families who have considerably fewer resources than those who are relatively privileged, who would fit more closely with the education levels and occupations of individuals in blue-collar working-class and lower white-collar middle-class strata, the private school can pass onto their children the cultural capital that has been unattainable for them. Clearly, these parents prefer private education for their children because they see it as a vehicle for educational and occupational access and opportunity. On this point, they are not terribly different from parents who either managed to climb into the professional middle class from lower white-collar middle-class or blue-collar working-class backgrounds or are themselves from solidly professional middle-class families. Whether parents have been able to scale the mobility structure to a small degree or by leaps, they continue to believe strongly in an open contest system and insist that the private school is an opportunity structure where, once students are admitted, they have available to them equal opportunity to compete and be rewarded for successful outcomes.[12] For Mrs. Rodriguez, a Hispanic whose daughter is first generation American, the private school is an enabling structure, promising educational access and occupational choices that were within reach neither for herself, who recently completed an Associates Degree and works as a teacher's aide nor her husband who went no further than the tenth grade in his education and currently does manual labor in a local factory.[13]

> A.P.: What do you say to your daughter about her goals for the future?
>
> Mrs. Rodriguez: We tell her that she could do it. I say, mamita, you could do it. You see how we are suffering now with bills, paying bills, everything for you to go to school, not only for her but everybody, [to be able] to buy you things. I don't want you to be suffering the same way [that we, as parents] did. I want you to study. I want you to be somebody in the future because I know you could do it. You could do it. If you get married someday, and the guy is no good for you, and you got kids or something, you are not going to be crying in the corner because you need money for this or that—no. You got a career, and you could do it. You could afford it, you can do it. And she [my daughter] said—mommy, I know what you are saying, and I understand what you are saying. So I know that she could do it.

Parents from blue-collar working-class and lower white-collar middle-class backgrounds who managed to work their way up the American class structure into the professional middle class hold similar views.

> A.P.: Do you think Best Academy prepares your daughter to meet her personal and professional goals for the future?
>
> Mrs. Foster: Sure. They give her the, the maturity and the tools to be independent and resourceful and [let her] know that if you work hard enough, you can get what you want. She has gotten that because they keep reinforcing that [in school]. And in a small environment, they are going to [do that].
>
> A.P.: What kind of image do you think the school is projecting as the "pot at the end of the rainbow?"

Mrs. Foster: If it's an obtainable goal, and you work hard, you will get there. You can be whatever you want to be. That's the American dream. They foster it, like I said, they have small goals that they have to obtain through the four years, and they have the team spirit and know-how to play together and to do things together.

A.P.: Do you as parents believe that if people work hard enough they will get what they want, and as parents, do you try to instill that in your daughter?

Mr. Foster: Yeah.

A.P.: Do you think this is possible?

Mrs. Foster: I think so. She sees us. I have worked almost all of her life. She was eighteen months old when I went back to work. She sees her father, struggling, going through school. I mean, we are making it and getting—our kids are getting what they want.

A.P.: As a parent, what does the American dream mean to you?

Mrs. Foster: To see our kids be happy and do what they want to do with their lives. When I was in seventh, eighth, and ninth grade, I wanted to, even junior high, I wanted to be a veterinarian. My parents had me, I had to go to work. College was for my brothers. I was the oldest, and I was not allowed to go to college. I had to go to work. When it got to my brothers who were four and five in the number of children, they dropped out of high school. So they didn't go to college either—which I always felt cheated—the fact that I didn't get to go to college.

*   *   *

A.P.: And what kind of young woman do you hope the school will produce in your daughter?

Mrs. Moore: Their part is to create, again, to give her that good academic background that she needs to carry forward, to give her leadership skills for her to excel. Everything that she does along this path at this point in time of her life is leading to her future and what it is going to be like down the road for her. She is coming from a lower income [family], but by no means has she been brought up to believe that will hold her back in any way.

A.P.: Do you see her being upwardly mobile in her future?

Mrs. Moore: I do, definitely. I always told the kids that you can do anything. There are ways to do whatever you would like to do, you know, or at least try. In other words, just because we don't have a lot of money, it doesn't mean you can't still go out and do what you want to in life. So, I guess I am looking for this opportunity to reinforce that in her, that she can go on and achieve.

For these parents, the private, independent high school picks up where structural conditions might very well have closed off more open-ended educational and occupational possibilities. This is no more clearly stated than in Mrs. Foster's observation that the private school is a place where a student can realize the "American dream" of open competition and just reward. These families wish for their daughters more than was possible in their youth and believe that the educational opportunities provided in a private school will help their daughters better control the direction and conditions of their live so that they will be able to "do what they *want* to do with their lives." As Mrs. Moore, a divorced parent raising two teenagers on a single income from her job as an administrative assistant, puts it, "I guess I am looking for this opportunity to reinforce in her [my daughter] that she can go on and achieve." Like Mrs. Foster, parents of private school students believe strongly "that if you work hard enough, you can get what you want." Their own experiences have told them that this is not an empty dream. It is important to remember that the effects of global restructuring and a diversifying economy had not yet touched youth coming of age in the 1960s and 1970s who would be the parents of this generation of Best Academy students. Collective memory fuels a measure of optimism here among parents fighting against challenges to the educational and professional barriers that the professional middle class has erected to separate itself from other class cultures and protect its own gains.

Professional middle-class families find themselves in a historical moment of "falling from grace" as they begin to discover that the class privileges that they have either inherited over generations or had conferred on them through their parents' gains in the post-war era are no longer guaranteed. The barriers that the middle class had built around itself to keep itself in and others out would no longer prove sufficient defense against the tide of economic change arriving in the early 1970s (Ehrenreich, 1989). Across the professional middle class, parents offer narratives that foreshadow impending social and economic loss as they look for ways to give their daughters that "edge" at a time when relative privilege is itself under siege. In a region that fell victim to economic retrenchment in the early 1980s, only 94,500 workers, less than one-fifth of the total regional workforce in the city, were left in manufacturing jobs at the decade's end (Perry and McLean, 1991). Parents see the impact of local economic decline most immediately on tightening standards of living in their own families and worry about their children's future financial security in the face of a widening service sector and narrowing job market overall.

> Mr. Falzone: I see an entire generation having a problem. [. . .] I see the entire generation, my daughter included in the generation. These kids are going to have a tough time. I can see it. I mean, being in business, I know they are going to have a tough time. Not all of them [but] the majority of them.

Mrs. Falzone: And I don't feel that we should hand them [things]. They have to work. We worked for where we are today, and we are still working.

*   *   *

A.P.: Do you see a future for your daughter in this city?

Mrs. Parks: I don't know. It is a rare thing where someone is still in the city anymore.

A.P.: You wouldn't discourage her from moving away?

Mrs. Parks: No, of course not. But I don't think they have any choice. You have to go where the work is now.

*   *   *

Mr. Graziano: I see a lot of effort [with respect to economic change in the city], but I am not too optimistic about tremendous change. I think we experienced tremendous appreciation in the 70s and people . . . salary increases that were disproportionate to what was happening. And when the bottom fell out in a lot of these companies and a lot of these savings and loans and a lot of these problems, it was all plastic. And we are paying for their sins. And the same thing in government. So I don't see, I see changes being made slowly, and I don't see any great changes. A lot has happened here with new buildings and stadiums and waterfront development and that, and that will continue. But I don't see any dramatic change. I don't think there is anything that could stimulate a northeast city and could stimulate a business to come into this area and start. The free trade was supposed to be the dramatic change for this city. That hasn't really caught on. It hasn't created the type of job opportunities that they thought it would. And I am concerned. It is sad for me to think that my daughter most likely would be better off in a profession in a different city as far as monetary gains and as far as career gains. And I am not afraid of that, but I would prefer that she could be in this city. But I don't see any dramatic changes [in the current situation].

Facing lengthening unemployment lines, working-class parents of Freeway High School students had no other recourse than to encourage their children to leave their community as a matter of their own economic survival (Weis, 1990). The economy kept them from envisioning a future for their children in Freeway, forcing parents to accept the fact that their children must relocate themselves and their families in more economically stable areas. Against the backdrop of a declining regional economy, the voices of professional middle-class parents sound strikingly similar. From this, it is possible to make yet another case for choosing private education as a buffer against downward mobility. It is documented that private school students on the whole attend more selective colleges than public school students even when academic achievement and family background are held constant (Cookson, 1981). A private education can, then, give students that extra "edge" in the competition for prized slots in these schools, most of which are far from this urban center. With a private education, students have a greater chance of moving out, and a college education at a reputable institution is a first step in that direction.

School Choice

The voices of proponents of school choice were heard loud and clear in the early 1980s as clarion calls for the radical restructuring of American education were sounded in response to claims from conservative foundations and policy groups that there was a profound "crisis in education." In recent decades, a series of national reports have drawn attention to the state of public education in the United States, the most significant report, A Nation at Risk (1983), attributing declining economic productivity and the slow pace of technological development to poor training in secondary schools. Policy analysts and educators backing these findings argue that mediocrity in education has put the United States behind in economic growth and cut into its being able to compete effectively on the international market. By forcing schools to compete among themselves for students, the school choice movement set the stage for market pressures whose immediate effects, this loose coalition argued, would show up in positive improvements in school practices and outcomes that would, in the end, situate the United States well to compete economically and technologically in the international arena.

While the crisis label attributed to U.S. schools is problematic for a number of reasons that continue as the focus of debate, it has managed to grab the popular imagination, holding great appeal for professional middle-class parents who want to shield their children against the effects of global structural change trickling down into their neighborhoods and homes.[14] As they see it, the public school hosts a set of problems that range from poorly trained teachers, students lacking discipline, and minimal academic standards, to violence and instrumental forms of presenting and delivering curriculm (Lesko, 1988). In a declining economy, professional middle-class parents want educational alternatives that they believe will prepare their children to be competitive in the marketplace. Maximizing educational and occupational outcomes join with a host of other factors to inform school choice for Best Academy parents who see the private school embodying many of the reforms that have been put forward for education in the 1980s. Self-selected students and faculty and small class size, typical characteristics of private, independent schools, are tremendously appealing for parents looking to find an educational climate that can individualize instruction to student needs as they come up.

Parents fold these pieces into their construction of the private school as different from and in opposition to the public school which they describe as unsafe, undisciplined, and not academically rigorous. That proponents of market-based reform have successfully coopted parents' support for their proposed reforms is evident in the many examples that parents draw on to rationalize their preference for private education.

> A.P.: Would it have mattered to you if your daughter had decided to go to a public high school rather than a private institution?

> Mrs. Parks: Well, I would rather private, just because I think that a little more is demanded. In the public, they can float a little bit, and they are teenagers, and they will. Or if they don't want to do the work, they won't. And if they don't want to be stimulated, no one forces them to look and listen or watch them and advance them. She could have gone to Knoll Park and absolutely thrived, but you are just taking more of a chance of them floating around a little bit and losing direction.

*   *   *

> Mrs. Fox: [. . .] And she came over and did a shadow day at Best Academy, and she loved it. She loved the atmosphere. She loved the students. There was this camaraderie between the students and just a very nice feeling with the students and with the faculty that she liked. She really liked it. And it was like nothing else. At that point, she knew that she was accepted at Central High [a public, magnet school] and, but she really, at that point, I'm not even sure that her Dad wanted her to go to Central High. There's something I think about the location of the school that turned him off, and he couldn't picture her coming home, in the dark, on the bus. And then the idea that he had gone to private high school, and he knew the benefits of a private high school.

> A.P.: From his perception, what would be the benefits of a private education for your daughter?

> Mrs. Fox: Small classroom, more individual attention. Subject matter. I think he perceived academically more challenging, and he wanted her to have it because he perceived her as having more ability, and he felt, I think at that time, she had a lot of talent that wasn't quite being tapped. He felt that she really wasn't being stretched all the way out, that she really had more to give academically. That she could perform beyond even the lowest that she was doing. And we both had agreed that we thought that she really could reach even more, reach farther than she was. She was an honors student. She was doing very well. She was, you know, in the gifted and talented program.

*   *   *

> A.P.: Did you want your daughter to go to a private school?

Mr. Falzone: Well, you see, maybe we had a problem with that because at the time, unlike when we [my wife and I] grew up, we just walked out the front door and went to a neighborhood school, which was fine. We couldn't just send our child where we thought—the public school in our neighborhood. She would have to be bussed halfway across the city [perhaps]. Well, I'm not, I don't have any say in where my kid is going to school or not. So we looked at private schools.

*   *   *

A.P.: How is it that you chose to send your daughter to a private, girls' school?

Mrs. Snyder: I guess discipline maybe. I always thought that the discipline was more structured in a private school.

Mr. Snyder: That was my primary reason. More is accomplished in a tighter environment. To me, that is how we decided, that St. John's [their daughter's Catholic grammar school] was a good school. It was clean, it was safe.

*   *   *

Mrs. Rodriguez: I found this school very different than other schools because of the way [of the] structures are different. In a public school, you don't got a place like this [room] to talk to somebody. You see classrooms, chairs, blackboards, books. This is like your home. That's a big difference. That's why I said that this school is a big difference from the public schools because when I send my daughter here, it's like sending her to another home. Even though I don't know everybody, [but] I know she is safe [here]. In public school, you see . . . I don't know how to say this. I don't know if you are here during the day, but in public school, it is too noisy, and kids [are] talking back to teachers, you know, that kind of thing, and I don't think she [my daughter] is seeing that kind of thing here.

*   *   *

A.P.: Now, you were going to support your daughter's decision [to transfer from Central High [a public, magnet school, where she was a freshman] to Best Academy?

Mrs. Bernstein: Maybe feebly, but I like Central High. She was hating it then. She was sick of the people [the students], so I could understand.

A.P.: Would you have sent your daughter to a public high school?

Mrs. Bernstein: Well, Central High is a public school.

A.P.: I realize that. But would you have sent your daughter to a school other than a magnet school?

Mrs. Bernstein: Oh my God. Do you know what they are like? [Places like] Riverview? Not my child. A magnet, but I don't know one person who sends their child to Bayview or Hilldale which is, when I was a kid, all the Jewish kids that didn't go to Best Academy or to Hartford School went to Hilldale and got a great education, and they had AP [Advanced Placement]. And they went to all of the same schools we did for college, and we were friends.

*   *   *

A.P.: Had your daughter previously gone to public school?

Mrs. Carpenter: No. She changed schools every two years in elementary [Mrs. Carpenter's husband was with the military and, therefore, the family frequently moved around the United States]. And she went mostly, well, I probably should say, fifty percent private and fifty percent to parochial schools, depending on where we lived and what was available. We lived in states where public education was just a baby-sitting service, and we would not tolerate her going to school where she was learning absolutely zero. [. . .] So now she has continued with private education because of those circumstances.

*   *   *

A.P.: How is it that you chose to send your daughter to a private girls' school?

Mrs. Snyder: I guess discipline, maybe. I always thought that the discipline was more structured in a private school.

Mr. Snyder: That was my primary reason. More is accomplished in a tighter environment. To me, that is how we decided, that St. John's [their daughter's Catholic grammar school] was a good school. It was clean, it was safe.

Positive descriptions of private schooling mark it as *different from* public schooling, in large measure shaping parents' decisions to choose private education for their children. Mrs. Parks is convinced that her daughter receives a qualitatively better education because a smaller, more structured context lends itself more to focused, rigorous, and challenging instruction. The public schools have a reputation for being no more than a "baby-sitting service," leading Mrs. Carpenter to decide on either private non-sectarian or parochial schooling for her daughter wherever the family happened to be living. Parents reach agreement on the matter of school discipline which they feel to be less of a problem in the private school. With his wife on this issue, Mr. Snyder concludes that "more is accomplished in a tighter environment," where disciplinary problems are less likely to bubble up in the first place in a smaller school where it is easier to monitor student behavior. Reports of rising levels of crime in urban centers and escalating incidences of violence growing at uncontrollable rates in U.S. public schools have fueled parents' distrust and disenchantment with public education. That their children will be safe and protected when they send them off to school each morning is one of their leading reasons for choosing alternatives to public schooling like Best Academy. An admissions officer explains this trend this way:

I think for the most part, parents want a safe environment for their daughters. Not that they want them to be cloistered, but they want them to be in an environment where they are free to walk the halls and not have somebody pull a knife out on them. That once they are here, they can concentrate on the academics because it is a safe environment. They like the idea of single-sex [education] because they don't think that their daughter is going to spend twenty hours coming to school in the morning and looking beautiful. They expect her to look good, but she doesn't need to put on tons of make-up or whatever. I had one parent who actually spent a whole year volunteering in the high school in her daughter's school district to see what it was like. She decided that there was no way that she would send her daughter to this high school where girls would sit in boys' laps during class, and people were making out quite a bit in the halls, all kinds of things that did not lend themselves to reading, writing, and arithmetic. A lot of the parents are educators themselves, and they know the difference, and I think that speaks to the issue as well, that teachers would send their child to a school like Best Academy versus a public school down the street. So I think that is one issue. Safety is definitely an issue. I think that academics are probably the priority, but safety has moved into the first notch, and academics are right behind it just because they don't feel that they can get the academics unless they are in a safe environment.

Shades of doubt surround problems that parents associate with public education. When I asked Mrs. Bernstein if she would have ever thought of sending her daughter to a public school other than a magnet, she is horrified at this suggestion and quickly shoots back—"do you know what they are like?" Motivated by similar concerns, Mrs. Rodriguez, who works as a school aide in a public elementary school in the city, knows that her daughter will be safe in Best Academy, a sense of security that she cannot depend on being in place in the public schools.

Single-Sex Schooling

The effectiveness of single-sex education has yet to be conclusively established, but there is strong empirical evidence that girls do experience a wide range of positive learning outcomes from going to school only with girls (OERI, 1993). Studies have documented higher academic outcomes among students in single-sex schools as compared to students in coeducational schools (Riordan, 1985; Lee and Bryk, 1986).[15] Best Academy students report feeling more comfortable and relaxed in a setting where they do not have to compete with boys for a teacher's attention, and with girls for boys' attention by overemphasizing their attractiveness, at least during school time (Sadker and Sadker, 1974; Holland and Eisenhart, 1990). Curricular forms and instructional practices in coeducational classrooms have not only been found to discourage equal educational attainments between boys and girls, but they have also proven to play a significant role in structuring unequal power relationships between male and female students which decidedly favor boys while putting girls at a distinct disadvantage as far as their social and cognitive development (MacDonald, 1980; Deem, 1984). Among girls in mixed-sex schools as compared to girls in single-sex schools, the "fear of success" seems to be a more persistent aspect of girls' culture (Winchel, Fenner, and Shaver, 1974). To protect themselves against social rejection, they avoid doing better than boys in the classroom. Girls' reluctance to speak out in class and to participate in classroom activities turns them into silent, passive, and invisible learners (Spender, 1982; Mahony, 1985). Curricular forms and school practices supporting unequal power relationships between girls and boys in school reinforce existing inequalities in the sexual division of labor at home and in the work place. In a bid to break this reproductive cycle, feminist educators have advanced the cause of single-sex education, seeing it as a powerful option for equalizing social relations and academic achievement between girls and boys.[16]

Parents have a general awareness of the advantages of all-girls' schooling for girls' attitudes towards school, academic outcomes, and socialization. Documented gains in girls' self-esteem, confidence, and achievement levels, particularly in math and science disciplines, findings that have identified instructional methods that best fit girls' relational learning styles, and the recent rise of trade books in the popular press that explore girls' loss of voice and identity as they enter adolescence have been published and broadly circulated in the media (Pipher, 1994; Mann, 1996). While the effectiveness of single-sex education has yet to be definitively established in the research, parents like what they hear, and search for educational options that will bring out the best in their daughters. On their decision to enroll their daughters in a girls' school, parents have this to say:

A.P.: How did you feel about a girls' school for your daughter?

Mrs. Peters: I think that was a big factor. I mean, I felt it was. To me, you're easily distracted when you have the boys around. To me, I'm interested in getting her an education, of [her] being self-reliant and being able to, you know. I mean, I hope she gets married too, if that's what she wants and has grandchildren for me. But, you know, never depend on anyone else or that, you know. But I thought it was helpful. I mean, she definitely has no intention on earth to go to an all-girls' college because she is interested in boys, and she's never had a boyfriend in high school or one brief little thing. But she wants that. She does miss that. She would like that now. [. . .]

*   *   *

Mrs. Moore: [. . .] She [my daughter] was always a good student all the way through [her grammar school training in a public magnet school]. But I think being at Best Academy, one of the main reasons I enrolled her, and I have read the studies about girls being left behind or losing the attention of teachers and instructors as the years go on. They have it in the early years, and not so much in the later years, and I didn't want to see that happen. I wanted to continue to see her grow and maintain her liking for school and education and want to progress and carry on with her education. So I didn't want to, to see it stifled in any way. So that was one of the factors why I decided to have her come to Best Academy, and I think that it has been very good in that regard. I think she has definitely blossomed and grown under the instruction that she has gotten here.

*   *   *

A.P.: What kinds of things did you hope for your daughter when she enrolled at Best Academy?

Mrs. Andrews: My daughter was extremely shy. And I saw her in her grammar school, even though she was probably brighter than anyone else there, I saw her stepping back and letting the boys do things. And I didn't want that to happen again. I wanted to make sure that she developed some leadership potential. And finally, I think last year was the first year she began exhibiting some ability to use her brain and make some decisions and influence other people. So I'm pleased with all of that.

*   *   *

A.P.: How will your daughter's life be different from yours?

Mr. Snyder: From a girls' school, she is going to be able to dominate situations when she wishes or assert herself when she wishes. She is not going to be as easily intimidated. She is going to have the opportunity to choose, and many people do not. And she will have the confidence.

*   *   *

A.P.: How about Best Academy? How did you learn about this school?

Mrs. Foster: My business partner went here. She was a graduate of this school. And I myself was a graduate of an all-girls' school, so I had a tendency to favor that type of education. I think that was better for me in high school.

A.P.: Why? What was your experience?

Mrs. Foster: It just, I, at first, I didn't realize how important it was until I was a junior in high school, and I went to summer school into a co-ed situation. I had to take a course that I couldn't get at my high school, and I was amazed at the difference going to school with boys and girls. Girls all of a sudden became very stupid. I didn't like that, and they didn't answer any questions. I used to raise my hand, and the girls would look at me like—why are you doing that? The boys are supposed to be the smart ones. So I mean, that type of thing I didn't care for. I didn't care for it at all. I mean, in an all-girls' school, you get to be the one who answers the questions, and you get to be the one who solves the problems.

A.P.: Mr. Foster, did you go to a co-ed high school?

Mr. Foster: No, I went to an all-boy's school.

A.P.: That is interesting. And your experience, how do you remember it?

Mr. Foster: I enjoyed my high school years, but I think, [with a] co-ed school, you get a more all-around idea of what the world is really like. I don't think you have the same experiences as you would have in an all-boys' or all-girls' school. There are men and women in the world, and we all have to interact together, work together. And I just feel that you miss things.

A.P.: But you, Mrs. Foster, don't feel like you missed anything?

Mrs. Foster: No. I gained from it. Confidence, if nothing else.

Clearly, parents are informed consumers, drawing on their own experiences in all-girls' schools and positive evidence documenting girls affective and cognitive development in single-sex settings. We do hear some hesitation on the part of Mr. Foster who is not altogether sure that he and his wife made the best decision in sending their daughter to a girls' school. Having attended a boys' school, he seems to think that a child is put at a disadvantage in their socialization by going to school with the same sex. Mr. Foster's argument is strikingly similar to those made by proponents of co-education who have spoken against separating the sexes during adolescence. Since this is a critical period of affective and cognitive growth, proponents of mixed-sex schooling submit that adolescents who do not have the experience of learning side by side with other youth will not reach full psychological and sexual development (Bicknell, 1979).[17] The hesitation we hear from this father is an exception, though, to the otherwise strong collective voice that carries the decisions these parents have made to send their daughters to a private, independent, single-sex high school. Interestingly, though, parents seem to weight more heavily concerns for discipline, safety, and academic excellence, while the benefits of single-sex education tend to be secondary in their decision-making. I argue this since parents appeared to address the advantages of educating girls together in a single-sex school in their conversations with me only after first turning to other overriding concerns like safety, discipline, and academic rigor. This is not to suggest that Best Academy parents are uninformed about the benefits of single-sex schooling since their narratives are strong on the many ways that their daughters will gain from the experience of single-sex schooling. My point is simply that gender-based outcomes, while important, are less salient determinants of school choice for parents who seem to be more invested in other defining characteristics of the private, independent high school. Sending their daughter to a private girls' school has the double-sided effect of protecting their child from negative and harsh elements on the outside and empowering them socially and intellectually as independent, confident, intelligent girls on the inside. There is no doubt that parents have chosen private education because of the appeal that more individualized instruction, a strong ethic of caring, and high academic standards holds for them. Even though they do not speak to the crisis in education, it is apparent that parents have also been influenced by the weight of exaggerated claims of a "crisis in education" and have jumped on the bandwagon of market-based educational reforms, first proposed in the 1980s and resurfacing again in the 1990s. The issue here is that while parents script a different set of reasons for choosing a girls' school, their arguments cannot be decontextualized from the broader climate of educational ills that they hear and see in urban settings, and the private, single-sex school appears to embody many of the proposed educational reforms that speak to parents' needs, preferences, and tastes at this structural moment.

Projections for the Future:
On Career, Marriage and Family

Working-class girls typically have not had many choices available to them after graduating from high school outside of marriage and semi-unskilled or unskilled labor in the secondary labor sector (Griffin, 1985; Lees, 1986; Valli, 1988; McRobbie, 1991). They assumed marriage and family as their next and only move up through the mid-1980s, a trend that would change as rising rates of inflation and economic downturns forecast relative instability for them and their families. In this context, working-class parents strongly encourage their children to go onto college and to develop skills that will make them more competitive in other employment markets (Weis, 1990). Higher education and professional credentialling are standard requirements of the professional middle class. Professionalism has been erected as a border around the middle class, keeping those on the inside in and others historically outside of the middle class out. Overall, parents are in general agreement that their daughters will go onto college immediately after they graduate from high school. In no instance do they suggest that their child should postpone college. While some parents do project the possibility that their daughter will marry during college or in graduate school, it remains highly unlikely as they see it that any one of their daughters will delay college and professional credentialling and choose marriage and children right after leaving Best Academy. Collectively, they position marriage and family in their daughters' distant futures and trust that the self-confidence, discipline, and motivation students receive at Best Academy will translate into professional goals and pathways for the immediate future.

A.P.: Five to seven years from now, what do you envision for your daughter's life in professional and personal terms?

Mrs. Foster: Basically I hope she is happy. I would like to see her pretty well settled. By then she should have made a choice as to what she wants to spend the rest of her life doing.

A.P.: Do you see marriage and family in her future?

Mrs. Foster: Yes.

A.P.: Would you like that for your daughter?

Mrs. Foster: Most definitely.

A.P.: If you could rank how you would like your daughter's life to get played out in terms of what she would most likely do after graduating from college, what would that look like?

Mrs. Foster: Knowing my daughter, she will get through college and probably working on her master's or something when she decides to settle down. And she may not get her master's right off the bat. Get married and have a couple of kids and maybe get it later on. I don't know. That depends on if and who she runs into. It is going to have to be a very special individual that she can finally settle down with.

A.P.: Do you think she would stop college to be married?

Mr. Foster: I don't think so.

A.P.: So you think that she would not stop her college education?

Mr. Foster: I hope not. I don't think she would.

Mrs. Foster: At least not the first four years. I think my daughter will get her degree. I don't know when graduate school will be.

*   *   *

A.P.: How do you envision your daughter's life five to seven years from now?

Mrs. Fox: Actually, I hope that she will still be in school. I hope that she will pursue a medical degree. She . . . we had a brief discussion about that recently, and I said to her that I, I said, if I had to do it over again, I would have gone ahead and pursued my degree. And I said a friend encouraged me to go ahead and do that, and I explained to her why. That MD after your name opens certain doors and offers certain authority behind it that you would not otherwise have, even with a Ph.D. after your name. And I said I didn't take that opportunity up. I changed fields. I'm happy with the field that I'm in, but I'm not so sure that I should not have gone ahead and finished that degree. [. . .]

A.P.: Do you see marriage and family in her future?

Mrs. Fox: I do. She said to me, and I was a little surprised, she said, I don't think that I will ever have children. And I said, well, you know something, I said that choice is yours. And I said there is nothing wrong with either decision. But I said, I think you are certainly capable and able to be able to have them both if you decide to. And I said you may want to pursue your career, and you may choose to put it aside for awhile and pursue your family. That's your choice.

       *   *   *

A.P.: Do you see marriage and family in your daughter's family?

Mrs. Carpenter: I do, yeah. But I think quite a ways off. But it wouldn't surprise me either if she got married when she was in college. She'll never, I like, I get teased by people who think that we are throwing our money away on a female, that it would be alright to spend this kind of money for college but not for high school. [They say] she's going to go off and get married, and you're going to lose your money. And I say, how do you lose your money?

A.P.: Your contemporaries say this to you?

Mrs. Carpenter: Oh yeah. You're out of your mind. You're paying all these taxes. Why not send her to public school. She would have a good education at this school or that school. We hear this all the time, and my comment to them is, just because you get married, you don't lose your brain. I mean, there's no reason why you can't work full-time, part-time, do whatever you want, just because you get married. And I don't think the people saying this are all a certain type of person, a traditional person who, where the woman has stayed home. We're getting this from a wide variety of ages and people.

A.P.: Professional women?

Mrs. Carpenter: Professionals. Perhaps they're not as happy with their little bailiwick as they think they are or something. It surprises me how often we hear this, how we're throwing our money away. But only time can tell. How can you throw away education?

       *   *   *

A.P.: How do you envision your daughter's life five to seven years from now?

Mrs. Moore: Success, in her terms.

A.P.: Which is what?

Mrs. Moore: Leadership. Decent money. So that she doesn't have to scrimp and scrap I suppose. Actually, you always want better. I guess it is true, you want better for your children then maybe what you were able to [have]. I would like to see all my children successful financially, simply because life is better that way. I suppose, if you don't have to worry about money, then you can put your attentions to other things, and you can experience many more things in life if you have money. Because our society is based on money. Those that have money can experience more of what life has to offer. I am sorry, not [to say] that things are impossible if you don't have money.

A.P.: Things are easier?

Mrs. Moore: Easier to experience. I hate to put a value on money, but the way our society is structured these days, you kind of have to. So I look for success in her terms so that she can experience what she wants to in life. I want for her what she wants. Her career goals—I am not this type of parent who has a plan in mind, that I want her to go to Harvard, and I want her to be a doctor, you know, I want for her what she wants. She seems to want for herself good things. She has goals. She has the desire to achieve, and that is what I want to see her do.

A.P.: Do you see marriage and family in her future?

Mrs. Moore: Oh yeah. Definitely, but down the line. I don't foresee her getting married right away nor having children right away. I think she will, but I don't see it for her immediately, and that is fine. When I was growing up, it was the thing to do, to come out of high school and get married which is basically what I did. I often think that is what led to the [my] first divorce because we were just too young. I wouldn't wish that on . . . I don't think that it is appropriate anymore, and I am glad to see the trend where women are waiting to get married and have families.

*   *   *

Mr. Gold: [. . .] I don't see her stopping at the bachelor's level.

Mrs. Gold: No. She will go on.

Mr. Gold: Particularly if she's looking into research science [for her future profession].

A.P.: And do you see marriage and family in her future?

Mrs. Gold: At some point. I think at some point. She loves to baby- sit for kids, and she does well with children. So, I mean she's definitely not ready for it yet, and that's fine with us.

Mr. Gold: Yeah, and I don't see her falling into something.

A.P.: You mean once she's in college?

Mr. Gold: Yeah, and then dropping everything just to do that. I think she's a little more independent.

Mrs. Gold: But if she meets "Mr. Right," and this is just one of those things that's meant to be, I think she would continue with her education after marriage.

Mr. Gold: Plus he would also be willing to share in bringing their life together and allowing freedom.

Mrs. Gold: That's true. Her married life will be fifty-fifty, or she will not have it. Because she will not be one who does everything. It's going to be a partnership.

Parents are clearly interested in seeing their daughters get a college education before they settle down, marry, and have a family. Thematically salient throughout these narratives is the privilege of choice, meaning that professional middle-class girls have a variety of options open to them, unlike working-class girls who still tend to be limited to marriage and waged labor primarily in service sector forms of employment. Playing an important role in intergenerational status transmission, Best Academy sets its graduates up to have personal and professional choices, creating windows of opportunity for the future. When asked whether she envisions marriage and family in her daughter's future, Mrs. Fox responds that she sees both for her child, strongly believing that her daughter should be able to choose one or both. Her point is that career should not necessarily offset the possibility of marriage and family and that her daughter should be able to exercise control over her options, one of which might include taking a detour from self-designed professional goals. But once again, this should be her daughter's choice and not forced on her, the point being that it *can* be her child's choice. It is worth noting that professional middle-class parents are hopeful that their daughters will be able to exercise choice specifically over their careers, so that they will not be forced into a job that they have neither been trained for nor are especially interested in doing. This suggests imminent restrictions on the choices that relative privilege opens up for these girls, reminding us through these parents' example, that the effects of global restructuring have not left the professional middle class untouched.

A.P.: What do you think about your daughter's [future] goals?

Mrs. Andrews: I think they are fine. I think she should be doing anything she wants to do that is going to make her happy. I mean the difference between . . . the girls see it everyday. I love my job [Mrs. Andrews is employed as an instructor in the English department of a local community college and also holds an administrative post in a related area], so I go to work, and I am happy. And I come home, and everything is wonderful. My husband hates his job.

A.P.: What does he do?

Mrs. Andrews: He is a project manager for a mechanical contractor. And so he goes to work, and he is miserable. And I tell the girls, what we want you to do is to find something that you like doing that is going to be a career rather than a job, something that will be challenging to you and rewarding. And I think they have accepted the fact that they don't have to be wealthy. [. . .]

*   *   *

A.P.: Do you see marriage and family in your daughter's future?

Mr. Henry: If she wants it. And I hope she finds happiness and does the things that she wants to do, whether it be married or not. Once she is enjoying herself and enjoying life and doing what she wants to do, that's what I would like to see.

A.P.: Do you have any insight as to how her life might be the same or different from the way your lives have played themselves out?

Mr. Henry: I just told you. I want her to just do what she wants to do and enjoy doing what she is doing. I can't do that.

Mrs. Henry: No, partially it's getting into a profession that she loves, something that she is going to love and get paid to do. He [my husband] hasn't had that luxury. And that would make a big difference. I think that would make a big difference to both of us. It is very sad when you have to go to a job everyday that you hate just so you can bring a paycheck home. And that's what we don't want her to have to do. But I don't think . . . I don't think that my daughter would ever do that. I think that she has seen what it has done to him [her father], for one thing.

*   *   *

Mrs. Peters: [My daughter] would like a family, get married to a wonderful man, do something she really [likes]. [. . .] She has a, I don't know, a natural love for animals. And she said, she can't imagine that she wouldn't work with them in some aspect. That is what is exciting. Or she will say, you know, I mean, I come home from work, and I enjoy my job [as a nurse] in some aspects, and other times, I am just dragging and complaining, and she will say, I am going to get a job that I love. I am going to have a job where I just love to go to work. That is what I hope you do. That is what it is all about. If you can find that in life, you have it made.

Mrs. Andrews points to the example of her husband who, unlike herself, is alienated from the work he performs daily. His experience stands in counterpoint to what he and his wife desire for their daughter's professional future. Generally unhappy with his work routine, Mr. Henry echoes his discontent on the job, leading his wife to say that "it is very sad when you have to go to a job everyday that you hate just so you can bring a paycheck home." Their wish is that their daughter will not be forced to compromise professional happiness for instrumental ends like a stable income. With Mrs. Peters, they would most likely conclude that if one has been able to avoid having to make this kind of compromise, then they "have made it."

In an earlier discussion of students' future projections around marriage, career, and family, Best Academy students filter their commentary on the importance of pursuing career first and marriage second through the lens of possible divorce. Close to half of this sample of thirty-four girls are children of divorced families. Spending most of their time outside school growing up in their mother's care, they have witnessed the firsthand effects of financial hardship and struggle among professional middle-class women and project the possibility that they will fall victim to this cycle later on in their adult lives. Fearing divorce in their futures, they weight heavily the financial security and autonomy a career can provide.

What mothers envision for their daughters in terms of career, marriage, and family grows out of the conditions of their own lives. Mothers who have been divorced filter their projections through the real experience of divorce, rather than the lens of possibility framing their daughter's narratives. Mothers who have not been divorced similarly narrate their wish that their daughters educate and professionalize themselves first so that they will have financial resources to draw on for themselves and their families *in the event of* divorce or spousal death later in their lives.

> A.P.: What kind of an influence do you think you have had on your daughter and her educational goals?
>
> Mrs. Peters: It's definitely played a role because I have always stressed in the situation, when I left my husband, I had to start nursing school like the next month, and it was very, very stressful. I didn't intend on stopping my education there, but my children were young, and I was . . . financially, it was rough. And emotionally just, I said, I wished now at my age that I had done it . . . I know I could still, people my age go back to school. But I just don't have the motivation for myself. I think I am living vicariously through my daughter. I hope she does fantastic. I have a, I mean, I don't stress that she has to be anything. I just tell her make sure it is something that you want, that you will enjoy, that is fulfilling, that is exciting because that is what it takes to want to get up and to go to work everyday. [. . .]
>
>   *   *   *
>
> A.P.: Would you like your daughter to be married before she enters college?
>
> Mrs. Rodriguez: No. I want her [to have] a career first. Then she could get married because if that doesn't work out the way that it is supposed to, she could support herself.

A.P.: Do you hope that your daughter will be able to have it all—career, marriage, and family?

Mrs. Fox: I hope that she would be able to make those choices and be able to decide that I can be a mother, and I can be a professional. I'm hoping, and it's interesting that you should ask that because we were talking on that subject recently. And some of the things—what were we talking about? We were talking about having an education and the value of pursuing that education before you decide to have children. We were talking about being able to bring more to your marriage, educationally, that, we were talking about, perhaps coming into your marriage with your master's or with your bachelor's or with your doctorate or whatever or with your MD. We were talking about not having to make a decision. [. . .] And I said, it's very, very hard to go back to school and have children and work. And it's easier if you finish off your academic program before you decide to go on with the family end of it. Because academically it's very demanding, and I think I may have said something to the effect of, I'm looking forward to going back now and doing my doctorate. I want to do that. But I said, I had to make a choice because it was very difficult finishing my master's program when I had a little girl. [. . .] And I also said to her that I would not do that again, that I would never do that. It was very hard, very difficult, very tiring. And I was very happy to finish it. But at the same time, it was urgent, it was important for me to finish my master's, and I didn't want to stop, but I also remember two females in my master's program who were of the, just the opposite mind, who said—oh, I think you are so persistent. Perhaps what you really should do is stop your master's program right now and just wait awhile longer while your daughter grows up a bit more and come back later. But they didn't understand the need. I needed to finish and have my master's because it was important to me to be able to rely on myself. Even though I was married, Amira, I needed to know that if anything happened, I could still support myself and my child. And I want my girls and my son to be independent of mind and of purpose, that you will have, I think, educationally and career-wise, you would have made and finished certain points in your life where if something happened, should your spouse die, should he decide to leave [you], you will always be able to take care of yourself, and I keep . . . kind of when the opportunity . . .

A.P.: Presents itself?

Mrs. Fox: Yeah, let them [my children] know. That's why it's important that you go ahead and you finish school. That's why it's important that if you want to be a doctor, you go ahead and do it.

A.P.: What kind of influence do you feel you have had, as a woman, on your daughter in terms of her sense of herself as a young woman?

Mrs. Moore: [. . .] As a woman, I think I have shown my daughter that as a woman, you can do things on your own. You don't have to be dependent on other people. You work with other people in your life, but you don't have to be dependent on somebody to take care of you and to do for you, that you can stand on your own two feet and achieve in your own right, and be independent. Not to say that she won't get married. Yes, you have a relationship, but you don't look to this man to take care of you and provide for you and think for you. In other words, I think I have taught her that as a woman, she can achieve in her own right.

Through tales told from their own experiences, divorced mothers like Mrs. Peters, Mrs. Rodriguez, and Mrs. Moore articulate the importance of cultivating self-reliance through education and professionalism as a buffer against the economic hardships and emotional setbacks that women, more so than men, tend to suffer in divorce or spousal death. Having left her husband, without a formal professional degree and means of supporting her family, Mrs. Peters knows firsthand the difficulties of balancing education and family. Sending her daughter to a single-sex high school carries a lot of weight for this mother who understands that a private, single-sex education can translate into self-sufficiency, autonomy, and independence for women. Concerned that her daughter have a means of being self-supporting, Mrs. Rodriguez urges her to develop herself professionally before marriage. Earlier, Mrs. Moore scripted education and professionalism through the personal experience of her divorce, arguing that the maturing effects of education may have staved off the breakup of her marriage had she waited to marry out of her twenties and after having completed a college education. Although Mrs. Fox is not divorced, she echoes the urgency running through these other mother's stories, recognizing that no woman is immune from the possibility of divorce and spousal death and their repercussions on family life. Ideal aspirations for her daughters' future are wrapped in unknown but realistic possibilities.

Born generally around and into the 1950s, these women were among the first generation to experience the beginnings of escalating divorce rates and the economic struggles following from the spiral of downward mobility within the middle classes. While few of the mothers in this sample make explicit reference to feminist principles and politics as a conceptual framework for their own experiences, it is worth considering Katherine Newman's (1989) contention that feminism did provide women of this generation with a language for shaping their lives in the aftermath of divorce. What these mothers envision for their daughters are working strategies that enable them to better control the conditions of their own lives so that they will not repeat the devastating effects of divorce and economic struggle in the future. The effects of social movements taking shape in the 1960s and 1970s are partially responsible for reshaping gender and class consciousness among this groups of parents, particularly the mothers. Despite the fact that mothers make no explicit mention of feminism and the feminist movement in articulating ideal aspirations for their daughters, the projections that they attach to their children's emerging public and private identities cannot be delinked and considered apart from the gains that women have made in second wave feminism and now into the third wave. For professional middle-class women, the effects of divorce on disposable income and resulting personal and professional hardships they incur as single parents and primary caregivers are more significantly felt than is the case among men. As the victims of this private assault, they are especially predisposed to direct their daughters toward education for confidence, independence, and autonomy.

Future studies of the professional middle class need to examine the role parents play in youth identity formation processes and probe further some of the issues that these narratives have only begun to uncover. Although new to independent education in many instances, parents of private school students are generally aware of the social and economic advantages that can follow from choosing this alternative to public instruction. They have made their decision to send their daughters to Best Academy out of a complex web of factors informed by economic change. These parents clearly see the private school facilitating their children's adjustment to and assimilation of upper middle-class cultural capital, providing them with that "edge" at a time when growing fiscal instability has deeply touched the professional middle class by narrowing its options in the educational and professional marketplace. Parents' narratives echo the felt impact of a changed economy on the conditions of their own lives. Filled with rising apprehensions over what their children have yet to face in the next generation, they voice ideal aspirations that sound very much like those that working-class parents in Freeway held out for their own children nearly a decade earlier. White, working-class mothers and fathers strongly encouraged their daughters' professional development as a means of their children being able to take control of their own lives in the face of growing economic hardship, urban dislocation, and the breakdown of family life. Parallel narratives coming from inside the professional middle class suggest that this class structure is not untouched by economic shifts either, forcing the realization that it can no longer depend on education and credentialling guaranteeing class-specific interests and investments. Poking through parents' narratives are deep worries that they will not be able to block a "second" fall from grace. Projections and aspirations wrapped around private, single-sex education stand in as hopeful visions for the next generation of relatively privileged youth where the odds of educational and occupational attainment are less and less stacked in their favor.

Chapter 7

Conclusions:
Repositioning Identities At/In the Center

A year from the time that I completed data collection, June 1994, I attended the Best Academy graduation, as the junior girls, now seniors about to graduate, prepared to leave the familiar world of the private school bound for any number of future experiences. The graduation ceremony is a theatrical spectacle of pomp and circumstance, not unlike that of any other public or private school, but this one at Best Academy is different because of the history and tradition that surrounds elite, private education for girls. Held in a local church, the ceremony resembles a group wedding where each young woman, as though she were about to leave her family, is given away. Dressed in long white gowns, one more elegant and detailed than the next, with white-gloved hands each clutching a dozen long-stemmed, blood-red roses, the graduates, one by one, take carefully measured steps down the long processional aisle leading to the church chancel where they will receive a diploma marking four years of rigorous academic work and time spent building lifelong friendships. Intelligent, poised, and polished in behavior and style, they appear to have accomplished all that the private school has promised for its graduates. As these girls proceed down the church aisle, I am taken back through my year-long journey with them, as they took me through the winding and unexpected turns of life as an adolescent girl in a private school. This moment, culminating four years of tremendous personal growth for each of them as they stand in anxious anticipation of what lies ahead, is time for added reflection as I gather together concluding thoughts about the intimacies and intricacies of female identity formation in a private girls' school.

Identity Production(s) in Context

As a critically informed investigation of youth socialization, this study has moved beyond the straight and narrow path of description to conceptual analysis of discursive forms and practices that students actively shape in school contexts. Reproductive models of youth socialization dominant in the sociology of education literature up until the early 1980s were based on the general premise that students are "framed" by institutional forms and distributed meanings and articulate their identities in relation to existing structures (Apple and Weis, 1983). Theorizing that students are simply shaped by available discourses has effectively denied youth creative agency over the process of "becoming somebody." Over the past two decades, the ways in which educators talk about and understand identity formation has radically changed, however, as ethnographic forays into educational sites have uncovered tactical marginalizing of students in/by schools and the strategies that students appropriate as counter-responses to silencing (Weiler and Mitchell, 1992; Weis and Fine, 1993; Davidson, 1996). With this, overdetermined accounts of youth identity construction have taken on a different cast as investigations of student culture increasingly capture students drawing on oppositional forms as they spin meaningful lives at the intersections of school, society, and culture (Giroux, 1992).

Studies of identity formation conducted during this same time frame focused almost exclusively on male youth cultural forms, either ignoring girls' subjectivities altogether or positioning girls in dependent relationships to boys. While research has established the relational construction of identity, it is still the case that girls' identity development has by and large not been portrayed as semi-autonomous and independent of boys. In effect, this has meant that girls have been denied the possibility of creative cultural critique on the level of their own lived cultural forms in schools. The groundbreaking work of feminist researchers emerging in the early 1980s would, however, call attention to multiple forms and possibilities for identity production among school-age girls. Re-envisioning the school as a cultural site, these theorists have made it possible to see the school as a location of active meaning making. Pioneering work by McRobbie (1982), Gaskell (1985), Valli (1988), Weis (1990), Raissiguier (1994) and others has taken the ethnographic lens into uncharted territory, entering the carefully guarded spaces of female youth cultures and asking overlooked questions about girls' attitudes and actions in schools around interrelated dimensions of class, race, ethnicity, gender, and sexuality. The power of their findings lies in the recommendation that girls' identity constructions can no longer be dismissed nor can they be described as simply dependent on the forms and practices that male youth enact in educational contexts. Their work makes clear that female identities are constructed discursively through active struggle and negotiation, pointing us in new theoretical directions that open up the possibility for girls to design complex discursive constructions of who they are becoming on a daily basis in school.

Youth order their lives in ways that make sense to them, and the logic of their constructions is only understandable to those of us on the outside looking in as they intersect with structural dynamics and broader social change. What happens in school is not divorced from fluctuations and shifts in society and culture at large, and private school officials are pointedly aware of this. Deindustrialization has hit hard many urban regions, and the northeastern city center in which Best Academy is located has not been immune from the devastating effects of declining market conditions. Corporate mergers and large-scale plant closings have displaced this city from the status that it once enjoyed as an independent center of manufacturing and commerce. Economic retrenchment and rising levels of crime and violence in urban centers nationwide have spurred the urban flight of professional middle-class families out of cities into the suburbs where they find that they can provide their children with a comparable education in a resource-rich, public, suburban high school. Against the backdrop of structural decline, the private school stands to lose significant ground as demographic shifts predict changes in what has been a relatively stable class base up to this point in time and with that, invite a new set of challenges for private education in the 1990s.

Private schools have conventionally served a homogeneous, privileged group of youth, yet there are strong indicators that the traditional population is changing to reflect greater diversification across class, race, ethnicity, and gender. Facing the pressures of public school reform and urban flight that have taken financial resources out of the local area, Best Academy, like many private schools, has had to tackle change head on by attracting students from a wider range of backgrounds (Kane, 1991). What happens in private school systems cannot be delinked from broader structural dynamics, and student identity processes reflect a private school culture in transition. Diversification of the student population across multiple dimensions casts a different light on the overdetermined portrayals of school life that have dominated research on private boarding and day schools. The important work of Cookson and Persell (1982), Lightfoot (1983), Connell (1985), Powell, Farrar, and Cohen (1985) and others reminds us that the culture of private education grows out of common norms, values, and traditions that give a school organizational coherence and identity. Shared pivot points are vital to the development of a rational culture binding students and faculty together in a joint educational mission. With this as a sound basis for community, students are brought from a place of individual to collective identification with an institution.

The cultural cohesion of private education around a common class culture through which other salient organizing dimensions of school life are filtered has, however, obscured complicated processes of contestation going on within school culture that paint a more dynamic picture of contested social relations and interactions inside the universe of private education. Mining

micro-processes at the level of youth subculture, this ethnography has provided strong and clear evidence that students are responding to discourses
made available to them in school in multiple and contradictory ways that cut
identity formation differently. The fact that private schools have traditionally
educated a homogeneous, affluent group has kept educational theorists from
seeing that students are actively repositioning themselves in dialectical
relationship to the intentional world (Shweder, 1991) at school and the
effects of structural change outside.

Beneath coherent school forms and practices, students are actively
engaged in the fracturing of self and other through dialectical constructions of
identity and difference that depend on positioning an "other" at the margins
of dominant cultural forms (Fine, 1994; Villenas, 1996). Peer group dynamics
in Best Academy sketch out a new set of tensions that have not been explored
in studies of private schooling up to this time. Problematizing social class as a
border zone of contested identity production, Best Academy students effectively de-center class culture, undertaking borderwork within and against the
dominant codes of upper middle-class privilege. Technologies of "othering" are
typically represented in terms of binary oppositions, embodying clear social
hierarchies—whites other blacks, boys other girls, the upper middle class
others the middle and working classes. What proves to be important about
class identity production[s] in Best Academy, though, are the exclusions and
differences that students script *horizontally* across the professional middle class.
From their peer groups, private school students sharpen differences between
peer networks by reappropriating elements of femininity as class signifiers that
help them to identify and articulate differences between students from families
with "more money" and others who are from relatively less affluent backgrounds. As illustrated earlier, girls identifying themselves with PG2, for
example, are notably othered as "material girls" by students in PG1 and PG3
who are critical of the conspicuous side of privilege that these students seem
to represent. Girls in PG1 and PG3, most of whom are from what I have
identified as professional middle-class backgrounds, although less relatively
privileged than other students, particularly girls in PG2, are othered by
members of PG2 as students perceived to be more conscientious about their
schoolwork because they have to work doubly hard to maintain the scholarships and grants-in-aid that have facilitated their being able to attend a
private school in the first place. Othering the girls in PG2, girls in PG1
remind us that "if you are wealthy, you can afford to sit around and eat bagels."
As they see it, this option following from class privilege, itself, is not available
to those who do not have the resources to back them up if they slip in their
level of academic performance.

Wide-ranging differences in social and cultural capital that professional
middle-class youth bring with them into school means that Best Academy

students do not all begin their time in private school on an equal playing field. Once students gain access to the private school, though, they are presented with the opportunity for equal competition and just reward for their achievements. Best Academy distributes messages supporting equal educational opportunity throughout its curriculum, and students fold these ideologies into their belief that they can and will achieve within the requirements of an elite, competitive, college preparatory environment. Shifting back and forth between the roles of othered object and othering subject, students draw borders around differences within the professional middle class, but they also skillfully work the boundaries of difference into border crossings. This is more easily facilitated against the backdrop of a culture wrapped tightly in liberal notions of equity, equality, and opportunity that works hard at containing and leveling differences along class lines. In an ironic turn, it is possible to argue that the underlying tension between sameness and difference in relation to operational class discourses in the private school keeps it intact and that the foundations of community are built on and solidified out of these contradictions.

Discourses of race privilege need to be brought to the surface and decentered as well in an institutional culture where white, liberal ideologies seemingly protect against the possibility of intolerance and exclusions on the basis of race differences. Social analysis of race has consistently called attention to the experiences of youth of color in schools, obscuring any suggestion that white is a racial category that structures white people's lives. In their interviews with me, white students repeatedly found it difficult to narrate what it means to be white, in general, and, more specifically, to describe the "white experience" in the context of a predominantly white school. Because whiteness has been obscured through its own naturalization, white girls struggle to find points of entry into a discourse that has simply been passed off as an objective racial location rather than a socially constructed site of experience and consciousness that needs to be deconstructed. Probing what it means to be white is a necessary and first step toward de-centering and de-naturalizing white privilege in order to decode the ways in which schools distribute, prop up, and reproduce discourses of privilege in their midst.

Not only does this study fill a notable gap in the literature on the social construction of race, but it draws important connections between the co-production of race and class discourses in private schooling. Through a polite and public language of naming race or silencing through omission, white girls take up talk about race through forms of race domestication that are decidedly shaped by liberal, upper middle-class values of tolerance and acceptance of difference and diversity. The private school bases its mission on a liberal commitment to transcending particularities and building a culture of inclusion. Assimilating discourses of universal sameness into daily routines and interactions, white girls and girls of color come to insist that despite differences, all students are equally valued and treated the same. Best Academy manages to contain race differences, leaving all students believing that they unequivocally share in a broader, universal identity and moral code. For white students, in particular, liberal ideologies provide them with guidelines for talking about race "safely," in ways that will not implicate them in white culture's inextricable ties to historical relations of domination. While liberal principles bind students together in spite of self-identified differences, they cannot quiet altogether the realities of racial negotiation beneath the surface as white students and students of color alike attempt to reconcile the persistent tension in American culture and its institutions between seeing race and structural relations of inequality and democratic discourse of equality and equity.

The centerpiece portrait of Mrs. Lyons hanging above the library fireplace, posters encouraging girls to pursue education and prepare for careers that have been historically dominated by men, and visits from accomplished women and alumnae to the school, remind Best Academy students through-out the year that they are part of a long history and tradition of educating upper middle-class women traceable back to the school's establishment in the mid-nineteenth century. Any conflicts between discourses of femininity and school achievement like the "fear of success" (Winchel, Fenner, and Shaver, 1974) are resolved by the focal platform and arch commitment Best Academy has had and continues to have toward girls' social, intellectual, and moral development. Full support for academic excellence creates a climate that fosters confidence, independence, and self-reliance among girls *because of* and not *in spite of* the fact that they are female. Through a curriculum that promotes values of individualism, academic excellence, moral behavior, and community service, female students are being prepared for their place in the class continuum. Put another way, the elite, private girls' school leaves a definite imprint on its graduates as gender and class intersect to shape educated, upper middle-class girls. In this context, girls are positioned to reflect certain norms, values, and expectations, yet their unique cultural productions tell the story of gender identities that grow out of their not simply being positioned by dominant meanings and practices but actively repositioning themselves through the lived contradictions of their own lives.

Assimilating parents' goals for their children and school messages steeped in the values and dispositions of upper middle-class privilege, students characteristically express strong desires for post-secondary education and professional credentialing. Parents see private education as a key factor in being able to provide their children with that extra edge in an increasingly competitive educational and occupational marketplace. As they see it, education and a career open up possibilities and choices that have not been previously available to women and buffer them from having to face the complications of early marriages, family responsibilities, and postponed careers that many of these parents experienced early in their own lives. Best Academy students attach importance to being educated and professionalizing themselves, and order their projections for the future around education and profession first with marriage and family a close second. The pattern they project unfolding in their futures, however, goes beyond expectations for educational and occupational attainments that dovetail with upper middle-class sensibilities. As I have argued, downward economic shifts have not escaped the professional middle class, and girls' future projections reflect the extent to which the effects of structural change have seeped into the minds and touched the lives of relatively privileged youth. Having a means of supporting themselves and their families in the future is an emergent concern among these girls, and education and a career, as they see it, will afford them greater control over the conditions of their own lives at a moment when they are beginning to see professional middle-class families losing ground. While girls from professional middle-class families have greater financial resources available to them as they leave high school bound for college, they are feeling the effects of economic decline in anxieties about the future that strikingly overlap in substance and tone with working-class girls' narratives (Weis, 1990). Upper middle-class girls look ahead into their future by looking backwards into their past and straight ahead into their present experience as children of separation and divorce. Given that many of these girls have experienced firsthand the financial setbacks of separation and divorce, they tend to script their desires for the future through the lens of the breakdown of the family structure. They do not dismiss these as possibilities in their future adult lives, given their own experience and awareness that separation and divorce are escalating at alarming rates in the United States.

From their narratives, it is possible to hear an emergent backlash as girls, reflecting on their own experiences growing up, express deep interest in becoming full-time mothers, yet are aware that economic realities prevail on the need for dual-income families. Indeed, choosing to stay at home as a full-time or even a part-time mom may not be a choice at all for them. In an ironic twist, professional middle-class girls' realistic appraisals of the future are framed by the structural barriers that they foresee pressing down on their lives, much like working-class girls who continue to make traditional choices in their lives because economic structures do not support their being able to participate in the labor force in a profitable enough way for women to be the primary breadwinners in their families (Gaskell, 1992). While salaried labor is an important priority for the reasons just mentioned, it appears as though upper middle-class, adolescent girls are just as interested in raising a family, if not more so, than they are in having a career. Educated in a school dedicated to showing girls that they have multiple and varied opportunities open to them, students begin to wonder how it will be possible to straddle competing pressures in traditionally oppositional domains. They have some evidence that they can manage career, marriage, and family from the women around them— their teachers, their mothers, and friends' mothers, but are not convinced that they will be able to have it all and to pull it off successfully without support from their husbands in the private domain and resources to help them meet their responsibilities in the public domain. At the same moment as their education opens up a number of choices for them, structural dynamics push down on and narrow their options. Projections for the future are fraught with the tensions that choice introduces, and the resolutions that might break girls' "fall from grace" are far from simple in the wake of a future whose present has already seen the *corporate* floor begin to shift beneath their feet.

Implications and Future Directions

The naturally unfolding character of ethnographic study lends itself to a spate of new questions that arise out of the limitations of this research site and research design and suggest fertile directions future studies of youth sub-cultures in educational contexts might explore. By definition, ethnographic research is partial and incomplete, gathering together tales individuals tell in the field where intentions change as quickly as the life cycle of a site moves ahead. Any story of school culture, like the one narrated here by Best Academy students, should be read in terms of particular contexts, time frames, and experiences that decide what a researcher sees in the field and the shape that collected narratives take.[1] It goes without saying that traveling into the field at another time and in another place would inevitably bring other issues of identity construction to the surface and out into the center.

Limitations notwithstanding, the portrait of school culture sketched out in this ethnography unearths contradictions that suggest that the private school is not as reproductive of identities as earlier studies have lead us to believe. Youth are an important group to study because they are at a particular juncture in their lives, just out of childhood and on the brink of young adulthood. As a new generation, their aspirations hold promise for the future. If youth are projecting life choices that are suddenly different from more traditional paths, educators need to examine what has produced this shift in their thinking because of the impact that this is bound to have on society and culture for the future. It is shortsighted to assume that students are not tackling these issues head on as agents directly implicated in processes of "becoming somebody."

On closer look, systems of power and privilege are played out in conflicted ways that are not explored sufficiently in class-reductionist models of schooling as they have been applied to both public and private educational domains. Reconfiguring identities in highly complex ways, the junior students of Best Academy narrate a story of negotiated boundaries and border crossings that together argue that class, race, and gender differences not only exist but also matter greatly in the private school. I encourage further field-based research of school culture along the lines of this ethnography that begins with the premise that students are struggling to live out the contradictions that class, race, gender, and other systems of representation present for them at the crossroads of school and society. Poststructural discourse is helpful here to the extent that it can inform ways of understanding school culture in its multiple and complicated forms, so that students are not seen as simply positioned by existing discourses but importantly reposition themselves in response to available meanings and practices in school and the broader society. Theoretical contributions from poststructural and feminist theorists amount to more fluid conceptualizations of the manufacture of culture as well as cultural productions in schools. For girls, in particular, these frameworks open up more spaces for re-envisioning students taking an active role in school life as they situate themselves rather than allow themselves to be situated subjects cast in the light of dominant practices. One becomes gendered not purely in relation to existing gender discourses but also by wrestling with and living through the contradictions that gender, as it intersects with class, race, ethnicity, and sexuality, can present for youth. As outsiders gain insight into the many and different ways that girls are positioned in school and society, opportunities for seeing how girls refashion and reinvent themselves multiply as well (Lather, 1991; Luke and Gore, 1992; Jones, 1993; Luke, 1996).

Where culturalists have found reproductive and productive processes taking place at one and the same time, they have failed to explore fully enough the possibility that conflicted social relations are being worked out beneath what appear on the surface to be relatively seamless communities. There is no question that systemic social inequalities are easier to see being reproduced in working-class schools. It is arguably more difficult to go into sites of structural dominance where privilege has a way of insidiously containing differences and masking power under the guise of equality of educational opportunity and racial diversity through harmony. This study brings into sharp relief the important point that studies of those at the social and cultural margins need to be balanced with critical inquiry into the cultural center. Studies of working-class youth's cultural expressions in school contexts, while important, have unfortunately edged other cultures out of the theoretical marketplace. "Studying down" has obscured other directions of inquiry, more than hinting at the mistaken assumption that majority cultures do not need to be problematized. Spending one year of field-based study in Best Academy is my response to the limitations that have narrowly defined research on school culture, ascribing value to "studying up" so that educators can fill a space that will help to build bridges across school systems that have historically been and continue to be in competition with each other, especially given the current climate of school choice politics and proposals for public education reform. Continuing to "study down" while neglecting to "study up" sets social analysis back in conceptual development and closes out possibilities for broadening our understanding of youth subcultures and socialization processes in educational contexts. Qualitative studies that disturb seemingly stable school sites need to be undertaken so that we can continue to theorize about schools and the ways in which power and privilege are prudently disguised and maintained in self-serving ways.

Support for the advantages of single-sex schooling for girls' socialization comes on the heels of wide-ranging evidence that coeducational schools perpetuate and reproduce sexual inequalities. Feminist scholars have looked to the single-sex school as an alternative to unequal power relationships and school outcomes (Arnot, 1983; Kenway and Willis, 1986). Taking their lead, I would like to argue that the single-sex school has a responsibility to educate girls to the ways in which power organizes social relations differently in private and public domains, sustaining social inequalities of class, race, ethnicity, gender, and sexuality in the classroom and in society at large. Put another way, this study of gender identity formation is not only a statement about why single-sex schools might be the preferred option for girls given existing empirical data, but it also raises the question of the pioneering work that can begin in these private educational contexts around broader initiatives for social reform and social justice. What I am proposing is urgent at a moment when sexual harassment of adolescent girls in our nation's schools is increasing at an alarming rate, leaving girls feeling more threatened than ever before in school spaces that no longer appear physically and emotionally safe for their bodies and their minds (AAUW, 1993; Pipher, 1994; Larkin, 1994).[2] If the single-sex school is going to be successful in keeping equal opportunities open to women, it needs to open itself up to more sustained communication with co-educational schools. All students, girls and boys, are part of the important work that has yet to take place in the direction of "dismantling the master's house" (Lorde, 1984). This book offers a strong recommendation that social analysis of all-girls' schooling move beyond a focus on those factors that contribute to girls' learning outcomes to examine possible ways that findings on educational effectiveness and girls' socialization in the private, girls' school can be instructive in coeducational settings for all students, both girls and boys. At a historical moment where private schooling is experiencing the effects of declining market conditions, there are fewer and fewer single-sex schools remaining. Many have merged with other private boys' schools, going co-ed at a time when depleted financial resources leave school officials with no other viable option for survival. Given this picture, it is that much more urgent that educators spend time in single-sex schools, evaluating learning outcomes and socialization processes whose understanding helps narrow the divide between public and private education and encourages joint participation in developing educational strategies that will serve boys and girls equally well.

Deepening understanding of gender identity construction depends just as much on exploring the penetrating influences of popular culture on girls' development. In her analysis of the discursive construction of femininity, Smith (1988) reminds us that gender relations are mediated by widely distributed cultural forms like the visual media and text-based print that deal a strong hand in denying women self-determination. Girls fold in expectations about their bodies, their minds, and their future roles from a recipe of cultural forms that signify and position them as girls. Doing gender is largely a matter of how femininity is imprinted on adolescent female. While examination of popular culture as it *impacts on* identity construction was only briefly touched upon in this study, I did catch glimpses of the ways in which popular texts make their way into girls' imaginations and become signifying practices in their subcultural lives. This was clearest in their talk about feminist principles and politics. Across the professional middle class, girls draw clear borders around feminism, choosing only partially to identify with the movement and its politics. Having assimilated incendiary images of 1960's bra-burning feminists, they hesitate to identify with the movement because of indelible attitudes and actions that they have come to associate with feminist ideology and practice. While the "fear of success" is overcome in the single-sex school as girls begin to see that high academic achievement is, indeed, compatible with their feminine roles, they are still not altogether comfortable identifying themselves with feminism which, for some of them, is seen as potentially compromising to their femininity. In their minds, feminist identity politics is partially out of character for professional middle-class girls, that it is essentially "unfeminine." What this suggests is the need for further studies of single-sex education that explore discourses of gender in the private, girls' school and probe structural phenomena in schools that collude to discourage girls from broadening the range of acceptable meanings and social practices tied to gender. If girls' expressed support for equality in the division of labor at home and at work is fractured by choosing more traditional roles, which became apparent in the narratives of some Best Academy students, we need to contextualize these decisions not only in light of current structural realities that frame and limit professional middle-class girls' lives but also in terms of prevailing social discourses of femininity and feminism operating inside and outside school and work these aspects into the school curriculum as the focus of social critique. Pinpointing otherwise "taken-for-granted" issues that are often overlooked in the curriculum of the all-girls' school creates space for theorizing about gender relations as they shape conditions at home and at work and provides a supportive context for students to begin to re-envision a democratic public sphere from out of the private school where they, as young women, can reposition themselves as "agents of public formation" (Giroux, 1995, p. 301), crossing cultural borders at the frontiers of emancipatory social change.

The beginning of ethnographic critique lies in looking at what is visible and then mining what is on the surface to look beneath and access what has been invisible up until now. This study has challenged class-reductive models of private school culture that have denied youth creative agency on the level of their own cultural critique, and has, in the process, reminded educators of the importance of critically appropriating schools as interpretive sites (Lesko, 1988). For those whose lives are shaped in fluid, shifting moments and spaces at the intersections of multiple cultures on/at the margins, the borderlands captures identity production out of lived contradictions (Anzaldua, 1987; Thompson and Tyagi, 1996). Private school students cannot escape having to wrestle with the contradictions that prevailing discourses of equality of educational opportunity and liberal ideologies of universal sameness create for them in a school context committed to and dependent on the maintenance of class privilege. Through their identity work, they have importantly transformed the cultural center into a border zone and reclaimed the private school as a place of constructive meaning-making.

This book has attempted to listen, hear and retell what was told as well as what was left unsaid, as thirty-four adolescent girls decided against seeking cover underground and, instead, came up to speak their voices and have them be heard. By breaking their silence, they show us that identity formation at the cultural center is more complicated than previous studies have allowed. The private, single-sex school is a critical site for seeing how girls engage discourses that have been presented to them in school as they reposition themselves in relation to pervasive meanings and practices built into the structure of the school and dominant in society. Field-based studies need to pry open spaces where students are actively resisting formal school culture and creating a range of expressive forms that are not as clean and controlled as social institutions have come to expect of and from girls in particular.[3] Educators are beginning to look to and theorize "that bit" that has remained hidden from their view, in many instances because they have chosen not to see it (Hurtado and Stewart, 1997). Best Academy has provided a first glimpse into parts and dimensions of schooling that haven't been seen before, and it is from this point that analysis of youth identity formation can move forward in new and meaningful directions.

Appendix

Methodology and Research Design

Framing Ethnographic Research

This study documents the complex and often highly contradictory forms that identities can take in school in the midst of defining moments of structural change. In order to capture identity production as it takes shape, researchers in the social sciences have utilized ethnographic techniques of data collection to explore the particularities of human experience across varied educational sites and settings (Van Maanen, 1995; Levinson, Foley, and Holland, 1996; Weis and Fine, 1996). Interpretive movements in the disciplines of anthropology and sociology emergent in the decade of the 1970s marked a signal shift away from positivist research designs based in empiricist assumptions and quantitative forms of data collection and analysis to a newfound focus on the cultural production of "local knowledges" in context (Geertz, 1973; Clifford and Marcus, 1986). While educational researchers focused on the relationship between structure and culture, they failed, for the most part, to explore the role that ideology and power played in shaping individual and collective responses to bounded conditions inside school classrooms and corridors as well as outside "the box." Ethnographic studies of school culture in context tended more toward traditional or descriptive representations of educational practice and process, favoring input-output analyses of schooling over studies of the relationship between human behavior, institutional structures, and broader social dynamics. This trend in educational research would change at the beginning of the 1980s as social science researchers began to document individual and collective expressions in the dialectical and emancipatory project of "inventing culture" (Rosaldo, 1993). Drawing on critical ethnographic research frameworks, educational ethnographers began to take a closer look at the ways in which students actively produced identities through mediation, negotiation, and reappropriation of school discourses that had been presented to them. Moving away from the conventions of ethnographic realism, critical ethnography dedicated research to examination of symbolic forms, social practices and rituals built into school structures and routines that served to create, legitimate, and maintain unequal distributions of power across social relations of race, ethnicity, class, gender, and sexuality (Anderson, 1989; Denzin and Lincoln, 1994; McLaren, 1994). Critical ethnographers set their sights on exposing structural forms of domination that place constraints and limitations on individual lives. This was no less than a signal development in ways of conducting and analyzing human experience in educational contexts. Schools were now re-envisioned as complex and dynamic institutions where students actively contested distributed meanings and social practices and re-fashioned them in ways that were meaningful to their own lived experiences.

For nearly three decades prior to the time that critical frameworks gained momentum in educational research, traditional, masculinist models of social science virtually ignored the sites and sounds of local knowledge production. Voices of lived experience taking shape at the intersections of race, ethnicity, class, gender, and sexuality were overlooked as focal points of meaning-making in context. As critical ethnographers began to conduct field research in ways that opposed colonizing discourses bent on representing the native as the exotic "other", voices that had, up until now, been marginalized and silenced, effectively left out of the identity literature, were provided a legitimating space in which to "go public" (Ganguly, 1991). It is here that critical ethnographic research benefits from the epistemological assumptions of feminist research methodology. Taking up the "science question in feminism," feminist social scientists have posed a challenge to traditional, positivist frameworks of scientific inquiry. Instead of designing and practicing science based on a transcendent, disembodied understanding of knowledge production, feminist critics of western science have recommended a more partial social analysis based on exploration of the lived moments of individual and collective experience. Arguing that conventional categories of scientific analysis be suspended, they have, instead, advanced examination of the lived details of the everyday (Harding and Hintikka, 1983; Bleier, 1985; Fox-Keller, 1985; Harding, 1987; Smith, 1987; Tuana, 1989). While varieties of feminisms obscure definition of one, single feminist research method, thus, leaving the question of what qualifies as feminist research open to debate, general consensus among feminist theorists is that feminist research shifts focus onto the concrete realities of women's everyday lives (Lather, 1991; Reinharz, 1992; Wolf, 1996). Women are located as social subjects whose partial perspective, that is, their own lived experience, becomes the basis for and source of knowledge production (Smith, 1987; Haraway, 1988; DeVault, 1990). Positioning women as producers of knowledge and interpreters of meaning, feminist research frameworks build on/from women's special knowledge for insight into the structures that both create possibilities and impose limits on women's experience. Attributing importance to local knowledge, social science inquiry informed by feminst epistemologies is driven by a concern to transform existing structures of oppression and relations of domination with the final goal of realizing greater social justice. These outcomes require no less than a full commitment to listen and hear the voices of the Other, but, this, feminist researchers argue, depends on restructuring hierarchical relationships between researcher and researched participant that have historically characterized inegalitarian and undemocratic practices in more traditional, positivist research designs (Roman, 1990; Olesen, 1994; Fine, 1994; Bloom, 1997).

> By dealing in voices, we are affecting power relations. To listen to people is to empower them. But if you want to hear it, you have to go hear it, in their space or in a safe space. Before you can expect to hear anything, worth hearing, you have to examine the power dynamics of the space and the social actors. Second, you have to be the person someone else can talk to, and you have to be able to create a context where the person can speak, and you can listen. That means we have to study who we are and who we are in relation to those we study. Third, you have to be willing to hear what someone is saying even when it violates your expectations or threatens our interests. In other words, if you want someone to tell it like it is, you have to hear it like it is (Reinharz, 1992, p. 215).

The challenge to masculinist research models is directed against epistemological claims for scientific objectivity. Feminist social scientists have suggested the opposite in their support for research models that depend on and validate intersubjectivity, reciprocity, and dialogue. What has all too often been the case in naturalistic ethnographic practice, for example, is that data collection techniques work against the discursive construction of narrative (Roman, 1993). Dimensions that shape the lives of researchers and researched participants are frequently omitted from the research process, providing little insight into the politics of social science research and the relational construction of knowledge (Ulichny and Schoener, 1996).

The shift in educational research approaches away from traditional empiricist paradigms toward postpositivist frameworks bent on capturing holistic portraits of culture in local contexts has invited debate around epistemological issues and modes of representation that have forced qualitative researchers into defending the rigor and scientific bases of their methods (Borman, LeCompte, and Goetz, 1986; Anderson, 1989). Whereas quantitative researchers enter a study with the intention of testing hypothetical statements or arriving at answers to direct questions, qualitative researchers view questions themselves as products of the research process (Bogdan and

Biklen, 1982). Qualitative researchers typically enter the field with exploratory questions that begin the process of uncovering and decoding human behavior in natural settings. While qualitative inquiry is based on particular research designs, the parameters and techniques of data collection and analysis are necessarily flexible and subject to change during the life cycle of a study. This characteristic flexibility in research design is often cited as grounds for questioning the disciplinary rigor or "goodness" of qualitative study (Peshkin, 1991). Since ethnographic research designs and techniques of data collection are responsive to the immediate context, any suggestion that there should be *rigid* guidelines structuring the design and conduct of research in the field is at odds with the bounded nature of this approach to inquiry. Nevertheless, there are standards and principles that have grown up in the qualitative community to insure methodological integrity and discipline (Wolcott, 1990; 1995).

In recent years, methodological discussions around the design and conduct of qualitative research have moved beyond a focus on matters of procedure to discourse that has problematized the research process itself. Within the past five to ten years, it has become acceptable and encouraged practice to share with peers both inside and outside of the formal research community common errors and successful strategies in field-based study (Metz, 1983; Peshkin, 1985; Lareau and Shultz, 1996; Weis and Fine, 1996).

> In most lines of work, including teaching, almost everyone is forced to admit to having made mistakes from time to time. But admitting mistakes in field work seems more difficult. Partly, this is because we often have an overly romantic notion of field work, which emphasizes the glory of 'going native' and glosses over the difficulties and problems of the endeavor. The implicit message is that mistakes are rare. Partly, this reluctance is an artifact of a scholarly tradition in which a public discussion of 'inner-workings' is considered unseemly and unnecessary. Finally, admitting to mistakes in field work raises questions about the quality of the body of research and the conclusions drawn from it. Given these considerations, it is hardly surprising that so little has been written about actual experiences in the field. Likewise, it is clear that all of us who are engaged in qualitative research could greatly benefit from a more frank sharing of our experiences (Lareau and Shultz, 1996, pp. 197–198).

Realistic descriptions of fieldwork demystify the research process, drawing out the complexities and potential complications that researchers face as they go about collecting data in both typical and atypical settings. By exposing the inner-workings of science, researchers also open up scientific procedure and process to the possibility of more impartial judgments from researchers working out of traditionally opposite paradigms. This is useful for helping researchers to move beyond the peaceful detente in which they found themselves in the early 1970s toward more comprehensive approaches to social science that involve mixing and merging methods across paradigms (Rist, 1977; Kidder and Fine, 1987). In the methodological discussion that follows, I describe key steps that were important to the design and conduct of this study of youth identity formation. By letting outsiders into my "journey through ethnography," it is my hope that those who are invested in educational research will become comfortable with the idea of venturing beyond the comfort zone into a space of relative instability that holds the promise of deepening our understanding of the human condition and the role that schooling plays in shaping individual and collective lives.[1]

Process in Research

Access

Burgess (1991) describes access as a social process that requires ongoing negotiation between principal investigators and researched participants not only at the beginning of a study when one first enters the field but importantly throughout the time spent on site. Negotiation of relatively unstable relationships in ethnography begins from the moment that contact is sought and then made with a potential research site and gatekeeper in charge there. The politics of access are played out daily in the field as relationships first begin, unfold, and change between researchers, gatekeepers, and informants.

My efforts to secure a viable site in which to undertake this study began in earnest six months prior to the start of the 1992–93 school calendar year at which time I began to investigate potential sites whose parameters might be a suitable fit with my guiding research question. Site selection often depends on a number of practical considerations that include choosing a site of reasonable size and manageability in the time allotted to complete the study; a convenient location, and one in which the researcher is not entirely immersed (Bogdan and Biklen, 1982). While Bodgan and Biklen identify conventional standards for selecting a site, they do not take this discussion far enough. Against the backdrop of growing interest in extending the generalizability of qualitative research, Janet Schofield (1990) argues that qualitative researchers should use a range of other criteria for site selection if they seek broader applicability of their research findings to other studies.[2] Notwithstanding the fact that site selection should not be an arbitrary decision, it is not always possible for researchers to land their preferred site. Since my study sought answers to the impact of economic restructuring on female youth subcultures in a private school, this meant that I needed to find a site in an urban region where meaningful connections could be made between girls' identity development, private school culture, and economic trends. My search for the most appropriate site was complicated by the fact that I was interested in finding a non-sectarian private school in a region where sectarian girls' schools far outnumber non-sectarian institutions. This research parameter, interestingly though, helped to narrow my focus since the urban area in which I lived only had one non-sectarian, single-sex high school from which to choose. In its purest sense, access is a matter of availability for the researcher, and ethnographers are often limited by physical location to the sites they identify and enter. The financial realities of conducting an ethnographic study are equally important and often further narrow criteria for site selection. In the end, a combination of these contingencies influenced my decision to target a school in a northeastern, urban location that housed one of the only non-sectarian, all-girls' private high schools in this region of the state. At the time, I was employed as a project assistant on a large-scale ethnographic study that required consistent and sustained contact with a local population for close to one year. In order to support myself financially, I needed to secure a research site for my study that would take into account the realities and responsibilites of my daily life as a graduate student.

At mid-summer, I identified a school that fit the parameters of my research question. Having targeted the institution I felt would best satisfy the boundaries of my study, I then arranged an appointment to meet with Mrs. Nicholson, the Head of School at Best Academy, in the remaining weeks of August prior to the start of the school year in September. Mrs. Nicholson was in her mid-fifties and had been newly appointed as Head of School only a few months prior to our first meeting. She replaced a headmaster who had administered the school's affairs for the past twenty-five years. The end of his tenure marked the beginning of a new phase in the history of Best Academy, signaled early on with her decision to call herself Head of School rather than Headmistress. I recall probing this decision in conversation with her not long after I was granted official access to the school since it indicated to me a beginning step toward institutional restructuring at Best Academy with potential implications not only for the inner-workings of daily life at the school but also for my role as an ethnographer on campus that year.

Prior to accepting the administrative post at Best Academy, Mrs. Nicholson had served as director of development and public relations at an elite, private, independent girls' school in a large, metropolitan center. As a graduate of an exclusive girls' college, she stood behind the philosophical mission of single-sex schooling and gave her full support for a project exploring identity formation processes of adolescent girls. As the school's gatekeeper, her greatest concern was that my presence as an observer not interrupt the flow of school life. The possibility for research, however well structured and ethically grounded, to disrupt school life is a constant and real concern for gatekeepers whose primary investment is in maintaining a unified school community. Having assured her that I would be as unobtrusive as possible, Mrs. Nicholson set certain conditions to the research, one of which was my promise that I would not only respect the day-to-day routines at Best Academy but that I would also share the findings of the data with the faculty and the students throughout the research process and certainly as a completed product.[3]

Mrs. Nicholson's insistence that she, students, faculty and any other interested participants in the study have access to the research findings draws on images of betrayal that schools have experienced at the hands of researchers whose personal goals have taken precedence over more public concerns for improving the quality of life in schools and communities (Gitlin, 1994). Schools have no doubt been abused by invasive researchers who have sacrificed integrity with students and school officials for their own professional ends (Patai, 1991). In such instances, the costs-benefits ratio decidedly favors the researcher rather than the study participants. As a researcher informed by principles of feminist research methodology, I was invested in more demo- cratic forms of research practice that took seriously the notion that knowledge is co-produced and sought non-exploitive relationships and mutually infor- mative alliances with students, faculty, administration, and staff throughout my stay in the field. Having assured her that my role was as an unobtrusive and peripheral observer, and that I would be more than willing to share my findings, she gave her complete endorsement of the project but could not grant full permission for me to begin until first presenting and discussing the proposed study with the full faculty at the first scheduled faculty meeting for the year. Mrs. Nicholson requested a letter of introduction from me outlining the focus, objectives, and goals of the study and promised to share it with the faculty at that time. Only with their approval would she issue her final decision to grant me unrestricted access to Best Academy for the research. While I offered to speak directly with the faculty at that time, Mrs. Nicholson made it clear that she preferred to introduce the matter herself. In my mind, this was a statement of her need to establish her role as institutional gate- keeper, with whom final authority over any school-related matter rested. As an outsider to the culture at Best Academy, her response was understandable and not unexpected. I feared, though, that her decision not to allow me to speak firsthand with the faculty might open my research project to misun- derstanding by faculty and staff who might subsequently be discouraged from supporting and participating in the study. I reclaimed some degree of control over the beginning stages of access in my repeated iterations that I would be available to answer any questions faculty might have and clarifications they feel need to be made in order to insure the smoothest possible transition of an outsider into the culture of Best Academy.

Three weeks after this initial meeting, Mrs. Nicholson's call came with
the assurance that the faculty had agreed to a yearlong study in the school.
From that point, she requested that I contact Mrs. Berson, a teacher on the
English faculty, who had been designated my "mentor." Mrs. Berson, herself,
had graduated from Best Academy over thirty years earlier and had been on
the school faculty for upwards of twenty years. As explained to me, the
decision to appoint a mentor was meant to facilitate smoother access to junior
class students. Equally important was the fact that Mrs. Berson would be more
available to me than would Mrs. Nicholson given her overwhelming
responsibilities as the new Head of School and that she would be able to
immediately address all questions and emergent concerns about school life at
Best Academy that might come up for me as I begin spending time there.

The politics of access dictate sustained negotiation of relations with the
gatekeeper on site who can choose either to facilitate or block a researcher's
introduction to and transition into the inner-life of the school. Mrs.
Nicholson's decision to present my project to the faculty and her insistence on
appointing me a "mentor" represented a strategic move on her part to establish clear lines of administrative control and power that set the boundaries for
and allowed her to better monitor my movements throughout the year. On
another level altogether, though, a "mentor" assisted my entry into the school.
It worked in my favor to have some way to hook more easily into the culture
of Best Academy if I had someone that I could directly contact for help. In the
end, I would need Mrs. Berson to "interpret" far less than I thought would be
the case, and most faculty and students proved willing to help and eager to
participate in whatever way they could.

This process did, however, bring the politics of negotiated access into
sharp relief where permission to enter and spend sustained time in school
significantly depended not only on the perceived merit of the study itself but
also on the implications of the findings for the public reputation of a school
whose finanical resources were threatened increasingly by growing competition from equally rigorous co-educational private and public institutions in
the local area. At the private school, the gatekeeper is invested in maintaining orderly social relations inside school and projecting that image onto
the public. Given restructuring of the local economy and demographic shifts
in the traditional class base of this private school, it is not surprising that Mrs.
Nicholson would be concerned about the potential for publicity to negatively
impact on school enrollment numbers that were already experiencing significant declines. Movement in this direction had significant implications for an
institution currently facing financial difficulties.

Mrs. Nicholson's decision to suspend approval until formal presentation
before the faculty was also predictable in light of the difficulties that surround
an administrative transition. A change in administrative regime after twenty-

five years of relative stability under one Headmaster was no doubt disruptive for students, teachers, and parents who had become comfortable with a certain style of leadership, and the presence of a researcher on site could add new tensions. Cultural context frames identity processes in highly complex ways, and the anatomy of a recent administrative transition could/would/should effect data collection. While institutional change has the potential to adversely impact data gathering, it can also lay the terrain for unexpected moments of meaning production that might otherwise not have emerged in a more stable setting.

Sample Parameters

At the start of the 1992–93 school calendar year, the upper-school population at Best Academy numbered 119 students.[4] I had proposed to track the junior class, made up of thirty-seven teenage girls. Only thirty-four of these students would agree to be part of the study sample; two declined to be interviewed, and one transferred to a local, public high school by the middle of the first semester of the junior year. That junior students would be the focus of this study was a conscious decision made on the basis of the critical and growing number of concerns and responsibilities that youth face at this level of schooling. No longer freshmen adjusting to the challenges of a new high school nor on the cusp of graduating, junior students find themselves in the middle of their high school careers. They face the standard battery of college entrance examinations, the SAT and ACT, generally required for application to competitive four year colleges and universities.[5] During this time, they customarily meet with guidance personnel who begin to help them target and identify their academic strengths and future career interests so that they can approach the college search and application process in a more systematic and focused way. For some of these students, responsibilities outside of school differ from previous years with the addition, in many cases, of an after-school job and community service. The challenges that junior students face then situate them best for a study of identity formation in peer subcultures where negotiation of a variety of responsibilities and decisions defines much of their academic and social development at this time in their lives.

Relationships in the Field

Penetrating what often remain impenetrable barriers between researcher and informants in the field depends, in part, on role-playing. In this scenario, the researcher puts forward an image that enables the cultural work that needs to be done, but not at the expense of developing authentic relations with informants in the field (Shaffir, 1991). Much of successful data collection depends on cultivating honest and engaged relationships with informants.

Ethnographers typically struggle to keep open the lines of friendship and protect them from the potentially exploitive directions that fieldwork can take. As Michelle Fine (1993) reminds us, the intimacies of data collection need to be carefully balanced against potential betrayals. In other words, personal and pragmatic interests in gathering data must be weighed and checked over against the trust that field researchers need to develop in order to see, hear, and listen on the face of it as well as beneath the surface and between the lines.

The field presents a potentially overwhelming set of challenges. It threatens to expose secrets of pleasure and desire along with well-kept pain, but it also presents an unexpected set of outcomes that foreground certain "subjective I's" while backgrounding others as researchers gain insight into who they are and who they have become along the way through their research endeavors (Peshkin, 1991). Because the field is an unwieldy and unstable place, it is all the more important that the researcher have a clear sense of who he/she is before entering a social context that is typically different from one's own experience. Ethnographers instruct their students who are about to enter the field to engage the field with a defined sense of self as a safeguard against becoming unraveled in the process of conducting research. The potential exists for researchers to become swept up into the whirl and confusion of lived narrative, in the process losing personal voice and identity. Lois Weis (1992) illustrates this point well in her description of the way that working-class informants positioned her as a white, upper middle-class researcher in a working-class high school. Informants will situate and attach certain identities to ethnographers who are essentially alone in the field with nothing left to their defense except their own honest intentions. It rests with the field researcher to negotiate these assigned roles over against the formal and latent roles that one brings with them to fieldwork (Metz, 1983). Alan Peshkin (1985) draws important attention to the fact that ethnographers enter the field recognizing that they play two separate yet overlapping roles. Subjectivity, split between the human self and the research self, plays a significant part in data collection and modes of representation. The lessons that are learned about self and other as subjectivity is layered onto and folded into the research process are invaluable to decoding meaning-making in social and cultural context. The human and the professional self continuously shift and interact as identities are, at times, foregrounded and, at others, backgrounded. The lines between both roles begin to run together as research informants become more and more familiar with the unfamiliar and the boundaries between insider and outsider status suddenly blur.

Building rapport with informants is one of the most significant predictors for the success of a study. My entrance to Best Academy and my ability to forge comfortable relationships with students, faculty, and staff would, no doubt, be complicated by the strain of administrative change. Students were quick to form impressions of me that appeared to be colored by the uncertainty of a new Head of School at the helm. Early in the school year around mid-October, Mrs. Nicholson had arranged a group meeting between junior students and a stress counselor in response to a spate of behavioral problems that included suicide threats by one or two students and related disciplinary problems concentrated mainly in the sophomore and senior class. A small private school cannot withstand disruptive behaviors by students who choose to "act out," and so the school administration sought appropriate counseling for students who seemed in need of help. That the Head of School had not yet earned the students' trust contributed to their fears that their conversations with the counselor would not be strictly confidential. They were cautious and decidedly on guard about newcomers to the school, and my presence became an understandable source of suspicion for them. Toward the end of my year in the field, I would learn from some students that they thought I might have been "planted" at the school at that particular time on behalf of the Head of School to monitor student stress levels and report my observations to school officials. Parents who had grown to understand and trust the former administration unsurprisingly were distrustful of the new Head of School. This added to their suspicions about me and my purpose for being at the school that year. I learned toward the tail end of the study that they carried impressions around with them about who I was and what I had been supposedly charged to do that were not unlike what their daughters had been thinking, that I was a "spy," and that what I learned at school would somehow be used against them. Students and parents had, then, positioned me early on as a pretender to the "new regime," leaving me with no recourse to self-defense other than time for the strange(r) to become familiar.

Admittedly, there were defining aspects of my identity that enabled easier entry into adolescent female subcultures at Best Academy. To begin with, the fact that my informants and I were of the same sex was decisive for my being able to more easily access girls' subcultures. That I was a female professionally committed to the project of all-girls' schooling and carrying out research that builds on and from girls' experiences undeniably facilitated the transition from outsider to insider status.[6] This was especially the case during those moments of what I choose to describe as "male-bashing" inside the private corridors of girl talk where girls looked for a forum for critique and complaint about boyfriends, male peers, and men in their families. Not only was I let into their private confessional tales, but I also represented the "feminist" whose identity politics and professional purpose provided a vocabulary and a sounding board as they struggled to negotiate gender relations on the cusp of young adulthood. That I was only fifteen years shy of adolescence and that several of the students had college-age siblings and relatives also enabled rapport-building with these girls early on. My age was a salient dimension of my subjectivity, a latent role that helped me slip into other roles as trusted friend and confidant. Interestingly though, I would learn after my time spent in the field drew to a close that some girls thought that I might be a lesbian because I had chosen to study gender identity construction among adolescent girls and had publicly discussed and expressed strong feminist sensibilities. In their minds, an articulated interest in gender and feminist identity politics for sure, meant that I was a lesbian. Despite the fact that I had talked to them about my friendships and relationships with men, and identified as a heterosexual, they were not able to delink feminism from lesbianism. Granted, this surfaced as a faint whisper at the very end of the study. Yet it is a significant gender dynamic that is telling of the ways that female informants position female researchers in uneasy sisterhood (Hull, 1984) with them, on one hand, as their ally, and on the other, a perceived threat to normative forms of sexuality.

As a female not more than twelve years older than most of my study sample, I remembered clearly enough the social, emotional and intellectural struggles that I first waged in early adolescence and carried with me into young adulthood (Gilligan, 1982; Pipher, 1994). Raised in a progressive, professional middle-class family, I received daily lessons on the value of women's intellectual and professional development and remember learning in my first women's studies course as an undergraduate that gender is a system of power and privilege that has to be contested and constantly redefined if women across class and racial lines, and sexual orientation were to gain control over the conditions that design the possibilities and limitations of their lives. On support for equality of opportunity and access, I can claim insider status. Liberal values of equality and opportunity swirled through my household through the example of two, highly educated, professional parents whose egalitarian attitudes spilled over to encourage me to follow my aspirations and fulfill my goals. As a young girl, I was taught and came to believe that I could be anything I wished to be and that I was not limited to gender roles and pursuits prescribed by the traditional sexual division of labor. I was, however, far removed from the experience of private schooling and stood very much outside the articulated class culture at this private institution. In an ironic twist, I was raised as the child of professional middle-class, Jewish parents among blue-collar working-class and lower white-collar middle-class families from largely Roman Catholic backgrounds and spent the first eighteen years of my life in a small, industrially depressed area adjacent to a regional college town. Professional families tended to populate this nearby town. New to this area in the early 1960s, my parents decided against living there, and, instead, settled into a quiet, well-maintained neighborhood mainly populated by teachers, nurses, secretaries, and factory workers where local taxes were considerably lower. Attending one of the seven local elementary schools and the single high school in the area, I remember sitting next to a cross section of students from diverse class and racial backgrounds for much of my first twelve years of schooling.

Early on, I learned that I would need to negotiate class and religious differences in my own life in order to avoid the inevitable alienation that can too easily fall on those who see themselves as different. Insider status enables clearer vision and understanding of some things, but it can also disable and block the researcher from seeing other things of equal importance (Peshkin, 1985). Shared identity dimensions do not necessarily translate into the "power to know everything" (Foster, 1994). While I shared the same gender with my informants at Best Academy, being female did not necessarily help me decode the culture of privilege at Best Academy. Up until I entered college, I had very little experience with upper middle-class culture. That would change, though, when I graduated from high school and entered the world of elite private education as a college student at one of the Seven Sister Schools. That experience would not only introduce me to the cultural norms, values, and codes of the upper middle class but would also help to crystallize in my mind that it is possible to be an 'outsider within' despite having benefitted from relative privilege in my own life (Cookson, 1991).

Ethnographic investigation of a private, independent school like Best Academy is complicated by the fact that it is an institutional site of dominance coded upper middle-class, all-female and white. Demographic characteristics give the impression that private school culture is relatively uniform and homogeneous, obscuring complexities and contradictions that tell another story of diversity across lived experience. As an institution whose coherence depends on building a solid cultural identity among its students, faculty and staff, the private school works to contain differences under the rubric of collective identification with institutional culture. Knitting the fabric of cultural life in Best Academy together are social relations of privilege that are thoroughly embodied in institutional forms and practices. The challenge of conducting research in a historically elite, private, independent high school for girls lies in being able to access and then mine surface forms that embody social relations of privilege, inequalities, and hierarchies that are typically invisible because they have been so thoroughly institutionalized. Neither a product of the private school nor from an upper middle-class background, I was positioned in this study as a researcher "studying up," that is, investigating those from family backgrounds with materially more power than myself. Insider status, no doubt, makes it easier to decode structures that frame cultural production in school. On the other hand, being an outsider foregrounds different subjective I's, enabling researchers to see things from one vantage point on the outside differently than if one were standing on the inside looking in. Whatever the case, fieldwork in a private school is complicated by the extent to which social relations of race, class and gender are carefully masked, making the ethnographers task of seeing through the veil of privilege that keeps upper middle-class culture from being interrogated all the more difficult.[7]

Methods and Practice in Research

Data collection began in the middle of September following final approval from the school. I would be on site from this point on, exiting at the end of the school calendar year in June. During this nine-month period of data collection, I would spend upwards of three to four days each week at the school, amounting to approximately 28–32 hours of contact time with students and school officials. My initial four months in the field were dedicated to building rapport and gaining the trust and confidence of students. Open lines of communication and beginning ties of friendship would prove central for access and willing participation of my informants in open-ended, in-depth interviewing scheduled to begin in the early part of the second semester.

Participant Observation

Data collection during the first phase of fieldwork relied mainly on participant observation. The focus of observation was the peer group as a site of identity production. Study of peer network formation and cohesion is particularly complicated by the tendency for youth to patrol the borders of their peer networks in order to keep outsiders from coming inside (Eder, 1985; Eckert, 1989). Adolescent girls are staunch defenders of the bonds of loyalty that unite them as friends, and the intrusion of a peripheral observer is threatening to the identity of the group. Observations of youth culture were conducted in the formal space of the classroom and the informal spaces of extracurricular and specially scheduled activities in otherwise "free spaces" like the cafeteria, library, study hall, corridors, bathrooms, and morning chapel assemblies. At times, I adopted the stance of the "fly on the wall" (Roman, 1993) as a removed, non-participatory observer, and at other points, found myself actively involved in class discussions and group exchanges outside of class. Data collected through participant observation were recorded as field notes that included direct observations of behaviors and narratives and on-site analysis driven by initial hunches.

Interviews

The second phase of the research process focused largely on data collection through semi-structured, in-depth interviews. Interviews were conducted with the faculty, exclusive of one teacher who declined to be interviewed, an auxiliary staff of twenty-nine in which I include administrators, thirty-four students and fifteen single and coupled parents. Rigorous social science requires informed consent of study participants (Bogdan and Biklen, 1982). In the case of minors, parental consent is sought before data collection can begin. At the beginning of January after the start of the second semester, consent forms for students to participate in interviews were issued to all students with an attached letter to parents introducing the research study. Students were asked to return the form within one week from the time that it was distributed. With the exception of two students comprising the initial sample, all agreed, with the consent of their parents, to participate.

Students

Interviewing was decided by the schedule of classes at Best Academy where some subject areas only met four times each week instead of five class periods. This permits flexibility in scheduling in a small private school and allows students additional time in which to complete class assignments and meet their extracurricular responsibilities. Interviews were scheduled during the school day, usually during free periods of no longer than a 42-minute scheduled class. All 34 participating juniors were interviewed at least twice during the school year; one-third of the sample were interviewed three times in the event that the interview schedule was not completed within two sittings.

Interview protocol was designed around a series of topics that would elicit data relevant to the questions framing the research study. Questions included a range of issues that would draw out the intersections of individual experience, school forms and practices and broader social dynamics. All interviews were tape-recorded. Prior to the beginning of the first interview session, each student was presented with a data sheet intended to gather background information that would better contextualize their narrative. The questionnaire solicited personal information about family background, parent[s]' education, neighborhood, and in-school and out-of-school responsibilities that constitute the typical lifestyle of an adolescent female. Before each interview session, students were instructed to turn the tape recorder off at any time during which they felt themselves uncomfortable with the process or wished a point of information be off the record. That students had upwards of four months to develop rapport with me meant that few of them found it necessary to hold themselves back during the course of an interview. Most fell easily into the role of interviewee and quickly took to open-ended conversation.

In addition to individual interviews with students, five focus group meetings, ranging in number from two to five students, were held in May, after the cycle of individual interviewing was complete. Because peer networks are tightly organized in the adolescent years, it is important to the success of the focus group to gather informants together who share the same friendship circles (Morgan, 1988). Therefore, girls from each of the peer groups, with the exception of PG3 [peer group 3], were able to meet me for a group interview. Group interviews were conducted in my apartment, a more comfortable space removed from the monitored environment of the school. The decision to convene the focus group interviews in my home gave the students a window into my life just as they had risked "going public" with me and marked a significant turning point in my being able to straddle and finally cross over the boundaries separating the human self and the research self (Fine, 1994). Focus groups lasted anywhere from one and one-half to three hours. Otherwise, individual interviews were conducted in a large room in a wing of the school reserved for alumnae events. The hall was not generally open to students, and they saw official permission to visit there for an interview a novelty as much as it was an opportunity to anticipate becoming part of the legacy of past and future graduates and supporters of Best Academy. They, too, would be alumnae in a long line of students to have attended this school, and their participation in this study contributed a piece to that history.

Teachers, Administrators and Auxiliary Staff

Teacher culture is central to the logic of school culture in both private and public institutions. While teachers were not the focus of this study, their perceptions are significant to a holistic portrait of school culture in context. In a small, private high school, teachers have an even greater opportunity than would be the case in a larger public school for more immediate involvement in their students' lives. Close relationships that went beyond the more formal boundaries of student-teacher relationships were frequent and sought after in Best Academy. As such, teachers played a central role not only in the delivery of school knowledge but also in the development of positive social relationships at the school. As part of data collection, faculty, auxiliary staff and administration were interviewed in two sessions of at least forty-five minutes to one hour in length. Interview sessions were conducted during available times in the course of the school day, or, at the request of some, outside school at a nearby restaurant or coffee house, generally decided on for reasons of confidentiality. Questions to the faculty were designed to gather information about their teaching role, relationships with students, other faculty, the administration, and parents. The absence of a tenure system in the organizational structure of private schooling coupled with the sensitive politics of a faculty renegotiating lines of communication with a new administration explained their initial hesitation and suspicion to participate in this project.

Like the students, faculty suspected that I might be employed as a spy for the new administration to monitor their support for the new Head of School. With the exception of one faculty member who declined to participate, twenty-three teachers complied with my request for interviews. More than half were interviewed twice in one-hour sessions each.

Parents

Parental involvement in schooling has been relatively unexplored in the field despite the fact that parents retain an important role in the interlocking relationship between school, home, and community. Parents' Association was open to all parents of students in Best Academy and provided them with a forum to voice concerns about the school curriculum, activities, special events, and policies. This group was a loosely constructed network of parents up until the first year of the current administrative transition at which time the Head of School sought to tighten school structures and encourage greater parental involvement. School officials saw this organization as a vehicle for opening up lines of communication with parents. Parents' interest in and willingness to involve themselves in the operation of the private school reflects the hand that parents want to have in their children's education and the control that they feel they have the right to exercise in a school that is driven by and responsive to market demands. Over the course of the academic school year, parents gradually became more familiar with my research through their children and through my consistent presence at the open monthly meetings of the Parents' Association. Parents' limited contact with me and the complications of work schedules would, however, work against the initial research design to interview more than half of the parents of junior students. The resulting twenty-two parents who agreed to be interviewed were stratified across class and racial lines in order to assemble a cross section of perspectives on a number of issues relevant to parental attitudes toward the school. Parents were interviewed in one sitting of from one to three hours in length during the summer months after the conclusion of the school year. Interviews were conducted in the school, family home, or my apartment at the parents' discretion.

Data Management

The technical requirements of ethnographic study demand immediate transcription of field notes and interview data (Bogdan and Biklen, 1982; Strauss, 1987). It is commonly the case, though, that the amount of data collected in a day's time spent in the field exceeds the time available for transcription on that very same day. Whenever possible, field notes were transcribed on the actual day of observation or interviewing. In those instances where time effectively got in the way of following technical procedure, field notes and interviews were transcribed as soon after interview or observation as possible. Where data could not be transcribed and immediately commented on, sidebar notes were jotted down on paper and/or spoken into a tape recorder and both were transcribed at a later time. On the surface, note-taking appears to be a rote activity, where the researcher simply records, verbatim, what is heard and what is seen. Data collection informed by the assumptions of critical ethnography and feminist research epistemologies take inter-subjectivity and the relational construction of knowledge very seriously. Beyond initial hunches and insights that emerge out of complex data, it is important to collect impressions of researcher subjectivity, what Peshkin (1991) has described as "situational subjectivity," that evolve and shift as a study unfolds. Who one is in the field at one stage is inevitably different from who one is at another, and research should include a record of one's own evolution in context.

Transcription of the entire data base monopolized the research process for close to six months. It was during this phase of the research that I began to familiarize myself with the data through numerous readings and rereadings of narrative and notes and to sketch out preliminary codes from which to generate a list of working codes that would assist in breaking down and managing the extensive data sets that traditionally grow out of qualitative inquiry. Data is only accessed by first breaking it down into its smallest component parts. With a coding strategy in place, it is possible to move onto secondary data analysis through development of themes that link data sets and collapse them under manageable categories for analysis (Strauss, 1987; Ely et al., 1991).

A computer-based program for Macintosh users called HyperQual more easily enabled analysis of observation and interview data (Tesch, 1990; Miles and Huberman, 1994; Richards and Richards, 1994). Conventional methods of qualitative data analysis traditionally involved "cutting and pasting" as the chosen method for sorting large bodies of information. Technological developments in information organization provide an attractive and user-friendly substitute for a painstaking and time-consuming manual process. As data is collected through interviews and observations, it is transcribed directly into the HyperQual program so that it can be properly coded. At the point that the data are transcribed into the HyperQual program, it is possible to tag or code portions of the text according to the set of working codes that emerged from successive readings and rereadings of the data set. Computer tagged data are processed into computer derived files named by code that stand in for a manual file system. This process cannot, however, eliminate such critical formative steps to data analysis as coding and thematization.

Supporting Documentation

The lack of a systematized archive for reconstructing the history of Best Academy required reference to past yearbooks and the private papers of former students, teachers, and administrators. Some of the faculty and staff had graduated from the school themselves, and their long association with Best Academy was a ready source of information filling in lost pieces of history. School and district records and policy statements directly related to the academic and administrative infrastructure of Best Academy were also examined in order to obtain information about the curriculum, internal organizational logic, philosophy, policies, and procedures. Regional demographics also factor into the representation of private school culture as they impact the production of identities in contemporary youth subcultures. Examination of data gathered for the SMSA [Standard Metropolitan Statistical Area] in which Best Academy is located provided hard evidence of demographic and economic trends that have impacted the local region.

Interview Protocol

Students

Background

1. How would you describe the neighborhood you live in?
2. What is your family like? What is your relationship like with your parents and your siblings?
3. How long have you attended Best Academy?
4. What factors influenced your decision to attend Best Academy?
5. What do you like best/least about attending a single-sex high school? What do you like best/least about attending Best Academy?
6. Do you have a job? If so, what do you do?

Inside School

1. What is your favorite subject? What do you think you are learning in your classes?
2. What do you think of when I say the word "knowledge"?
3. Do you create knowledge or do you feel that it is given to you in your classes?
4. Do you feel what you are learning in school is relevant to your life?
5. How do you feel about your teachers?

6. Do you feel that the school avoids teaching you certain things in your classes? If you could teach your classes for a week, is there anything that you would do differently?
7. Do you play an important role in the school? What contribution do you feel you make to the school?
8. How have things changed in this school since you've been a student here?
9. Do you feel that Best Academy is a community? In what sense?
10. If you could change anything about your school, what would you change and why?
11. How would you describe the students in Best Academy? In the junior class? How would you describe relationships between students in the junior class?
12. How do you think the other students/teachers in school view you?
13. How have you changed since you've been a student here?

Gender Relations

1. How important are your friendships with other women? Are these friendships more important than school? If so, why? Who do you turn to in school when you have a problem?
2. What kinds of relationships with students/teachers have you developed in school?
3. What do you see as your role as a young woman in the 1990s? Does anyone influence what you think your role as a woman should be? Are there things that you would like to see changed about relationships between men and women? About women's and men's roles? Do you think these roles will change?
4. How would you characterize the women's movement?
5. What do you understand as feminism? Do you see yourself as a feminist?

Class Relations

1. What social class do you think you belong in? Why?
2. Do your friends belong to the same social class as you? Does social class make a difference in your friendships? To what extent do you interact with girls from different social class backgrounds at school? How do you feel about your relationships with these girls?
3. In English and history class, you have been learning about the American dream. What does the American dream mean to you? Do you have a dream as a white/African-American/Hispanic/Native-American?

Race Relations

1. In what racial group do you locate yourself?

2. [White students] How do you see the experience of being white in Best Academy? Can you think of a time when being white made a difference for you in school? How did you deal with this? [Same set of questions repeated with students who are African-American, Hispanic, and Native-American].

3. To what extent do you interact with girls from different racial backgrounds at school? How do you feel about your relationships with these girls?

Future Projections

1. What do you see yourself doing 5–7 years from now? What factors influenced your decision?
2. Do you think it is possible to have it all—career, marriage, and family?
3. Do you have an important role model in your life?
4. Do you think Best Academy prepares you to meet your goals?
5. What do you think the school would like you to be?
6. Do you think your relationships will change after leaving high school? How do you feel about this?
7. If you were to look back on your high school experience ten years from now, what do you think will have been the most valuable part for you? What would you like to be remembered for?

Family Life

1. Do you speak to your parents about school?
2. What do you think your parents would like you to be learning in school?
3. Can you tell me what your parents think about their own lives? Their work?
4. Is anything going to be different between your life after high school and that of your parents?

Student Focus Groups[8]

1. What is a typical Friday night or weekend evening like for you and your friends? How do you spend your private time? Do you ever get together exclusively with your girlfriends for a girls' night out? What do you do in these meetings?
2. How do other students in school view you as a group? What are the major tensions between different students or groups of students in school?
3. What do you see for yourselves and your friends in the future? What do you hope your lives will be like after graduation? In 5–7 years? What do you hope for and what do you fear for yourselves and your friends?

4. When do you notice your race/class/gender either inside or outside of school? Can you think of a time when your race/class/gender made a difference in a situation you were in either inside or outside school? What was the situation and how did you handle it?

5. Do you feel that issues of race/class/gender are discussed in school? Does the school bring adequate attention to these issues? If so, in what ways? What contribution do you feel you bring to these discussions? [Non-white students] What role do you feel you play in bringing attention to issues of race/class/gender?

6. How do you feel about interracial friendships and relationships? How do you feel about dating a man from a different racial/ethnic and/or social class background? How would your friends feel about this? How would your parents feel about this?

7. As young women in the 1990s, would you like to see anything changed about gender roles and relationships between men and women? How might you play a role in bringing about these changes?

8. Was there ever a time when you felt that a boy had control over you either physically, emotionally, or intellectually? If so, what did you do about it? If not, imagine a situation where this would be the case. What would you do about it?

9. How do you feel about your body? Does the school have any influence on the way you feel about your body?

Faculty[9]

Background

1. How would you describe who you are as a person?
2. What social class do you locate yourself in?
3. When did you first consider teaching in a high school? What circumstances brought you to teach at Best Academy? How many years have you been a teacher at Best Academy?

Inside School

1. How would you describe Best Academy?
2. How has the experience of teaching in a single-sex school been for you? Has it had any impact on your teaching?
3. What subject[s] do you teach and in which grades? Did you always teach this content area?
4. How would you define "knowledge"? What knowledge would you say is the most appropriate for girls in your classes to be learning?

5. What do you look for in choosing a text and designing assignments?

Student Culture

1. How would you describe the students in Best Academy in general and in the junior class in particular? How would you describe relationships between students here?
2. Do you see any differences [academic; relational] between your students? Between students of different racial backgrounds? Social class backgrounds?

Teacher Culture

1. What are your goals as a teacher?
2. Has the experience of teaching at Best Academy changed for you over the years? If so, in what ways? To what do you attribute the changes?
3. How have you changed since you've been a teacher at Best Academy?
4. How do you define success in teaching at Best Academy? Is there anything that prevents you from being as successful as you would like to be?
5. Is there anything that you especially like or dislike about teaching at Best Academy or would like to see changed? Are there any changes that you would like to see made in your department or in your curriculum?
6. What is your relationship like with the new administration? What has been the effect of the change of administration on the faculty?
7. What is your relationship with the faculty? How has it changed during your years of teaching at Best Academy?
8. Would you like to change careers at some point in the future? To what and why? Is there anything that prevents you from doing this?

Parents

1. How long have you lived in this community? What is your profession? Are you married? If so, how long?
2. How would you define yourself in social class terms?
3. How did you learn about Best Academy? Why did you choose to send your daughter here? Could anything have prevented your daughter from attending Best Academy? If you didn't send your daughter to Best Academy, where would you have sent her and why?
4. How would you characterize the educational experience at Best Academy? What would you like your daughter to learn while a student here?
5. What kinds of women do you feel that Best Academy is interested in producing? Has your daughter changed during the time she has attended Best Academy? If so, in what way[s]?

6. What are your daughter's goals? What do you think of them? Does the school encourage students in their educational and professional goals for the future? When your daughter graduates from Best Academy, what do you envision her doing immediately after high school? What would you like her life to look like 5–7 years from now? Would you like to see your daughter get married and have a family in her future? Do you think she will have a future in this city?

7. In what ways do you think your daughter's life will be the same or different from your life and why? Do you feel that your daughter will be upwardly or downwardly mobile in her future? Do you feel that Best Academy plays a role in influencing her future in this way?

8. How do you feel about the teachers at Best Academy? What kind of influence do you feel that they have had on your daughter and her education?

9. How do you feel about the change in school administration this year? What would you like to see changed in the school? How do you think the new school administration views parents?

10. Do you feel that Best Academy is a community at this point in time? Are you involved with the school in any way? If so, how? What role do you feel parents play in the school community? To what extent is this role encouraged or discouraged by the school? If your daughter had gone to public school, would you have been as involved as you are at Best Academy?

11. Do you think that the school should teach students values? Which values should the school teach and why? Do you share these values?

12. If you had to do it all over again, would you send your daughter to Best Academy?

Data Sheet[10]

Name:

Date:

Time:

Age:

Ethnicity:

Neighborhood:

Grammar School:

Profession:

Mother:

Father:

Education:

Mother:

Father:

Number of children in family:

Highest level of education completed:

Profession:

School club membership:

After-school Activities / Job:

Notes

Chapter 1

1. The name of the school has been changed to protect the privacy of my informants. Independent schools are a subset of private schools mainly supported by tuition, charitable contributions, and endowment monies rather than tax or church dollars. Independent schools share a number of common characteristics that include: self-governance, self-support, self-defined curriculum, self-selected students, self-selected faculty, and small size (Kane, 1991, p. 397). Private schools in the United States numbered at 27,700 in 1993 of which 1,500 were independent schools. The NAIS [National Association of Independent Schools] reports that the number of single-sex schools has decreased by 12.1 percent over the past decade while the number of co-educational schools has increased by 15.6 percent since 1982-83. Of the 915 independent schools of 24,690 [23 percent] existing private schools in the United States, only 97 or 11 percent of them are girls' schools (p. 5). For detailed statistical analysis of independent education in the United States, see *National Association of Independent School Statistics* (1993).

2. Upper middle class and professional middle class are categories that are used interchangeably throughout the text. Varieties of class culture at Best Academy will be explored in detail in chapter 3.

3. Newman (1989) points out that both the blue-collar working class and the lower white-collar middle class have felt equally threatened by the losses of downward mobility beginning in the mid 1970s, following from rising inflationary rates and the escalation of economic de-industrialization.

4. As Reich (1992) and others point out, the shift in the organization of work relations in the new economy is less in the form of structured bureaucracy than it is in the development of a series of weblike relationships between workers. It is, however, still the case that a hierarchical and bureaucratic structure basically describes the social relations of production in American work culture.

5. *Census of Population and Housing* (1990).

6. By the end of the 1980s, only 94,500 workers, less than one-fifth of the total regional work force in the city, remained in manufacturing jobs. More than 400,000 people are employed in the service sector of this regional economy while the overall unemployment rate stands at under five percent (Perry and McLean, 1991). The unemployment rate in this urban center reached as high as 12.2 percent in 1982, precipitously declining over the next eleven years to a rate of 7.3 percent in 1993, the year during which data was collected for this study (XXX PMSA, 1993).

7. Information about parent income is confidential. It is not publicly circulated and so it was not available for use in this study. School data on 1992–93 parental income sets the mean family adjusted income at 32,074 dollars, understood as parents' disposable income after tax deductions and major household expenses. The mean adjusted family income only applies to financial aid recipients. The fact that the tuition for the 1993–94 academic year was set at 7,800 dollars in relation to the mean family adjusted income brings into sharp relief the difficulties that parents from the professional middle class face in funding a private education.

8. Social theorists (Roman, Christian-Smith, and Ellsworth, 1988; Apple, 1993; Farber, Provenzo, and Holm, 1994; Kincheloe, 1995; McLaren, 1995) have turned to examination of the impact of hyper-mediated culture on identity formation. Schools bear the imprint of popular cultural forms with obvious implications for identity formation processes among youth subcultures. Examination of the influence of popular culture on emergent notions of self among the students in Best Academy was outside the scope of this study. Therefore, I do not explore the ways in which popular culture explicitly impacts on the manufacture of identities.

9. I single out race, social class, and gender here as central categories of analysis since they set the boundaries for the current study. Ethnicity and sexuality are treated as they arise in the data, but they were not working categories throughout this analysis.

10. Reproduction theory is also referenced in the sociology of education literature as structuralist theory, social transmission theory, economic and cultural reproduction theory, and correspondence theory.

11. For one of the earliest and arguably most definitive discussions of the structuralist paradigm as applied to analysis of school forms, see Parsons (1959).

12. Weiler (1988) uses the term "critical educational theory," under which she subsumes the new sociology of education, radical education theory, and feminist social and cultural theory. Giroux (1983) uses "resistance theory" to refer to the same theoretical framework.

13. Socialist feminist scholars identify gender as the central organizing principle of social relations in schools and explore the linkages between gender, structure, ideology, and power. Weiler (1988) points out that much of the research focused on the relationship between women and schools has come from liberal feminist circles where inquiry has tended to center on issues of sex stereotyping and bias in school curriculum and practice. Unlike socialist feminist arguments, liberal feminist analyses generally exclude class analysis of gender experiences in school.

14. hooks (1990) is eloquent on the matter of triple jeopardy and the extent to which race, class, and gender interpolate to configure specific identity forms for girls of color. For further discussion, see King (1989).

15. In their recently published study of the role that ideology plays in shaping middle-class mothers' educational interests for their children, Brantlinger, Majd-Jabbari, and Guskin (1996) note the tendency for researchers to study historically marginalized groups rather than groups in positions of greater power and privilege. There is much need for further study of elite groups at/in the cultural center.

16. Connell makes the point that the ruling-class school does not consist of a homogeneous student body but, rather, draws from a wider class base than would be expected. In large measure, however, ruling-class schools draw families from the Australian establishment who live mainly in upper-class, wealthy, prestigious suburbs, where fathers tend to hold jobs associated with the professional or entrepreneurial class, have university degrees, and private education in their backgrounds. Mothers also tend to have been educated in private schools.

17. Kingston and Lewis (1990) similarly note that elite institutions of higher education aim to shape in their students a collective identity based in the common class culture of the school.

18. One the most comprehensive and in-depth discussions of the cognitive and social/affective development and learning outcomes of girls in schools is found in the AAUW Report (1992).

19. At the same time as feminists find the postmodern project useful to their critique of subjectivity, they also recognize inherent problems in linking the two discourses together. Further discussion of this tension appears in Nicholson (1990); Giroux (1991); and Luke and Gore (1992).

20. It is not my intent to devalue the serious work of post-colonial critics who acknowledge the highly specific struggles of those whose multiple and marginal identities have created for them a condition of non-identity. While I respect these highly specific struggles, I argue throughout that the borderland is a powerful concept for understanding the complexities and contradictions of identity formation for those historically located at the cultural center who are also actively repositioning themselves in relation to others inside and outside cultural privilege. On the concept of the borderland as a site for "critical analysis, experimentation and possibility," see Grossberg, Nelson, and Treichler (1992).

Chapter 2

1. Hannaway and Abramowitz (1985) observe that commitment, active participation, and cohesion are less evident in public schools than is the case in private schools.

2. While socialization is a critical element in both public and private school culture, Kapferer (1981) finds that rituals and ceremonies play a more central role in cultural formation in the private school in contrast to public institutions where teachers and parents see these practices interfering with the private interests of family life.

3. Although race is not unrelated to the central arguments in this chapter, I have chosen to focus only on social class in this discussion. Race will be analyzed in detail as a separate yet interrelated aspect of school life in chapter 4.

4. By curriculum-in-use, I assume a conceptualization of curriculum that departs from rigid definitions that restrict curriculum to instructional materials to a broader notion of curriculum as a social process, taking into account the whole school context—materials, content, and delivery of school knowledge and relationships between students and teachers.

5. In chapter 4, I will submit that girls are raced by definition of class as well.

6. Best Academy School Archives, unpublished documents. The establishment of the academy predated by ten years efforts in the area to provide a quality collegiate education for women. The school moved to its current location in 1909.

7. See *An Address Delivered Before the Patrons and Pupils of Best Academy of XXX Hall* (1852). Female seminaries were established in the early nineteenth century for women's professional preparation. They were often modelled after the structural design and organization of asylums. One building encompassing nearly all of the physical plant of the school was typical of the design of early women's seminaries and, later, colleges where facilities were either located in one large building or several adjoining buildings. Mary Lyon, one of the founders, along with Zilpah Grant, of Ipswich Seminary [later renamed Mount Holyoke], emphasized punctuality and constructive use of time. Regulatory codes of this nature would remain part of the culture of girls' schooling through the nineteenth and well into the twentieth centuries. For further discussion of schooling for girls, specifically at the collegiate level, see Horowitz (1984).

8. Best Academy consists of a single building housing all school facilities with the exception of a separate building whose grounds are often utilized for gym classes held outside during the fall and the spring. This separate property, purchased and renovated for school use, not only provides additional space for outside sports activities but also services meetings, school-related events, and private affairs. Up until 1992, it doubled as housing for the Head of School.

9. On the relationship between the organization of space in school and gender and class codes, see Masemann (1974).

10. The physical arrangement of space inside nineteenth-century female seminaries reflected a respect for authority and rank so much so that it was common practice to locate the major public rooms of a school on both sides of the main entrance.

11. This is not to suggest a homogeneous class culture at Best Academy since this is certainly not the case. Faculty note in their interviews that class culture noticeably

began to shift in the 1970s as the school began to aggressively recruit students from different racial, ethnic, and class backgrounds in response to the pull of a local, competitive private school that had chosen to become co-educational and was perceived by parents in the local community as a more rigorous academic environment, and as a reaction to the flight of white, upper middle-class families to more affluent suburbs.

12. Pseudonyms with the prefix "Ms." indicate informants who might either be single or married but have chosen not to go by the title "Mrs."

13. It is noteworthy that up until the 1992 school year, school policy, although inconsistent on this matter, dictated that students were not allowed to enter the school through the front door. Veteran faculty explain that this regulation was put in place to control the flow of students into the main vestibule, an area not equipped to accommodate numbers of students hovering at close to two hundred in earlier decades. With the reduction in enrollment in the past five years to nearly half of what it was and the turn of administration after a twenty-five year period of relative stability, this policy was reversed. While this policy was recently withdrawn, it is striking to consider the ways that private school culture is contained, so much so that it becomes nearly invisible to the local neighborhood that it has and continues to serve.

14. As part of the formal interview schedule, students were asked to describe themselves in social class terms. This data appears in chapter 3.

15. For further discussion of the symbolic role of ritual, see Geertz (1973). Amplification of the role of ritual and the variety of forms it takes in the private school occurs in Kapferer (1981), Varenne (1981), and McLaren (1986).

16. With the change in school administration in the 1992–93 academic year, a schoolwide decision was made to replace the name "Chapel" with "Morning Meeting" because of implied religious connotations. The time set aside for morning assembly "Chapel" is a carryover of the period scheduled for private devotion and communal worship in girls' seminaries in the wake of religious revivalism in early nineteenth-century New England.

17. Before reinstating Morning Meeting at the beginning of the 1992–93 school calendar year, it was standard for the school to formally convene as a community only during specially designated Chapel days.

18. See the *Best Academy School Catalogue* (1852). This excerpt was reprinted in the bulletin prepared by the Best Academy Art Department on the occasion of the school's 125th year anniversary.

19. *Best Academy Information Bulletin*, 1993–94.

20. Because of school size, relative absence of disciplinary problems and physical layout of the private school, students face fewer restrictions on their use of time and access to school spaces than is the case in the public school where structures and governance are less conducive to students having these kinds of privileges.

21. The student handbook notes that students are able to choose where and how they spend their free periods, except in those instances where they have been either assigned or have volunteered for a teacher supervised study hall. Free periods were structured into the school day to facilitate smoother course scheduling. Students also have special privileges that include use of the grassed Boulevard adjacent to the school during free periods for study or recreation. This practice is open to all students during the spring, provided they are in good academic standing with the school administration and faculty.

22. The Study Center is a large, open room where students are each assigned a school desk in areas sectioned off for each class. Students do not have lockers nor are their desks locked. Any expensive items that they wished to protect are handed over to the Head of School for safe keeping.

23. My appropriation of the notion of "free space" is necessarily different from the definition of free space as both an objective and subjective place where individuals are active participants in shaping identities that have been denied and increasingly stripped away in their communities and the broader public. For further discussion, see Boyte and Evans (1992), and Fine and Weis (forthcoming, 1998).

24. Wilson (1992) debates the validity of the claim that independent schools are at a significant advantage over public schools in terms of curriculum development and academic outcomes, arguing, instead, that they are at a particular disadvantage with regard to limitations on their willingness and ability to experiment with different instructional approaches and curricular content.

25. As an independent high school, Best Academy does not depend on the Regents of the University of the State for accreditation. Accreditation is granted through the State Association of Independent Schools and the Middle States Association of Colleges and Secondary Schools.

26. In 1990–91, the average earned income of a secondary, public school teacher was 35,384 dollars while the average earned income of a secondary, private school teacher was 21,864 dollars (*National Center for Education Statistics*, 1993).

27. These contradictions are clarified in later analysis of the social construction of class and race relations in the school.

28. Observations were conducted across content areas in the junior curriculum. Teaching styles vary throughout any school, but it is evident that less instrumental forms of instruction, particularly those I observed in the Advanced Placement History classes, are related to the fact that students in Advanced Placement subjects are thought to be better able to deal with more critical approaches to material.

29. For further discussion of curricular forms, see Anyon (1979) and Sleeter and Grant (1991).

30. Instruction is, however, framed by the standardized Advanced Placement test administered to all junior students in college preparatory courses in public and private school systems and so there is equal emphasis placed on students learning facts and

information in preparation for the test. This also raises a number of questions about secondary levels of tracking in college preparatory high schools where the assumption is that all students will go onto college. Most, if not all students, will go onto college after they graduate. What is left out of the discussion is the fact that not all students will go on to equally competitive schools. A secondary tracking system within the school legitimates different ability levels and serves to channel students into schools of higher education appropriate to their abilities.

31. Henry (1993) makes a similar point in her analysis of the curriculum in a private, college preparatory high school. Students in private schools are generally very literate in Western culture though this is changing as multicultural initiatives force necessary restructuring of existing curriculum to reflect more interdisciplinary and post-disciplinary approaches to teaching and learning.

32. As part of a new five year, comprehensive, strategic plan for school restructuring, the school administration brought an external consultant into the school during the 1992–93 academic year whose recommendations for program development included fostering more interdisciplinary collaboration between faculty as part of a wide ranging initiative to implement a culture of academic excellence at Best Academy.

33. This strikingly parallels the attitudes of working-class youth in schools who see the school as important for the diploma that it will give them. For amplification of this point, see Weis (1990).

34. It is not accurate to generalize economic privilege to the entire school population at Best Academy nor to private schools in general. Despite gradual growth in economic diversity in private schools throughout the twentieth century, private school demographics have remained relatively stable (Newman, 1995). While financial aid packages are increased to meet the fiscal hardships that families incur, it is more commonly the case that soaring college tuition costs put many families out of the private education market, essentially reserving the option of private schooling for families of relatively privileged means.

Chapter 3

1. Here, I refer to multiculturalism as a broad social movement. This is not to suggest that there is a single-overarching definition or all-encompassing category of multicultural discourse. Sleeter and Grant (1988), Banks (1991), McCarthy (1993), Nieto (1995), Jackson and Solis (1996) and others have pointed to clear differences between multicultural frameworks. Analysis of these nuances is beyond the scope of this discussion.

2. It is not my intention to provide a thoroughgoing analysis of postmodernity since this ethnography is not based on an explicit postmodern framework. Postmodern constructs will, however, inform various points of discussion throughout the text.

3. The crisis of representation brought on by postmodernity challenges struc-turalist frameworks that draw meaning, including what is meant by identity, through binary oppositions between and among individuals and groups. Postmodern under-standings of meaning-making processes are openly critical of such binarisms, offering in their place the possibility of multiple and situated perspectives as sites of knowl-edge production. For further discussion and analysis of this last point, see Haraway (1988).

4. Sieber (1982) draws important attention to the fact that ethnographic research has tended to focus examination on high rates of academic failure among minority, working-class and poor youth while leaving the academic success of middle class and elite school populations relatively unexplored. Over a decade later, it is still the case that ethnographic research in schools continues to dedicate itself to exam-ination of school forms, processes and bases for academic success among relatively disadvantaged populations, reflecting the tendency for ethnographers to study "down" rather than "up."

5. While this might be the case for non-sectarian private schools, Newman (1995) points out that private Catholic schools, accounting for eighty percent of private school enrollment from the early decades of the twentieth century up through the early 1970s, served a less economically privileged group of students than public school students (U.S. Department of Education, 1994).

6. Brint does not define the professional middle class in terms of an income index as there is no standard income measure for this group. Instead, he defines each of the categories that he has named as part of the professional middle class in terms of their social purpose, considering the type of knowledge that is produced and whose ends it is designed to serve.

7. In this occupational category, Reich (1992) includes individuals who tend to function as scientists, engineers, executives, bankers, lawyers, developers, consultants, producers, publishers, and university teachers. While wide ranging in responsibilities, symbolic analysts share in common the manipulation of symbols from which others benefit from the development of new resources.

8. Forty-seven percent of junior students receive financial assistance in the form of grants-in-aid based on financial need or merit scholarships.

9. In 1943, the U.S. Bureau of the Census devised occupational categories that reflected the prestige and income associated with certain jobs. With the shift toward a global economy and the development of new occupational categories, this classifica-tion system no longer holds true. New categories of work raise important questions about the extent to which the blue-collar working class and the occupations that have conventionally fallen under that category could be considered middle class as a func-tion of shared beliefs and expectations (Halle, 1984). The occupations of the parents that I refer to here include, but are not limited to, bus driver, truck driver, school cafeteria aide, and teacher aide.

10. It is noteworthy that most of the prestigious private schools [both sectarian and non-sectarian] in this region are located in the urban center rather than outlying suburbs. That Best Academy has a relatively traditional curriculum coupled with the growing incidence of crime in the city contributed to significant declines in student enrollment beginning in the early 1990s.

11. This is in no way meant to overlook important studies of peer group formation that have found evidence that class operated as a determining factor in selection of peers within racial groupings (Shimahara, 1983). There are a fair number of studies linking social class to peer identification and stratification (Brantlinger, 1993), but further research needs to be done along these lines.

12. My analysis in this chapter centers on class only. I have strategically decided to do this as a way of working through rather dense data. The treatment of class, race/ethnicity and gender in discrete chapters is in no way meant to suggest that these are distinct categories that are neither interrelated nor interdependent.

13. Because the culture of a small, private school lends itself to making friendships easily, students are less likely to name themselves and others categorically in stereotypical terms. For further discussion of this point, see Eckert (1989).

14. Magnet schools vary in their focus and orientation. They were established by order of the federal court to integrate the public school system as part of a city-wide desegregation initiative designed to achieve integrated schools. Magnet schools were also aimed at reducing white, middle-class flight from school districts in the process of desegregating.

15. It is arguable that some of the students included in this peer group, approximately four girls, come from families whose parents' occupations would fall within the lower white-collar middle class and blue-collar working class.

16. The tuition for the 1993–94 academic year was listed at 7,800 dollars.

17. From the student descriptions of their families' lifestyle outside of school, parents' occupations and knowledge that I had of some of the families in the community, I was able to surmise that some of the students in PG2 came from families where parents' occupations would most likely put them in the top income bracket of the professional middle class.

18. Oppositional and internally fractured peer cultures are more likely to develop in the public high school where issues of size and racial, ethnic, and socioeconomic diversity, relative to the private school, make it more difficult to contain differences as easily as might be the case in a smaller private institution. I am grateful to Lois Weis for this insight.

19. Student reflections on social class are largely absent from the socialization literature.

20. Although I did not have access to information on parent income or financial aid, I gathered from interviews with Beth and her parents that the family faces financial hardship. Beth attends Best Academy on full scholarship. In her interviews with low-income adolescents, Brantlinger (1993) found that three-quarters of this group self-identified as "in-between" rich or poor (p. 59).

21. It is noteworthy that Lisa comes from one of the more affluent families in the junior class. Her father is a well-known lawyer in the area and her mother is a nurse. Two of her siblings attended Best Academy before her. Despite the fact that she clearly benefits from privilege, she describes herself as middle class and provides a critique of privilege at the same time.

22. The recent emergence of a small but growing body of literature on the social construction of whiteness furthers our understanding of the ways in which "othering" keeps those who benefit from race privilege from seeing their own privilege. The ways in which white privilege goes unrecognized among whites is instructive for parallel examination of the relative invisibility of class privilege in the United States. This discourse is explored in greater depth in chapter 4.

23. Interview segments with Mrs. Nicholson suggest that there was an unwritten practice of admitting students to the school on the basis of financial backing. To this effect, Mrs. Nicholson observed that prior to her assuming the role of Head of School that the previous administration "let in for a long time anybody that could either pay the tuition or that would fill a classroom." Simply put, she stated that, in the past, "we" [the school administration] bought them."

24. Oakes (1986) speaks of schools as sites of inegalitarian stratification around the persistent practice of tracking which perpetuates the illusion of an open contest system in U.S. public schools.

25. While I do not know for a fact that such practices are in place, I would think it highly doubtful for the school to support unethical policies of the type that students describe.

26. Thorne (1994) notes that she borrows the term "borderwork" from Barth (1969).

Chapter 4

1. Roman (1993) points out that the phrase "people of color" intimates that white culture is the norm against which all other groups are positioned and judged. For further discussion of this point, see Carby (1990). I do not intend this as it would contradict my project to critique whiteness as a standpoint of racial privilege. Although I recognize that there is no representative experience of women of color, I have chosen to appropriate this as a category because of the small number of underrepresented groups in the study sample. Where possible, I draw ethnic and racial distinctions among students.

2. Nowhere is this more apparent than in the white media where hyper-mediated representation of black people has kept the focus away from seeing and interrogating whiteness. For further discussion along these lines, see Hall (1988) and hooks (1992).

3. Hurtado and Stewart (1997) make the point that whites look to define white identity through comparisons of whites and non-whites. McIntosh (1992) demonstrates the many "invisibile" privileges that being white affords in a powerful essay that lists several privileges that whites benefit from that non-whites do not equally participate in. The point is that theoretical analysis of white identity depends on comparisons with people of color.

4. I should note that the tendency to direct attention away from whiteness and project it onto ethnic, religious, and cultural categories was not a common finding in my data. In one other instance, a student responded to my question about her race identity by identifying herself as Jewish. This single instance, however, is instructive for understanding other categories that white youth draw on as a substitute for identifying as white.

5. Frankenberg (1993) notes that color evasion has also been referred to as "color-blindness." She chooses the term "color evasion" rather than "color-blindness" because the latter term carries with it negative connotations for differently enabled people and implies that one literally does not see racial differences whereas she argues that white women do recognize and name race in strategic ways that suggest, on the surface, that they do not see race differences at all.

6. Mrs. Berson does not currently teach the junior girls English. She has had them as freshmen and could have them as seniors. Since she has been on the school faculty for nearly twenty years, her comments provide us with insight into a part of Best Academy's history.

7. When asked to describe the focus of the play that she had written, Lucy provided this summary of its contents: "The play is about black women, African women, West African women, to be more specific, from about the fourteen or fifteen hundreds until present. It basically shows scenes from the past. A lot of people think that all black history starts with slavery, but it doesn't. It started back in Africa, just everything that we were. It started then. And the play brings out kind of a, it just shows that we weren't ignorant, we weren't ignorant people. We just didn't understand their [Europeans] language, the way that they spoke. It shows that the people that were slaves, they still kind of, some of them bought into it, and some of them didn't. And the ones that didn't were the ones that survived and were able to acept freedom. Then it goes to the twenties, to the working-class black people who were trying to get their children to have a better life than they did and taking some of the same crap that they took when they were slaves. Then it goes to the forties, just basically saying, not letting black people get ahead, not saying—well, you can't have an education, but saying that you can get an education, and you can then be my maid. And then the past meets the present, and that's the play."

8. This incident was relayed to me as secondhand information in student interviews. I was not present in the classroom on the day of this incident and only learned

about it after the fact. The inability for a researcher to be in two places at once speaks to the limitations of a single ethnographic investigator studying school culture.

9. There are a number of interpretations of Du Bois's notion of double-consciousness. It is not my intent here to explore this except to point out the particularity of the African-American struggle to transform the double self into a unified self-consciousness, resolving the conflict experienced at the interface of the Black and American (coded white) worlds.

10. Scheurich (1993) makes the point that popular cultural forms, particularly the media, capture overt and crude expressions of racism commonly associated with white, working-class culture. Willis (1977) and Weis (1990) respectively describe the overt and noticeably raw racism of the white working class as distinct from less overt forms of middle-class racism where discrimination and prejudice tend to be less visible, carefully managed, and contained.

11. In his analysis of recent developments in public and private education in this century, Newman (1995) notes that racial and ethnic diversity has grown consistently in private schools, particularly from the mid-1980s up to the present time. Roman Catholic schools have historically enrolled significant numbers of ethnic, immigrant, and poor children, and it is in Roman Catholic schools that we see minorities making up nearly twenty-two percent of total enrollments, broken down as ten percent representation of Hispanics, nine percent representation of African-Americans, and three percent representation of Asians (p. 14).

12. It was common to hear white students use words like "sister," "fat," and "dukey," a vocabulary that they borrowed from students of color and appropriated as their own.

Chapter 5

1. Fox-Genovese (1994) notes that women currently make up approximately half (45 percent) of the U.S. labor force. See U.S. *Department of Labor, Women's Bureau, "Facts on Working Women,"* 92–93 (June 1993).

2. Research studies have challenged the assumptions of the dual-career model for their tendency to idealize middle-class family norms. For further discussion, see Ferree (1984).

3. Recent studies provide evidence of sexist education in single-sex schools where limited course offerings, especially the number and nature of electives, have the effect of narrowing girls' academic preparation and occupational choices for the future. For further discussion, see Kenway and Willis (1986).

4. Drawing on Lather's (1990) distinction between the 'postmodern' and the 'poststructural,' Jones (1993) understands the first to mean the "cultural shifts of a post-industrial, post-colonial era" while the second term is appropriated to mean the "working out of those shifts within academic theory" (p. 158). I do not intend a formal

poststructural analysis of gender constructions around marriage, career, and family in this discussion but only use it as a helpful framework for understanding the ways in which gendered subjectivities are actively constituted through discursive practices that shape girls as girls. In other words, feminist poststructuralism allows us to reenvision girls' active participation in the construction of discourses of femininity. For thoughtful discussion of the movement toward poststructural work in education, see the introduction to Luke and Gore (1992).

5. Smith (1988) calls attention to the double power of social texts, like the printed media and other visual images, to appeal to women as subjects and to consume them as objects.

6. Examination of student files archived over the past three decades reveals that Best Academy graduates, for much of the decade of the 1960s and into the early years of the 1970s, were more likely to attend two-year programs at community colleges, a pattern of college attendance historically viewed as prestigious. From the mid-1970s and onward, the tendency was for students to move into four-year colleges or universities immediately after high school graduation.

7. In only two instances did girls couch their opportunity to go to college as a class-based privilege. For the most part, students virtually overlooked any connection between class and educational opportunity. All thirty-four students interviewed as part of this study went directly onto college and were accepted at a wide range of institutions, both public and private. Eight students chose to attend colleges in the local area.

8. For discussion of the institutionalization of gender inequalities in school, see Sadker and Sadker (1994).

9. Defending the rigor of these early female academies, Solomon (1985) points out that most did not offer courses in housewifery or domestic science, what we know today as home economics.

10. Okely (1978) makes a similar point in her study of boarding school education for girls, that the girls' school served more to prepare girls for lived dependence in marriage while boys' boarding schools sought to prepare young men for independence and positions of power. Women were also encouraged to participate in volunteer work in the form of community social service, a tradition that continues today to be important, particularly in the lives of upper-class women. For further discussion, see Ostrander (1984).

11. While I speak briefly to this emergent theme in this discussion, it is evident, for several of the girls, that the culture of professionalism emphasized at school and the pursuit of careers looked upon by school officials as successful are key factors in sustaining the reputation and drawing in funding to support the school financially.

12. Lees (1986) found in her study of gender identity production in interviews with approximately one hundred fifteen- and sixteen-year-old, working-class and middle-class girls from different ethnic backgrounds that girls are interested in delaying marriage until a later time so that they can get the necessary education and training

that they need to avoid having to take a "dead end job" (p. 95). This theme did not appear in any of my interviews with Best Academy students, suggesting that class privilege, in some measure, protects girls against this.

13. Over the past decade and a half, national statistics document that slightly more than one-half of all marriages end in divorce. See *Statistical Abstracts of the United States* (1993).

14. The postfeminist perspective finds women embracing aspects of feminist ideology and practice at the same time as they hesitate to identify politically with the feminist movement. For further discussion, see Rosenfelt and Stacey (1987).

15. Machung (1989) found that senior women at the University of California–Berkeley expected equal sharing of household chores in their visions of family but that these same women also responded that women are better suited to stay at home and raise children, reflecting the traditional sexual division of labor.

18 Although I speak of feminism rather than feminisms, I do not intend to suggest that there is a singular, unifying definition of feminism. I agree with Delmar (1994), though, that, even though there are many different feminisms, it is possible to design a broad definition of feminism.

19. From their perspective, taking on any feminist affiliation implied that they were also lesbian. This theme runs through the data.

20. Griffin (1989) points out that studies of feminist identification conventionally overlook discussion of those forces that create potential roadblocks to political affiliation.

21. Defining issues in third wave feminism include equal pay for women in the work place, parental leave after childbirth and adoption, provisions for child care in the work place, and flexible work schedules to better accommodate dual-working families.

Chapter 6

1. Status attainment studies, prominent in the 1960s, sought answers to the impact of family background and parental attitudes and aspirations on educational and occupational attainment and intergenerational status mobility. Although there are limitations to the status attainment research, there is no question that quantitative studies have brought us closer to understanding those factors that mediate life chances and outcomes. Specifically, it has failed to explore why families from different social classes maintain and pass on certain goals to their children and has also overlooked the impact labor market conditions have on life chances. On this point, see Persell (1977).

2. Increasing numbers of jobs at lower income levels widen the wage gap and lower the economic standard of living for the middle class (Leigh, 1993).

3. Weis (1990) makes this point in accounting for the relative lack of existing ethnographic research on the family as an important site of education and socialization.

4. Parents' work commitment did, in fact, prove to be a significant obstacle to obtaining a broader cross section of parent interviewees. Mothers tended to be more available to speak with me than fathers. Where both parents were present for the interview, mothers tended to dominate the conversation and were more actively involved in their daughter's schooling.

5. The Head of School and select faculty informally recommended parents to me who they thought would be willing candidates for interviews. This initial list included approximately twenty-five single and coupled parents. All of these parents were contacted more than once. If parents did not respond after two attempts at making contact, their names were deleted from the list. The final list consisted of twenty-two parents. The sample was stratified across race, level of education, and occupation. A year of administrative transition found parents renegotiating styles of communication that they had grown accustomed to with the previous Headmaster of twenty-five years. Exercising caution with the new administration spilled over into parents' initial hesitation to talk with me and to be interviewed for the study. Knowing that interviews with parents were an important piece of being able to draw as complete a portrait of private school culture as possible, I expanded my fieldwork to include Parent Association Meetings held once a month at the school with the Head of School in attendance.

6. Chubb and Moe (1990), two of the foremost spokespeople for market-based school choice plans, argue that large bureaucracies, found mainly in public school systems, work against effective school organization and have the end result of holding students back from producing at higher levels of achievement.

7. Cookson (1994) notes that few school choice plans include private schools. There is a wide body of literature on the school choice movement. For a more expansive and detailed discussion of the main debates, see Coombs (1985), Cookson (1991, 1992) and Clune and Witte (1990)

8. Channel One is a commercially sponsored and produced television program where students watch short segments of national and international news, punctuated by commercial spots by business sponsors. For a penetrating critique of the implications of commercial supported material being entered into school curriculum, see Apple (1993).

9. Investigating parents' and students' attitudes toward public schools of choice, Driscoll (1992) found that parents and students felt that they had fulfilling school experiences, in large part due to the fact that they believed that the school they attended was more selective. Commenting on this study, Cookson (1994) observes that parents surround the private school with a qualitative specialness simply because the school they are choosing has control over who it selects for enrollment.

10. I borrow this play on language from Fine (1993).

11. It is worth speculating that Best Academy school officials are apprehensive about the introduction of parents new to private schooling because they are invested in preserving class privilege and keeping the lines between public and private education hard and clear.

12. This is not to overlook the fact that private schools also have tracking systems that sort and select students. Cookson (1994) notes that the simple fact that a student attends a private school can protect average or below-average achieving students from downward educational mobility.

13. There exists a wide and growing body of literature on the experiences of first generation immigrant families with schooling in the United States. Mrs. Rodriguez's attitudes toward the school are inflected by her immigrant status. Her narrative at this point in the discussion is instructive for understanding what the private school represents for immigrant and first generation ethnic groups who have been a representative population in private, parochial schools.

14. Cookson (1994) finds the "crisis" label attached to assessments of school culture in the United States problematic, particularly since there are sufficient questions around research designs and data analysis to be able to argue conclusively for a "crisis" in the American education system proposed by proponents of educational reform in the 1980s. Assessments based on national trends tend to obscure positive developments in public elementary and secondary schools. National reports are more inclined to focus on national trends rather than small-scale developments.

15. Studies conducted outside of the United States measuring girls' achievement in single-sex schools as opposed to students in co-educational settings have found that students in girls' schools outperformed girls in co-educational schools (Carpenter and Hayden, 1987; Jimenez and Lockheed, 1989).

16. Feminists differ in the positions they take in support of single-sex education. Liberal feminists argue that girls do not achieve at levels that are comparable to boys academic performance in co-educational settings because existing curricular forms and school practices do not favor equal educational opportunities. Radical feminists, on the other hand, contend that unequal power relationships traceable to patriarchal systems of domination are responsible for lower levels of achievement among girls as compared with boys in mixed-sex schools.

17. Historically, co-education was endorsed by its proponents as a way to prevent any urge toward homosexuality, seen as unnatural. Since heterosexuality was defined as the norm, educating girls and boys together in school supported the most natural sexual arrangement. On this point, see Brehony (1984).

Chapter 7

1. Unlimited time and funding significantly influence time able to be spent in the field, with implications for the breadth and depth of data that is collected. Had I not faced these limitations, common in the experience of most field researchers, I might have tracked this student cohort from the beginning of the junior year up through the end of their senior year. This might have illuminated issues that could have helped further my understanding of emergent categories of girls' experiences in a

single-sex school. While this research was not framed this way, it does suggest the need for longitudinal studies that track development and change over time, not so much to arrive at conclusions that can be transferred and applied from one ethnography to another, but, rather, to be able to develop a deeper understanding of the complexities of youth identity production in school as they play themselves out over time.

2. Studies of sexual harrassment of women have looked closely at women's victimization in the work place and in higher education. Girls' "going public" about their experiences of harassment in school have recently been the focus of media attention. A recent study conducted by the American Association of University Women (1993) documents significant percentages of girls experiencing sexual harassment in school.

3. A recent body of literature has begun to explore forms of resistance within girls' subcultures across racial and class lines. For amplification of this potent body of work, see Fine (1992), Fordham (1993), Leadbeater and Way (1996), and Brown (1996).

Appendix

1. I am indebted to Sandra Jackson and Jose Solis for their articulation of the need to move beyond the comfort zone in critical multicultural discourse.

2. Qualitative researchers have responded to the charge, generally lodged by the quantitative research community, that qualitative research has limited external validity, by redefining the construct of generalizability as it has been traditionally understood in positivist research frameworks so that it fits the assumptions of naturalistic inquiry. For further discussion of alternative definitions of generalizability in qualitative research, see Goetz and LeCompte (1984); Lincoln and Guba (1985); Stake (1978, 1986); Wolcott (1990).

3. Gatekeepers and informants are distrusting of researchers who have conventionally exploited the research-researched relationship, gathering information in the field for self-interested purposes without fully integrating researched participants in more democratic ways into the research process.

4. Since 1992–93, the student population has declined due to increases in tuition costs. One year later, the student population numbered one hundred.

5. The SAT [Standardized Achievement Test] and the ACT [American Collegiate Test] are first taken in the junior year. These tests are required as part of the admissions process to competitive, four-year colleges and universities.

6. I am not making an essentialist argument that women are by nature better suited to undertaking research on women. I argue, though, that this facilitates access but does not necessarily lead to insider status across multiple dimensions. For an instructive discussion and analysis of the limits of shared subjectivity, see Foster (1994).

7. "Studying down" represents the power relationship that has defined traditional approaches to qualitative inquiry. Postcolonial feminist scholars and feminist field researchers have actively questioned inequities structuring top-down approaches, arguing for more democratic research designs based on epistemological assumptions that knowledge is mutually informative, co-constructed and co-produced in the research encounter. For further discussion, see Lather (1988), Reinharz (1992), Wolf (1996), and Bloom (1997).

8. Focus group interview protocol was derived from salient themes that began to emerge in initial interviews with students. Issues warranting further exploration were targeted and explored in greater depth in the context of these group meetings.

9. A variation of this protocol was used to interview administrative and staff personnel.

10. This information sheet is adapted from Raissiguier (1994).

References

Aggleton, P. (1987). *Rebels without a cause: Middle class youth and the transition from school to work*. London: Falmer Press.

Aggleton, P., & Whitty, G. (1985). Rebels without a cause? Socialization and subcultural style among the children of the new middle class. *Sociology of Education*, 58, 60–72.

Alcoff, L. (1989). Cultural feminism versus post-structuralism: The identity crisis in feminist theory. In M. Malson, J. O'Barr, S. Westphal-Wihl & M. Wyer (Eds.), *Feminist theory in practice and process*. Chicago: University of Chicago Press.

Almquist, E., Angrist, S., & Mickelsen, R. (1980). Women's career aspirations and achievements: College and seven years later. *Sociology of Work and Occupations*, 7, 3, 367–384.

Anderson, G. (1989). Critical ethnography in education: Origins, current status and new directions. *Review of Educational Research*, 59, 3, 249–270.

Anderson, K., Armitage, S., Jack, D., & Wittner, J. (1987). Beginning where we are: Feminist methodology in oral history. *Oral History Review*, 15, 103–127.

Anyon, J. (1979). Ideology and United States history textbooks. *Harvard Educational Review*, 49, 3, 361–386.

———. (1980). Social class and the hidden curriculum of work. *Journal of Education*, 162, 1, 67–92.

———. (1981). Elementary schooling and distinctions of social class. *Interchange*, 12, 2–3, 18–32.

———. (1981). Social class and school knowledge. *Curriculum Inquiry*, 11, 1, 3–42.

———. (1984). Intersections of gender and class: Accommodation and resistance by working-class and affluent females to contradictory sex role ideologies. *Journal of Education*, 166, 1, 25–48.

Anzaldua, G. (1987). *Borderlands/La frontera*. San Francisco: Aunt Lute Book Company.

Apple, M. (1982). *Cultural and economic reproduction in education: Essays on class, ideology and the state*. London: Routledge & Kegan Paul.

————. (1982). *Education and Power*. London: Routledge & Kegan Paul.

————. (1983). Curricular form and the logic of technical control. In M. Apple and L. Weis (Eds.), *Ideology and practice in schooling*. Philadelphia: Temple University Press.

Arnold, K. (1995). *Lives of promise: What becomes of high school valedictorians*. San Francisco, CA: Jossey-Bass Publishers.

Arnot, M. (1982). Male hegemony, social class and women's education. *Journal of Education*, 164, 1, 64–89.

Aronowitz, S. (1992). *The politics of identity: Class, culture, social movements*. New York: Routledge, Chapman & Hall, Inc.

Aronowitz, S., & Giroux, H. (1991). *Postmodern education: Politics, culture, & social criticism*. Minneapolis: University of Minnesota Press.

Baker, C. (1982). The adolescent as theorist: An interpretive view. *Journal of Youth and Adolescence*, 11, 3, 167–181.

————. (1983). A 'second look' at interviews with adolescents. *Journal of Youth and Adolescence*, 12, 6, 501–519.

Balsamo, A. (1990). Rethinking ethnography: A work for the feminist imagination. *Studies in symbolic interaction*, 11, 45–57.

Banks, J. (1993). The canon debate, knowledge construction, and multicultural education. *Educational Researcher*, 22, 5, 4–14.

Barton, L., Meighan, R., & Walker, S. (Eds.). (1980). *Schooling, ideology and the curriculum*. Lewes: Falmer Press.

Belenky, M., Clinchy, B., Goldberger, N., & Tarule, J. (1986). *Women's ways of knowing: The development of self, voice, and mind*. New York: Basic Books.

Bellah, R. (1985). *Habits of the heart: Individualism and commitment in American life*. Berkeley: University of California Press.

Bennett, K., & LeCompte, M. (1990). *The way schools work: A sociological analysis of education*. New York: Longman.

Bernstein, B. (1977). *Class, codes and control: Towards a theory of educational transmission*, Vol. 3. London: Routledge & Kegan Paul.

Bicknell, R. S. (1979). *Self-concept and sex-role attitudes among single-sex and coeducational, independent, residential secondary school students*, Ph.D. diss., University of Massachusetts.

Biklen, S., & Pollard, D. (Eds.). (1993). *Gender and education: Ninety-second yearbook of the national society for the study of education*. Chicago: University of Chicago Press.

Bleier, R. (Eds.). (1985). *Feminist approaches to science*. New York: Pergamon Press, Inc.

Bloch, R. (1978). Untangling the roots of modern sex roles: A survey of four centuries of change. *Signs: Journal of Women in Culture and Society*, 4, 237–268.

Bloom, L. R. (1997). Locked in uneasy sisterhood: Reflections on feminist methodology and research relations. *Anthropology & Education Quarterly*, 28, 1, 111–122.

Bluestone, B., & Harrison, B. *The deindustrialization of America: Plant closings, community abandonment, and the dismantling of basic industry*. New York: Basic Books, 1982.

Bogdan, R., & Biklen, S. (1982). *Qualitative research for education: An introduction to theory and methods*. Boston: Allyn & Bacon, Inc.

Bolotin, S. (1982). Voices from the postfeminist generation, *New York Times Magazine*, 17 October, 28-31, 101–117.

Borman, K., Le Compte, M., & Goetz, J. (1986). Ethnographic and qualitative research design and why it doesn't work. *American Behavioral Scientist*, 30, 1, 42–57.

Boston, T. (1988). *Race, class and conservatism*. Boston: George Allen & Unwin.

Bourdieu, P. (1974). The school as a conservative force: Scholastic and cultural inequalities. In J. Eggleton (Ed.). *Contemporary research in the sociology of education*. London: Methuen and Company, Ltd.

Bourdieu, P., & Passeron, C. (1977). *Reproduction in education, society and culture*. London: Sage.

Bowles, S., & Gintis, H. (1976). *Schooling in capitalist America*. New York: Basic Books.

Boyte, H.C., & Evans, S. M. (1992). *Free spaces: The sources of democratic change in America*. Chicago: University of Chicago Press.

Bradbury, K. (1986). The shrinking middle class. *New England Economic Review*, 41–55.

Brake, M. (1980). *The sociology of youth culture and youth subcultures*. London: Routledge & Kegan Paul.

Brantlinger, E. (1985). What low-income parents want from schools: A different view of aspirations, *Interchange*, 16, 4, 14–28.

———. (1993). *The politics of social class in secondary school: views of affluent and impoverished youth*. New York: Teachers College Press.

Brantlinger, E., Majd-Jabbari, M., & Guskin, S. Self-interest and liberal educational discourse: How ideology works for middle-class mothers. *American Educational Research Journal, 33*, 3, 571–597.

Brehony, K. (1984). Co-education: Perspectives and debates in the early twentieth century. In R. Deem (Ed.), *Co-education reconsidered.* London: Open University Press.

Brint, S. (1994). *In an age of experts: The changing role of professionals in politics and public life.* Princeton: Princeton University Press.

Broad, D. (1986). *Upper class cohesion: The Nichols School of Buffalo, 1892–1977.* Ph.D. diss., State University of New York at Buffalo.

Brown, L. (1996). Educating the resistance. *High School Journal, 79*, 3, 221–229.

Bryk, A., & Driscoll, M. (1988). *The high school as community: Contextual influences and consequences for students and teachers.* National Center on Effective Secondary Schools.

Burgess, R. (1991). Sponsors, gatekeepers, members and friends: Access in educational settings. In W. Shaffir & R. Stebbins (Eds.), *Experiencing fieldwork: An inside view of qualitative research.* Newbury Park: Sage.

Burke, P. (1989). Gender, identity, sex, and school performance. *Social Psychology Quarterly, 52*, 2, 159–169.

Cairns, E. (1990). The relationship between adolescent perceived self-competence and attendance at single-sex secondary school. *British Journal of Educational Psychology, 60*, 207–211.

Canaan, J. (1991). Passing notes and telling jokes: Gendered strategies among American middle class teenagers. In F. Ginsburg & A. Tsing (Eds.), *Uncertain terms: negotiating gender in American culture.* Boston: Beacon Press.

Carger, C. (1996). *Of Borders and dreams: A Mexican-American experience of urban education.* New York: Teachers College Press.

Carpenter, P., & Hayden, M. (1987). Girls' academic achievements: Single-sex versus coeducational schools in Australia. *Sociology of Education, 60*, 156–167.

Chang, H. (1992). *Adolescent life and ethos: An ethnography of a US high school.* London: Falmer Press.

Christman, J. (1988). Working in the field as the female friend. *Anthropology & Education Quarterly, 19*, 2, 70–85.

Chubb, J., & Moe, T. (1990). *Politics, markets, and America's schools.* Washington, DC: Brookings Institution.

Cibulka, J. (1989). Rationales for private schools: A commentary. In W. Boyd & J. Cibulka (Eds.), *Private schools and public policy: International perspectives.* London: Falmer Press.

Clarricoates, K. (1981). The experience of patriarchal schooling. *Interchange*, 12, 2–3, 185–205.

Clifford, J., & Marcus, G. (1986). *Writing culture: The poetics and politics of ethnography.* Berkeley: University of California Press.

Clune, W. H., & Witte, J. (Eds.). (1990). *Choice and control in American education, Vol. 2: The practice of choice, decentralization and school restructuring.* New York: Falmer Press.

Code, L. (1991). *What can she know?: Feminist theory and the construction of knowledge.* Ithaca: Cornell University Press.

Cohen, J. (1993). Constructing race at an urban high school: In their minds, their mouths, their hearts. In L. Weis & M. Fine (Eds.). *Beyond silenced voices: Class, race and gender in United States schools.* Albany: State University of New York Press, 1993.

Coleman, J. (1961). *The adolescent society.* New York: Free Press.

Coleman, J., & Hoffer, T. (1987). *Public and private schools: The impact of communities.* New York: Basic Books.

Coleman, J., Hoffer, T., & Kilgore, S. (1982). *Public, catholic and private schools compared.* New York: Basic Books.

———. (1991). Public, catholic, single-sex, and catholic coeducational high schools: Their effects on achievement, affect, and behaviors. *American Journal of Education*, 99, 3, 320–356.

Conforti, J. (1992). The legitimation of inequality in American education. *The Urban Review*, 24, 4, 227–238.

Connell, R. (1987). *Gender and power: society, the person and sexual politics.* Sydney: George Allen & Unwin.

Connell, R., Dowsett, G., Kessler, S., & Ashenden, D. (1981). Class and gender dynamics in a ruling-class school. *Interchange*, 12, 2–3, 102–117.

———. (1982). *Making the difference: Schools, families and social division.* Sydney: George Allen & Unwin.

Cookson, P. (Ed.). (1992). *The choice controversy.* Newbury: Corwin.

Cookson, P. (1991). Race and class in America's elite preparatory boarding schools: African Americans as the 'outsiders within'. *Journal of Negro Education*, 60, 2, 219–228.

Cookson, P. (1994). *School choice: The struggle for the soul of American education.* New Haven: Yale University.

Cookson, P., & Persell, C. (1985). *Preparing for power: America's elite boarding schools.* New York: Basic Books.

Coombs, P. (1985). *The world crisis in education: The view from the eighties.* New York: Oxford University Press.

Cooper, B. (1984). The changing demography of private schools: Trends and implications. *Education and Urban Society,* 16, 4, 429–442.

Cooper, B., & Dondero, G. (1991). Survival, change, and demands on America's private schools: Trends and policies. *Educational Foundations,* 5, 1, 51–74.

Cornbleth, C. (1990). *Curriculum in context.* New York: Falmer Press.

David, M. (1993). Parents, gender, and education. *Educational Policy,* 7, 184–205.

Davidson, A.L. (1996). *Making and molding identity in schools: Student narratives on race, gender, and academic achievement.* Albany: State University of New York Press.

Davidson, N. (1988). *The failure of feminism.* New York: Prometheus Books.

Davies, L. (1983). Gender, resistance and power. In S. Walker & L. Barton (Eds.), *Gender, class and education.* Barcombe: Falmer Press.

Deal, T. (1991). Private schools: Bridging Mr. Chips and my captain. *Teachers College Record,* 92, 3, 415–424.

Deem, R. (1978). *Women and schooling.* London: Routledge & Kegan Paul.

Deem, R. (Ed.). (1980). *Schooling for women's work.* London: Routledge & Kegan Paul.

Delamont, S. (1989). *Knowledgeable women: Structuralism and the reproduction of elites.* London: Routledge.

de Lauretis, T. (Ed.). (1986). *Feminist studies/critical studies.* Bloomington: Indiana University Press.

Delmar, R. (1994). What is feminism? In A. Herrmann & A. Stewart, (Eds.). *Theorizing feminism: Parallel trends in the humanities and social sciences.* Boulder: Westview Press.

Delpit, L. (1993). The silenced dialogue: Power and pedagogy in educating other people's children. In L. Weis & M. Fine (Eds.), *Beyond silenced voices: Class, race, and gender in United States schools.* Albany: State University of New York Press.

De Mott, B. (1993). *The imperial middle: Why Americans can't think straight about class.* New Haven: Yale University Press.

Denzin, N., & Lincoln, Y. (Eds.). (1994). *Handbook of qualitative research.* CA: Sage.

DeVault, M. (1990). Talking and listening from women's standpoint: Feminist strategies for interviewing and analysis. *Social Problems,* 37, 1, 96–116.

Domhoff, G. (1967). *Who rules America?* New Jersey: Prentice-Hall, Inc.

Driscoll, M. (1992). *Changing minds and changing hearts: Choice, achievement and school community*. Paper delivered at "Choice: What role in American education?" Sponsored by the Economic Policy Institute, Washington, D.C.

Du Bois, W.E.B. (1989). *The souls of black folk*. New York: Bantam, 1989.

Dyer, R. (1988). White. *Screen*, 29, 4, 44–64.

Eckert, P. (1989). *Jocks & burnouts: Social categories and identity in the high school*. New York: Teachers College Press.

Eder, D. (1985). The cycle of popularity: Interpersonal relations among female adolescents. *Sociology of Education*, 58, 154–165.

Eder, D., & Parker, S. (1987). The cultural production and reproduction of gender: The effect of extracurricular activities on peer-group culture. *Sociology of Education*, 60, 200–213.

Ehrenreich, B. (1989). *Fear of falling: The inner life of the middle class*. New York: Pantheon Books.

Eisenstein, Z. (1979). *Capitalist patriarchy and the case for socialist feminism*. New York: Monthly Review Press.

Ellsworth, E. (1992). Why doesn't this feel empowering? Working through the repressive myths of critical pedagogy. In C. Luke & J. Gore (Eds.), *Feminisms and critical pedagogy*. New York: Routledge.

Ely, M., Anzul, M., Friedman, T., Garner, D., & Steinmetz, A. (1991). *Doing qualitative research: Circles within circles*. New York: Falmer Press.

Epstein J.L., & Karweit, N. (1983). *Friends in school: Patterns of selection and influence in secondary schools*. New York: Academic Press.

Esman, A. (1990). *Adolescence and culture*. New York: Columbia University Press.

Esty, Jr., J. (1991). Independent schools: What, whither, and why. *Teachers College Record*, 92, 3, 485–490.

Faludi, S. (1991). *Backlash: The undeclared war against American women*. New York: Doubleday.

Farber, P., Provenzo, Jr., E., & Holm, G. (Eds.). (1994). *Schooling in the light of popular culture*. Albany: State University of New York Press.

Ferree, M. (1984). Sacrifice, satisfaction, and social change: Employment and the family. In K. Sacks & D. Remy (Eds.), *My troubles are going to have trouble with me*. New Jersey: Rutgers University Press.

Finch, J. (1984). 'It's great to have someone to talk to': The ethics and politics of interviewing women. In C. Bell & H. Roberts (Eds.), *Social researching: Politics, problems, practice*. London: Routledge & Kegan Paul.

Fine, M. (1992). *Disruptive voices: The possibilities of feminist research.* Ann Arbor: University of Michigan Press.

Fine, M. (1993). [Ap]parent involvement. *Equity and Choice, 9*, 3, 4–8.

Fine, M. (1994). Working the hyphens: Reinventing self and other in qualitative research. In N. Denzin & Y. Lincoln (Eds.), *Handbook of qualitative research.* California: Sage Publications, Inc.

Fine, M., Weis, L., & Addelston, J. (1994). What does it mean to be white? The construction of whiteness and masculinity. Mimeo.

Fine, M., Weis, L., Powell, L., & Wong, L. Mun. (1997). *Off white: Readings on race, power, and society.* New York: Routledge.

Finn, J., Dulberg, L., & Reis, J. (1979). Sex differences in educational attainment. A cross-national perspective. *Harvard Educational Review, 49*, 477–503.

Finn, J. (1980). Sex differences in educational outcomes: A cross-national study. *Sex Roles, 6*, 1, 9–26.

Flax, J. Postmodernism and gender relations in feminist theory. In R. Malson et al. (Eds.), *Feminist theory in practice and process.* Chicago: University of Chicago Press.

Fonow, M., & Cook, J. (Eds.). (1991). *Beyond methodology: Feminist scholarship as lived research.* Bloomington: Indiana University Press.

Foon, A. (1988). The relationship between school type and adolescent self-esteem, attribution styles, and affiliation needs: Implications for educational outcomes. *British Journal of Educational Psychology, 58*, 44–54.

Fordham, S. (1988). Racelessness as a factor in black students' school success: Pragmatic strategy or pyrrhic victory? *Harvard Educational Review, 59*, 1, 54–84.

———. (1993). "Those loud black girls": (Black) women, silence, and gender passing" in the academy. *Anthropology & Education Quarterly, 24*, 1, 3–32.

Fordham, S., & Ogbu, J. (1986). Black students' school success: Coping with the 'burden of acting white'. *Urban Review, 18*, 176–206.

Foster, M. (1994). The power to know one thing is never the power to know all things: Methodological notes on two studies of black American teachers. In A. Gitlin (Ed.), *Power and method: Political activism and educational research.* New York: Routledge.

Foucault, M. (1972). *The archaeology of knowledge and the discourse on language.* New York: Pantheon Books.

———. (1980). *Power/knowledge: Selected interviews & other writings. 1972–1977.* New York: Pantheon Books.

Fox-Genovese, E. (1996). *"Feminism is not the story of my life".* New York: Anchor Books.

Fox-Keller, E. (1985). *Reflections on gender and science*. New Haven: Yale University Press.

Frankenberg, R. (1993). *White women, race matters: The social construction of whiteness*. Minneapolis: University of Minnesota Press.

Frazer, E. (1993). Talk about class in a girls' public school. In G. Walford (Ed.), *The private schooling of girls: Past and present*. England: The Wobrun Press.

Frye, M. (1992). *Willful virgin: Essays on feminism*. Freedom: The Crossing Press.

Fuller, M. (1980). Black girls in a London comprehensive school. In R. Deem (Ed.), *Schooling for women's work*. London: Routledge & Kegan Paul.

Gallagher, C. (1994). White reconstruction in the university. *Socialist Review, 1–2*, 165–187.

Ganguly, K. (1991). Ethnography, representation and the reproduction of colonialist discourse. *Studies in Symbolic Interaction, 11*, 69–79.

Gaskell, J. (1985). Course enrollment in the high school: The perspective of working-class females. *Sociology of Education, 58*, 48–59.

———. (1992). *Gender matters from school to work*. Buckingham: Open University Press.

Gatlin, R. (1987). *American women since 1945*. Jackson: University Press of Mississippi.

Geertz, C. (1973). *The interpretation of cultures: Selected essays*. New York: Basic Books.

Gilbert, P., & Taylor, S. (1991). *Fashioning the feminine: Girls, popular culture and schooling*. North Sydney: George Allen & Unwin.

Gilligan, C. (1992). *In a different voice: Psychological theory and women's development*. Cambridge: Harvard University Press.

Gilligan, C., Lyons, N., & Hanmer, T. (1990). *Making connections: The relational worlds of adolescent girls at Emma Willard School*. Cambridge: Harvard University Press.

Giroux, H. (1981). *Ideology, culture, and the process of schooling*. Philadelphia: Temple University Press.

———. (1983). Theories of reproduction and resistance in the new sociology of education: A critical analysis. *Harvard Educational Review, 53, 3*, 257–293.

———. (1988). *Teachers as intellectuals: Toward a critical pedagogy of learning*. South Hadley: Bergin & Garvey.

———. (Ed.). (1991). *Postmodernism, feminism, and cultural politics: Redrawing educational boundaries*. Albany: State University of New York Press.

———. (1992). Resisting difference: Cultural studies and the discourse of critical pedagogy. In L. Grossberg, C. Nelson & P. Treichler (Eds.), *Cultural Studies*. New York: Routledge.

Gitlin, A. (Ed.). (1994). *Power and method: Political activism and educational research.* New York: Routledge.

Gluck, S., & Patai, D. (Eds.). (1991). *Women's words: The feminist practice of oral history.* New York: Routledge.

Goetz, J.P., & LeCompte, M.D. (1984). *Ethnography and qualitative design in education research.* Orlando: Academic Press.

Goldberg, D. T. (1993). *Racist culture: Philosophy and the politics of meaning.* London: Basil Blackwell.

Goffman, E. (1990). *Asylums: Essays on the social situation of mental patients and other inmates.* New York: Doubleday.

Granfield, R. (1991). Making it by faking it: Working-class students in an elite academic environment. *Journal of Contemporary Ethnography, 20, 3, 331–351.*

Grant, L. (1992). Race and the schooling of young girls. In J. Wrigley (Ed.), *Education and gender equality.* London: Falmer Press.

Griffin, C. (1985). *Typical girls? Young women from schools to the job market.* London: Routledge & Kegan Paul.

———. (1989). 'I'm not a women's libber, but . . .': Feminism, consciousness and identity. In S. Skevington & D. Baker (Eds.). *The social identity of women.* Newbury Park: Sage.

Grossberg, L. (1996). Identity and cultural studies: Is that all there is? In S. Hall & P. du Gay. *Questions of cultural identity.* London: Sage.

Grossberg, L, Nelson, C., & Treichler, P. (1992). *Cultural studies.* New York: Routledge.

Guba, E.G., & Lincoln, Y.S. (1981). *Effective evaluation: Improving the usefulness of evaluation results through responsive and naturalistic approaches.* San Franciso: Jossey-Bass.

———. (1982). Epistemological and methodological bases of naturalistic inquiry. *Educational Communication and Technology Journal, 30, 233–252.*

Hall, S. (1991). Ethnicity: identity and difference. *Radical America, 23, 4, 9–20.*

Hall, S., & du Gay, P. (Eds.). (1996). *Questions of cultural identity.* London: Sage.

Hall, S., & Jefferson, T. (Eds.). (1976). *Resistance through ritual: Youth subcultures in post-war Britain.* Birmingham: Center for Contemporary Cultural Studies.

Halle, D. (1984). *Work, home, and politics among blue-collar property owners.* Chicago: University of Chicago Press.

Hannaway, J., & Abramowitz, S. (1985). Public and private schools: Are they really different?. In G. Austin & H. Garger (Eds.). *Research on exemplary schools.* Orlando: Academic Press.

Haraway, D. (1988). Situated knowledge: The science question in feminism and the privilege of partial perspective. *Feminist Studies*, 14, 3, 575–599.

Harding, S. (1985). *The science question in feminism*. Ithaca: Cornell University Press.

———. (1986). The instability of the analytical categories of feminist theory. *Signs: Journal of Women in Culture and Society*, 11, 4, 645–664.

———. (1987). *Feminism and methodology*. Bloomington: Indiana University Press.

———. (1991). *Whose science? Whose knowledge?: Thinking from women's lives*. Ithaca: Cornell University Press.

———. (1994). Thinking from the perspective of lesbian lives. In A. Herrmann & A. Stewart (Eds.), *Theorizing feminism: Parallel trends in the humanities and social sciences*. Boulder: Westview Press.

Harding, S., & Hintikka, M. (Eds.). (1983). *Discovering reality: Feminist perspectives on epistemology, metaphysics, methodology, and philosophy of science*. London: D. Reidel Publishing Co.

Harvey, D. (1992). *The condition of modernity: An inquiry into the origins of cultural change*. Cambridge: Blackwell Publishers.

Haug, F. (1986). *Female sexualization: A collective work of memory*. London: Verso.

Haymes, S. (1995). White culture and the politics of racial difference: Implications for multiculturalism. In C. Sleeter & P. McLaren (Eds.). *Multicultural education, critical pedagogy, and the politics of difference*. Albany: State University of New York Press.

Hebdige, D. (1979). *Subculture: The meaning of style*. London: Methuen.

Hemmings, A. (1996). Conflicting images? Being black and a model high school student. *Anthropology & Education Quarterly*, 27, 1, 20–50.

Henry, M. (1993). *School cultures: Universes of meaning in private schools*. Norwood: Ablex Publishing Corporation.

Herek, G., & Berrill, K. (Eds.). (1992). *Hate crimes: Confronting violence against lesbian and gay men*. CA: Sage.

Hicks, E. (1988). Deterritorialization and border writing. In R. Merrill (Ed.), *Ethics/ aesthetics: Post-modern positions*. Washington, DC: Maissoneuve Press.

Hoffman, D. (1996). Culture and self in multicultural education: Reflections on discourse, text, and practice. *American Educational Research Journal*, 33, 3, 545–569.

Holland, D., & Eisenhart, M. (Eds.). (1990). *Educated in romance: Women, achievement, and college culture*. Chicago: University of Chicago Press.

Hollway, W. (1984). Gender difference and the production of subjectivity. In J. Henriques, W. Hollway, C. Urwin et al. (Eds.), *Changing the subject: Psychology, social regulation and subjectivity*. London: Methuen & Co., Ltd.

hooks, bell. (1992). *Black looks: Race and representation*. Boston: South End Press.

————. (1984). *Feminist theory: From margin to center*. Boston: South End Press.

————. (1989). *Talking back: Thinking feminist, thinking black*. Boston: South End Press.

————. (1990). *Yearning: Race, gender, and cultural politics*. Boston: South End Press.

Horowitz, H. (1984). *Alma mater: Design and experience in the women's colleges from their nineteenth-century beginnings to the 1930s*. New York: Alfred A. Knopf.

Horowitz, R. (1986). Remaining an outsider: Membership as threat to research rapport. *Urban Life*, 14, 4, 409–430.

Hostile hallways: The AAUW survey on sexual harassment in America's schools. (1993). Washington, DC: American Association of University Women Educational Foundation.

How schools shortchange girls: The AAUW report, a study of major findings on girls and education. (1992). Washington, DC: American Association of University Women Educational Foundation and National Education Association.

Howe, C. (1992). *Political ideology and class formation: A study of the middle class*. Westport: Praeger.

Hull, G. (1984). Alice Dunbar-Nelson: A personal and literary perspective. In C. Archer, L. DeSalvo & S. Ruddick (Eds.), *Between women: Biographers, novelists, critics, teachers and artists*. Boston: Beacon Press.

Hunter, M. (1991). *The family experience: A reader in cultural diversity*. New York: Macmillan Publishing Company.

Hurtado, A., & Stewart, A. (1997). Through the looking glass: Implications of studying whiteness for feminist methods. In M. Fine, L. Weis, L. Powell, & L. Mun Wong (Eds.), *Off white: Readings on race, power, and society*. New York: Routledge.

Ilon, L. (1994). Structural adjustment and education: Adapting to a growing global market. *International Journal of Educational Development*, 14, 2, 95–108.

Jackson, S., & Solis, J. (Eds.). (1995). *Beyond comfort zones in multiculturalism: Confronting the politics of privilege*. Westport: Bergin & Garvey.

Jaggar, A. (1988). *Feminist politics and human nature*. London: Rowman & Littlefield Publishers, Inc.

James, T. (1987–88). Totality in private and public schooling. *American Journal of Education*, 96, 1–17.

James, T., & Levin, H. (1988). *Comparing public and private schools*. New York: Falmer Press.

Jimenez, E., & Lockheed, M. (1989). Enhancing girls' learning through single-sex education: Evidence and a policy conundrum. *Educational Evaluation and Policy Analysis*, 11, 2, 117–142.

Johnson, D., (ed.). (1982). *Class and social development: A new theory of the middle class*. New York: Sage.

Jones, A. (1993). Becoming a 'girl': post-structuralist suggestions for educational research. *Gender and Education*, 5, 2, 157–166.

Jones, J. (1990). Outcomes of girls' schooling: Unravelling some social differences. *Australian Journal of Education*, 34, 2, 153-167.

Jones, S. (1988). *Black culture, white youth: The reggae tradition from JA to UK*. London: Macmillan Education Ltd.

Kane, P. (1991). Independent schools in American education. *Teachers College Record*, 92, 3, 397–408.

———, (Ed.). (1992). *Independent schools, independent thinkers*. San Francisco: Jossey-Bass Publishers.

Kapferer, J. (1981). Socialization and the symbolic order of the school. *Anthropology & Education Quarterly*, 11, 3, 258–274.

Kelly, G., & Nihlen, A. (1982). Schooling and the reproduction of patriarchy: Unequal workloads, unequal rewards. In M. Apple (Ed.), *Cultural and economic reproduction in education: Essays on class, ideology and the state*. London: Routledge & Kegan Paul.

Keohane, N. (1990). Educating women students for the future. In J. Antler & S. Biklen (Eds.). *Changing education: Women as radicals and conservators*. Albany: State University of New York Press.

Kessler, S., et al. (1985). Gender relations in secondary school. *Sociology of Education*, 58, 1, 34–48.

Kidder, L., & Fine, M. (1987). Qualitative and quantitative methods: When stories converge. In M. Mark & R. L. Shotland (Eds.), *Multiple methods in program evaluation*. San Francisco: Jossey-Bass, Inc.

Kincheloe, J., & Steinberg, S. (Eds.). (1995). *Thirteen questions: Reframing education's conversation*. New York: Peter Lang Publishing, Inc.

King, D. (1989). Multiple jeopardy, multiple consciousness: The context of a Black feminist ideology. In M. Malson et al. (Eds.), *Feminist theory in practice and process*. Chicago: University of Chicago Press.

King, J. 1991. Unfinished business: Black student alienation and Black teachers' emancipatory pedagogy. In M. Foster (Ed.), *Readings on equal education*. New York: AMS Press.

Kingston, P., & Lewis, L. (Eds.). *The high status track: Studies of elite schools and stratification*. Albany: State University of New York Press.

Kohn, M. (1977). *Class and conformity: A study in values*, 2d ed. Chicago: University of Chicago Press.

Ladner, J. (1971). *Tomorrow's tomorrow: The black woman*. Garden City: Doubleday.

Laosa, L. M. (1982). School, occupation, culture and family: The impact of parental schooling on the parent-child relationship. *Journal of Educational Psychology*, 74, 6, 791–827.

Lareau, A. (1987). Social class differences in family-school relationships: The importance of cultural capital, *Sociology of Education*, 60, 73–85.

———. (1989). *Home advantage: Social class and parental intervention in elementary education*. New York: Falmer Press.

Lareau, A. & Shultz, J. (Eds.). (1996). *Journeys through ethnography: Realistic accounts of fieldwork*. Boulder: Westview Press.

Larkin, J. (1994). *Sexual harassment: High school girls speak out*. Toronto: Second Story Press.

Larkin, R. (1979). *Suburban youth in cultural crisis*. New York: Oxford University Press.

Lather, P. (1986). Research as praxis. *Harvard Educational Review*, 56, 3, 257–277.

———. (1988). Feminist perspectives on empowering research methodologies. *Women's Studies International Forum*, 11, 6, 569–581.

———. (1991). *Getting smart: feminist research and pedagogy with/in the postmodern*. New York: Routledge.

Leadbeater, B. & Way, N. (Eds.). (1996). *Urban girls: Resisting stereotypes, creating identities*. New York: New York University Press.

Leahy, T. (1994). Taking up a position: Discourses of femininity and adolescence in the context of man/girl relationships. *Gender & Society*, 8, 1, 48–71.

LeCompte, M., & Preissle, J. (1993). *Ethnography and qualitative design in educational research*, 2d ed. Academic Press, Inc.

Lee, S. (1996). *Unraveling the "model minority" stereotype: Listening to Asian American youth*. New York: Teachers College Press.

Lee, V.E., & Bryk, A. S. (1986). Effects of single-sex secondary schools on achievement and attitude. *Journal of Educational Psychology*, 78, 5, 381–395.

Lee, V. E., & Marks, H.M. (1990). Sustained effects of the single-sex secondary school experience on attitudes, behaviors and values in college. *Journal of Educational Psychology*, 82, 578–592.

———. (1992). Who goes where? Choice of single-sex and coeducational independent secondary schools. *Sociology of Education*, 65, 226–253.

Lees, S. (1986). *Losing out: Sexuality and adolescent girls*. London: Hutchinson.

Leigh, N. (1993). Regional change in middle class earnings and standards of living. *Growth and Change*, 24, 3–31.

Lerman, R., & Salzman, H. (1988). Deskilling and declassing: Whither the middle stratum. *Social Science and Public Policy*, 25, 6, 60–66.

Lesko, N. (1988). The curriculum of the body. In L. Roman, L. Christian-Smith, & E. Ellsworth (Eds.), *Becoming feminine: The politics of popular culture*. Lewes: Falmer Press.

———. (1988). *Symbolizing society: Stories, rites and structure in a catholic high school*. Lewes: Falmer Press.

Levin, H. (1989). Education as a public and private good. In N. Devins (Ed.), *Public values, private schools*. New York: Falmer Press.

Levinson, B., Foley, D., & Holland, D. (1996). *The cultural production of the educated person: Critical ethnographies of schooling and local practice*. Albany: State University of New York Press.

Lightfoot, S. (1983). *The good high school: Portraits of character and culture*. New York: Basic Books.

Lincoln, Y., & Guba, E. G. (1985). *Naturalistic inquiry*. Beverly Hills: Sage.

Lorde, A. (1984). *Sister outsider*. Freedom: The Crossing Press.

Luke, C. (Ed.). (1996). *Feminisms and pedagogies of everyday life*. Albany: State University of New York Press.

Luke, C., & Gore, J. (Eds.). (1992). *Feminisms and critical pedagogy*. New York: Routledge.

MacDonald, M. (1980). Schooling and the reproduction of class and gender relations. In L. Barton, R. Meighan, & S. Walker (Eds.), *Schooling, ideology and the curriculum*. Lewes: Falmer Press.

Machung, A. (1989). Talking career, thinking job: Gender differences in career and family expectations of Berkeley seniors. *Feminist Studies*, 15, 35–58.

MacLeod, J. (1995). *Ain't no makin' it: Aspirations and attainment in a low-income neighborhood*. Boulder: Westview Press.

Mahony, P. (1985). *Schools for the boys: Co-education reassessed*. London: Hutchinson.

Mann, J. (1996). *The Difference.* New York: Warner Books.

Mann, P. (1994). On the postfeminist frontier. *Socialist Review,* 1-2, 223–241.

Mascia-Lees, F., Sharpe, P., & Cohen, C. (1989). The postmodernist turn in anthropology: Cautions from a feminist perspective. *Signs: Journal of Women in Culture and Society,* 15, 1, 7–33.

Masemann, V. (1974). The 'hidden curriculum' of a West African girls' boarding school. *Canadian Journal of African Studies,* 8, 3, 479–494.

Mason, K., & Lu, Y. (1988). Attitudes toward women's familial roles: Changes in the United States, 1977–1985. *Gender & Society,* 2, 1, 39–57.

McCarthy, C. (1988). Marxist theories of education and the challenge of a cultural politics of non-synchrony. In L. Roman, et al. (Eds.), *Becoming feminine: The politics of popular culture.* Lewes: Falmer Press.

———. (1993). After the canon: Knowledge and ideological representation in the multicultural discourse of curriculum reform. In C. McCarthy & W. Crichlow (Eds.), *Race, identity and representation in education.* New York: Routledge.

McCarthy, C., Rodriguez, A., David, S., et al. (1994). Danger in the safety zone: Notes on race, resentment, and the discourse of crime, violence and suburban security. Mimeo.

McCarthy, C., & Apple, M. (1988). Race, class, and gender in American educational research: Toward a nonsynchronous parallelist position. In L. Weis (Ed.), *Class, race, & gender in American education.* Albany: State University of New York Press.

McEwen, C. (1980). Continuities in the study of total and nontotal institutions. *Annual Review of Sociology,* 6, 143–185.

McLaren, P. (1986). *Schooling as ritual performance.* London: Routledge & Kegan Paul.

———. (1991). Decentering cultures: Postmodernism, resistance, and critical pedagogy. In N. Wyner (Ed.), *Current perspectives on the culture of schools.* Cambridge: Brookline Books.

———. (1991). Field relations and the discourse of the other: Collaborations in our own ruin. In W. Shaffir & R. Stebbins (Eds.), *Experiencing fieldwork: An inside view of qualitative research.* Newbury Park: Sage.

———. (1994). White terror and oppositional agency: Towards a critical multiculturalism. In D. Goldberg (Ed.), *Multiculturalism: A critical reader.* Cambridge: Basil Blackwell.

———. (1995). White terror and oppositional agency: Towards a critical multiculturalism. In C. Sleeter & P. McLaren (Eds.), *Multicultural education, critical pedagogy, and the politics of difference.* Albany: State University of New York Press.

———. (1997). Unthinking whiteness, rethinking democracy: Or farewell to the blonde beast; towards a revolutionary multiculturalism. *Educational Foundations*, 11, 2, 5–39.

McNeil, L. (1983). Defensive teaching and classroom control. In M. Apple & L. Weis (Eds.). *Ideology and practice in schooling*. Philadelphia: Temple University Press.

McRobbie, A. (1982). The politics of feminist research: Between talk, text and action. *Feminist Review*, 12, 46–57.

———. (1991). *Feminism and youth culture: From Jackie to Just Seventeen*. Boston: Unwin Hyman.

McRobbie, A., & McCabe, T. (Eds.). (1981). *Feminism and girls: An adventure story*. London: Routledge & Kegan Paul.

McRobbie, A., & Nava, M. (Eds.). (1984). *Gender and generation*. London: Macmillan Publishers, Ltd.

Mendelsohn, J. (1990). The view from step number 16, girls from Emma Willard School talk about themselves and their futures. In C. Gilligan et al. (Eds.), *Making connections: The relational worlds of adolescent girls at Emma Willard School*. Cambridge: Harvard University Press.

Metz, M. (1983). What can be learned from educational ethnography? *Urban Education*, 17, 4, 391–418.

Mickelson, R. Why does Jane read and write so well? The anomaly of women's achievement. *Sociology of Education*, 62, 47–63.

Miles, M., & Huberman, A. (1993). *Qualitative data analysis: A sourcebook of new methods*. Newbury Park: Sage.

Min, M. (1991). *Relative effects of coeducation and single-sex schools on students' schooling, affection, and career choice: Exploring conventional and feminist perspectives*. Ph.D. diss., University of Illinois at Urbana-Champaign.

Mohanty, C. (1988). Under western eyes. Feminist scholarship and colonial discourses. *Feminist review*, 30, 60–88.

Mohanty, C. (1990). On race and voice: Challenges for liberal education in the 1990s. *Cultural Critique*, 179–208.

Morgan, D. (1988). *Focus groups as qualitative research*. Newbury Park: Sage Publications.

National association of independent schools statistics. (1993). Washington, DC: National Association of Independent Schools.

Nieto, S. (1995). From brown heroes and holidays to assimilationist agendas: Reconsidering the critiques of multicultural education. In C. Sleeter & P. McLaren, (Eds.), *Multicultural education, critical pedagogy, and the politics of difference*. Albany: State University of New York Press.

Newman, J. (1995). Comparing private schools and public schools in the 20th century: History, demography, and the debate over choice. *Educational Foundations*, 9, 3, 5–18.

Newman, K. (1989). *Falling from grace: The experience of downward mobility in the American middle class*. New York: Vintage Books.

———. (1993). *Declining fortunes: The withering of the American dream*. New York: Basic Books.

Nicholson, L. (Ed.). (1990). *Feminism/postmodernism*. New York: Routledge.

Noddings, N. (1988). An ethic of caring and its implications for instructional arrangements. *American Journal of Education*, 96, 2, 215–230.

Oakely, A. (1981). Interviewing women: A contradiction in terms. In H. Roberts (Ed.), *Doing feminist research*. London: Routledge & Kegan Paul.

Oakes, J. Tracking, inequality, and the rhetoric of reform: Why schools don't change. In H. S. Shapiro, & D. Purpel (Eds.), *Critical social issues in American education: Toward the 21st century*. New York: Longman.

Ogbu, J. (1988). Class stratification, racial stratification, and schooling. In L. Weis (Ed.), *Class, race, & gender in American education*. Albany: State University of New York Press.

Ogbu, J., & Fordham, S. (1986). Black students' school success: Coping with the "burden of 'acting white'". *The Urban Review*, 18, 3, 313–334.

Okely, J. (1978). Privileged, schooled and finished: Boarding education for girls. In S. Ardener (Ed.), *Defining females: The nature of women in society*. New York: John Wiley & Sons.

Olesen, V. (1994). Feminisms and models of qualitative research. In N. Denzin & Y. Lincoln (Eds.), *Handbook of qualitative research*. CA: Sage.

Omi, M., & Winant, H. (1994). *Racial formation in the United States*. 2d ed. New York: Routledge.

Ortner, S. (1991). Reading America: Preliminary notes on class and culture. In R. Fox (Ed.), *Recapturing anthropology: Working in the present*. Santa Fe: School of American Research Press.

Ostrander, S. (1980). Upper-class women: Class consciousness as conduct and meaning. In G. W. Domhoff (Ed.), *Power structure research*. Newbury Park: Sage.

———. (1980). Upper class women: The feminine side of privilege. *Qualitative Sociology*, 3, 1, 23–44.

———. (1984). *Women of the upper class*. Philadelphia: Temple University Press.

Parsons, T. (1959). The school class as a social system: Some of its functions in American society. *Harvard Educational Review*, 29, 4, 297–318.

Patai, D. (1991). U.S. academics and third world women: Is ethical research possible? In S. Gluck & D. Patai (Eds.), *Women's words: The feminist practice of oral history*. New York: Routledge.

Perry, D. (1987). The politics of dependency in deindustrializing America: The case of Buffalo, New York. In M. Smith & J. Feagin (Eds.), *The capitalist city: Global restructuring and community politics*. Basil Blackwell, 1987.

Perry, D., & McLean, B. (1991). The aftermath of deindustrialization. *Buffalo Law Review*, 39, 2, 345–383.

Perry, I. (1988). A black students' reflection on public and private schools. *Harvard Educational Review*, 58, 3, 332–336.

Persell, C. (1977). *Education and inequality*. New York: Free Press.

Pershkin, A. (1985). Virtuous subjectivity: In the participant observer's 'I's. In D. Berg & K. Smith (Eds.), *Exploring clinical methods for social research*. Beverly Hills: Sage.

Peshkin, A. (1991). *The color of strangers, the color of friends: The play of ethnicity in school and community*. Chicago: University of Chicago Press.

Peterson, W. (1994). *Silent depression: The fate of the American dream*. New York: W.W. Norton & Company.

Peterson's annual guide to independent secondary schools. (1993). Princeton: Peterson's Guide.

Phelan, P., & Davidson, A. (Eds.). (1993). *Renegotiating cultural diversity in American Schools*. New York: Teachers College Press.

Phelan, P., Davidson, A., & Cao, H. (1991). Students' multiple worlds: Negotiating the boundaries of family, peer, and school cultures. *Anthropology & Education Quarterly*, 22, 3, 224–250.

Phillips, K. (1993). *Boiling point: Republicans, democrats, and the decline of middle class prosperity*. New York: Random House.

Pipher, M. (1994). *Reviving Ophelia: Saving the selves of adolescent girls*. New York: Ballantine Books.

Powell, A. (1987). Private school responsibilities, private school rights. *Independent School*, 47, 1, 51–54.

Powell, A., Farrar, E., & Cohen, D. (1985). *The shopping mall high school: Winners and losers in the educational marketplace*. Boston: Houghton Mifflin.

Raissiguier, C. (1994). *Becoming women, Becoming workers: Identity formation in a French vocational school*. Albany: State University of New York Press.

Ravitch, D. (1991). Different drummers: The role of nonpublic schools in America today. *Teacher College Record*, 92, 3, 409–414.

Reich, R. (1992). *The work of nations: Preparing ourselves for the 21st century.* New York: Vintage Books.

Reinharz, S. (1992). *Feminist methods in social research.* New York: Oxford University Press.

Ribbens, J. (1989). Interviewing—an 'unnatural situation'? *Women's Studies International Forum, 12,* 6, 579–592.

Rich, A. (1980). Compulsory heterosexuality and lesbian existence. *Signs, 5,* 4, 631–660.

Richards, T., & Richards, L. (1994). Using computers in qualitative research. In N. Denzin & Y. Lincoln (Eds.), *Handbook of qualitative research.* Newbury: Sage.

Richardson, L. (1988). The collective story: Postmodernism and the writing of sociology. *Sociological Focus, 21,* 3, 199–208.

Riordan, C. (1985). Public and catholic schooling: The effects of gender context policy. *American Journal of Education, 23,* 518–540.

———. (1990). *Girls and boys in school: Together or separate?* New York: Teachers College Press.

Rist, R. (1977). On the relations among educational research paradigms: From disdain to detente. *Anthropology & Education Quarterly, 8,* 2, 29–42.

Roman, L. (1993). Double exposure: The politics of feminist materialist ethnography. *Educational Theory, 43,* 3, 279–308.

———. (1993). White is a color! White defensiveness, postmodernism, and anti-racist pedagogy. In C. McCarthy & W. Crichlow (Eds.), *Race, identity and representation in education.* New York: Routledge.

Roman, L., Christian-Smith, L., & Ellsworth, E. (Eds.). (1988). *Becoming feminine: The politics of popular culture.* Lewes: Falmer Press.

Rosaldo, R. (1993). *Culture & truth: The remaking of social analysis.* Boston: Beacon Press.

Rosenfelt, D., & Stacey, J. (1987). Review essay: Second thoughts on the second wave. *Feminist Studies, 13,* 2, 341–361.

Russell, S. (1986). The hidden curriculum of school: Reproducing gender and class hierarchies. In R. Hamilton & M. Barrett (Eds.), *The politics of diversity: feminism, marxism and nationalism.* Montreal: Book Center, Inc.

Ryan, B. (1992). *Feminism and the women's movement: Dynamics and change in social movement, ideology and activism.* New York: Routledge.

Sadker, M., & Sadker, D. (1994). *Failing at fairness: How America's schools cheat girls.* New York: Charles Scribner's Sons.

Sarup, M. (1996). *Identity, culture and the postmodern world.* Athens: The University of Georgia Press.

Scheurich, J. (1993). Toward a white discourse on white racism. *Educational Researcher*, 22, 8, 5–10.

Schofield, J. (1990). Increasing the generalizability of qualitative research. In E. Eisner & A. Peshkin (Eds.), *Qualitative inquiry in education: The continuing debate*. New York: Teachers College Press.

Scott, J. (1988). *Gender and the politics of history*. New York: Columbia University Press.

———. (1994). Deconstructing equality - versus - difference: Or, the uses of post-structuralist theory for feminism. In A. Herrmann & A. Stewart, (Eds.), *Theorizing feminism: Parallel trends in the humanities and social sciences*. Boulder: Westview Press.

Scott, E. & McCollum, H. (1993). Making it happen: Gender equitable classrooms. In S. Biklen & D. Pollard. (Eds.), *Gender and education*. Chicago: University of Chicago Press.

Seller, M., & Weis, L. (1997). *Beyond Black and White: New faces and voices in U.S. schools*. Albany: State University of New York Press.

Shaffir, W., & Stebbins, R. (Eds.). (1991). *Experiencing fieldwork: An inside view of qualitative research*. Newbury Park: Sage.

Shimahara, N. (1983). Polarized socialization in an urban high school. *Anthropology & Education Quarterly*, 14, 109–130.

Shujaa, M., (Ed.). (1994). *Too much schooling, too little education: A paradox of black life in white societies*. New Jersey: Africa World Press, Inc.

Shweder, R. (1991). *Thinking through cultures: Expeditions in cultural psychology*. Cambridge: Harvard University Press.

Sieber, R. T. (1982). The politics of middle-class success in an inner-city public school. *Journal of Education*, 164, 30–47.

Single-sex schooling: Perspectives from practice and research, I-II. (1993). Washington, DC: Office of Educational Research and Improvement, U.S. Department of Education.

Sleeter, C., & Grant, C. (1988). *Making choices for multicultural education: Five approaches to race, class, and gender*. Columbus: Merrill.

Sleeter, C. & McLaren, P. (Eds.). (1995). *Multicultural education, critical pedagogy, and the politics of difference*. Albany: State University of New York Press.

Smith, D. (1987). *The everyday world as problematic: A feminist sociology*. Boston: Northeastern University Press.

———. (1988). Femininity as discourse. In L. Roman et al. (Eds.), *Becoming feminine: The politics of popular culture*. London: The Falmer Press.

Solomon, B. (1985). *In the company of educated women: A history of women and higher education in America.* New Haven: Yale University Press.

Spelman, E. (1988). *Inessential woman: Problems of exclusion in feminist thought.* Boston: Beacon Press.

Spender, D. (1982). *Invisible women: The schooling scandal.* London: Writers and readers publishing cooperative.

Spring, J. (1996). *American Education.* New York: McGraw-Hill.

Stacey, J. (1991). *Brave new families: Stories of domestic upheaval in late twentieth century America.* New York: Basic Books.

———. (1991). Can there be a feminist ethnography? In S. Gluck & D. Patai (Eds.), *Women's words: The feminist practice of oral history.* New York: Routledge, Chapman & Hall, Inc.

Stake, R.E. (1978). The case-study method in social inquiry. *Educational Researcher, 7,* 5–8.

———. (1986). An evolutionary view of educational improvement. In E.R. House (Ed.), *New directions in educational evaluation.* London: Falmer Press.

Stanlaw, J., & Peshkin, A. (1988). Black visibility in a multi-ethnic high school. In L. Weis (Ed.), *Class, race, & gender in American education.* Albany: State University of New York Press.

Statistical abstracts of the United States. (1993). Washington, DC: United States Department of Commerce.

Strauss, A. (1987). *Qualitative analysis for social scientists.* NY: Cambridge University Press.

Strobel, F. (1993). *Upward dreams, downward mobility: The economic decline of the American middle class.* Maryland: Rowman & Littlefield Publishers, Inc.

Tesch, R. (1990). *Qualitative research: Analysis types and software tools.* NY: Falmer.

Thomas, C. (1980). *Girls and counter-school culture.* Melbourne Working Papers, Sociology Research Group in Culture and Educational Studies. Melbourne: University of Melbourne.

Thomas, J. (1993). *Doing critical ethnography.* Newbury Park: Sage Publications.

Thompson, B. & Tyagi, S. (1996). *Names we call home: Autobiography on racial identity.* New York: Routledge.

Thorne, B. (1993). *Gender play: Girls and boys in school.* New Brunswick: Rutgers University Press.

Tuana, N. (Ed.). (1989). *Feminism and science.* Bloomington: Indiana University Press.

Turner, P. (1984). *Campus: An American planning tradition.* Cambridge: The MIT Press.

Tyack, D., & Hansot, E. (1990). *Learning together: A history of coeducation in American schools*. New Haven: Yale University Press.

Ulichny, P., & Schoener, W. (1996). Teacher-researcher collaboration from two perspectives. *Harvard Educational Review*, 66, 3, 496–524.

Valdes, G. (1996). *Con respeto: Bridging the distances between culturally diverse families and schools*. New York: Teachers College Press.

Valli, L. (1988). Gender identity and the technology of office education. In L. Weis (Ed.), *Class, race, & gender in American education*. Albany: State University of New York Press.

Van Maanen, J. (1988). *Tales of the field: On writing ethnography*. Chicago: University of Chicago Press.

Van Maanen, J. (Ed.). (1995). *Representation in ethnography*. Thousand Oakes: Sage.

Varenne, H. (1981). Symbolizing American culture in schools. *Character*, 1–9.

Villenas, S. (1996). The colonizer/ colonized Chicana ethnographer: Identity, marginalization, and co-optation in the field. *Harvard Educational Review*, 66, 4, 711–731.

Walker, S., and Barton, L. (Eds.). (1983). *Gender, class & education*. Oxford: Falmer Press.

Weedon, C. (1987). *Feminist practice and poststructuralist theory*. New York: Basil Blackwell.

Weiler, K. (1988). *Women teaching for change: Gender, class & power*. South Hadley: Bergin & Garvey Publishers, Inc.

Weiler, K., & Mitchell, C. (1992). *What schools can do: Critical pedagogy and practice*. Albany: State University of New York Press.

Weinberg, I. (1968). Some methodological and field problems of social research in elite secondary schools. *Sociology of Education*, 141–155.

Weis, L. (1990). *Issues of disproportionality and social justice in tomorrow's schools: A symposium presented at the annual meeting of the AERA*. Buffalo: Graduate School of Education Publications.

———. (1990). *Working class without work: High school students in a de-industrializing economy*. New York: Routledge.

———. (1992). Reflections on the researcher in a multicultural environment. In C. Grant (Ed.), *Research and multicultural education: From the margins to the mainstream*. New York: Falmer Press.

Weis, L., & Fine, M. (Eds.). (1993). *Beyond silenced voices: Class, race, and gender in United States schools*. Albany: State University of New York Press.

Weis, L., Proweller, A., & Centrie, C. (1997). Re-examining "a moment in history": Loss of privilege inside white working-class masculinity in the 1990s. In M. Fine, L. Weis, L. Powell & L. Mun Wong (Eds.), *Off white: Readings on race, power, and society.* New York: Routledge.

Weitzman, L. (1985). *The divorce revolution: The unexpected social and economic consequences for women and children in America.* New York: Free Press.

Wellman, D. (1993). *Portraits of white racism.* 2d ed. Cambridge: Cambridge University Press.

Wellman, D. (1996). Red and black in white America: Discovering cross-border identites and other subversive activities. In B. Thompson & S. Tyagi, (Eds.), *Names we call home: Autobiography on racial identity.* New York: Routledge.

West, C., & Fenstermaker, S. (1995). Doing difference. *Gender & Society,* 9, 1, 8–37.

Wexler, P. (1988). Symbolic economy of identity and denial of labor: Studies in high school number 1. In L. Weis (Ed.), *Class, race, & gender in American education.* Albany: State University of New York Press.

———. (1992). *Becoming somebody: Toward a social psychology of school.* London: Falmer Press.

Whitty, G., & Young, M. (Eds.). (1977). *Explorations in the politics of school knowledge.* England: Nafferton Books.

Willis, P. *Learning to labor.* (1977). New York: Columbia University Press.

———. (1981). Cultural production is different from cultural reproduction is different from social reproduction is different from reproduction. *Interchange,* 12, 2–3, 48–67.

Willis, S., & Kenway, J. (1986). On overcoming sexism in schooling: To marginalize or mainstream. *Australian Journal of Education,* 30, 2, 132–149.

Wilson, Z. V. (1992). How independent is independent school curriculum? In P. Kane (Ed.), *Independent schools, independent thinkers.* San Francisco: Jossey-Bass Publishers.

Winchel, R., Fenner, D., & Shaver, P. (1974). Impact of coeducation on "fear of success": Imagery expressed by male and female high school students. *Journal of Educational Psychology,* 66, 5, 726–730.

Wolcott, H. (1990). On seeking—and rejecting—validity in qualitative research. In E. Eisner & A. Peshkin (Eds.), *Qualitative inquiry in education: The continuing debate.* New York: Teachers College Press.

———. (1995). Making a study "more ethnographic." In J. Van Maanen (Ed.), *Representation in Ethnography.* Thousand Oakes: Sage.

Wolf, Diane L. (1996). *Feminist dilemmas in fieldwork.* Boulder: Westview Press.

Woloch, N. (1984). *Women and the American experience*. New York: Alfred A. Knopf, Inc.

Wolpe, A. (1981). The official ideology of education for girls. In M. McDonald, R. Dale, G. Esland & R. Fergusson (Eds.), *Politics, patriarchy and practice*. Lewes: Falmer Press.

Yudice, G. (1993). Neither impugning nor disavowing whiteness do a viable politics make: The limits of identity politics. Mimeo.

Zweigenhaft, R., & Domhoff, G. W. (1991). *Blacks in the white establishment: A study of race and class in America*. New Haven: Yale University Press.

Index

the Other: delegitimizing, 106, 122; discourses of, 95; and identity, 62; and self, 62, 93; voices of, 211; and white privilege, 99, 112–118
Othering, 77, 81, 93, 200, 244n22
Otherness, 113; language of, 98–99

Parents: access to, 167; "consumer mentality" among, 168–170; demands on schools, 170–174; dual-career, 133, 169–170, 203; educational interests for children, 237n15; expectations of private schooling, 15, 165–196; incomes, 71; occupational status, 64, 67, 68; relationships with schools, 171; school choices, 179–183, 249n7; working-class, 165, 166
Patriarchy, 250n16; inequalities in, 153; norms of femininity in, 139, 156; and sexual division of labor, 7; structures of, 162; women's experiences of, 136
Peer group: borderwork in, 84; and class background, 67–69, 85–87; cohesion in, 67; culture, 3; differences in, 72–76; dynamics of, 200; formation, 243n11; legitimating function, 67; minority comfort with, 123; networks, 67, 68, 84, 87; racially mixed, 123; as safe space, 67; stratification, 243n11
Power: asymmetrical relations of, 104; class, 81; culture of, 114, 118; discourse of, 131; distribution, 5, 210; exercise of, 56; inequalities, 250n16; institutional, 65; markers of, 10; and multiculturalism, 61; reclamation of, 81; relationship to knowledge, 3; of social texts, 247n5; traditional forms of, 36; unequal allocations of, 4; white, 95, 109
Privilege, 24, 81, 119, 148; claiming benefits of, 83; class, 3, 15, 18, 26, 95, 146, 167, 177, 200; decentering, 93; deconstructing, 76; discourses of, 14; gender, 3; guarding, 127; heterosexual, 156; institutionalization of, 104, 112; invisibility of, 130, 244n22, 245n3; location of, 76, 101, 102; maintenance of, 56, 167; markers of, 10; and multiculturalism, 61; negotiating, 29; protection of, 83; race, 3, 104, 109, 112, 120, 126, 201, 244n1, 244n22; reproduction of, 26; social relations of, 100, 131; student blindness to, 81; transmission of, 18; whiteness as, 95, 96–118

Race, 1; and achievement, 128; border work in, 119, 122; and "color blindness," 128, 245n5; and color evasiveness, 100, 101, 102, 110, 111, 112, 122, 128, 245n5; consciousness, 112, 131; discourse, 18, 201; dominant, 9; double-consciousness in, 246n9; identity forms of, 9; language of, 115; management, 103, 104, 105, 106, 116; privilege, 3, 104, 109, 112, 120, 126, 201, 244n22; relations, 107; seeing, 102, 105, 106, 109, 110; silence on, 107, 110, 111; social analysis, 201; social construction of, 9; social relations of, 95, 210; structural dimensions of, 96; subjectivities, 114; token celebrations of, 104; visibility of, 114, 116
Racial: accommodation, 9; conflict, 105, 107; differences, 15, 95, 100, 103, 105, 110, 114, 115, 117, 127, 128, 129, 130, 201, 205; discourse, 69, 96, 107, 109, 110, 112, 116; diversity, 103–104, 246n11; experience, 109; identity, 10, 15, 95–131, 95–132; privilege, 244n1; respect, 116; signifiers, 96; stratification, 9; tension, 106, 107, 131; tolerance, 116
Racism, 100, 102, 105, 106, 110, 246n10; invisible, 246n10
Relationships: achievement/race, 128; among students, 2; building, 26, 27; class/education, 11, 66; class/gender, 7; classroom, 120; egalitarian, 141; with friends, 48–51; gender, 162, 208; identity/difference, 95; knowledge/power, 3; peer, 3, 67–69, 72–76, 79; power/control, 35; production of, 2; racial, 107; school/class structure, 5; school/parent, 171; self/other, 95; social, 14, 17–60; with teachers, 48, 141; work, 2
Resistance: countercultural, 7; expressions of, 8; to formal school culture, 8; to sex stereotypes, 8

School(s): adjustment to, 5; attitudes toward, 84; choices of, 179–183, 249n7; class inequalities in, 5; cultural advantages in, 5; culture, 6, 7, 9, 24, 105, 113, 119, 136, 143, 204; cultures of opposition in, 9; curriculum organization in, 5; and development of relational communities, 2; executive elite, 31; financial assistance in, 2, 67, 78, 80; independent, 21, 35, 63, 168, 174, 235n1, 240n24, 240n25; magnet, 67, 243n14; non-